The Complete Investment Guide

The Complete Investment Guide
Create Your Path to Wealth

Kévin Poncelet

Copyright © 2023 Kévin Poncelet

Published by
  Bulan Press
  Unit 1.01, Ground Floor
  Menara Boustead 39
  Jalan Sultan Ahmad Shah
  10050 George Town
  Penang, Malaysia
  Email: hello@bulanpress.com
  Website: www.kevinponcelet.com
        www.bulanpress.com

All rights reserved. No part of this publication may be reproduced, stored in a retrieval system, or transmitted in any form, or by any means, electronic, mechanical, photocopying, recording, or otherwise, without the prior written permission of the author and publisher.

Cataloguing-in-Publication Data

Perpustakaan Negara Malaysia

A catalogue record for this book is available from the National Library of Malaysia

ISBN 978-967-25626-1-0

Edited by Gareth Richards and Eryn Tan
Cover design by Patsy Yap
Typesetting and layout by Janice Cheong

Printed in Malaysia by
Phoenix Printers Sdn Bhd
6 Lebuh Gereja
10200 George Town
Penang, Malaysia

Disclaimer
The information provided in this book is for educational and informational purposes only. As such, the information contained here does not constitute legal or financial advice. You should never make any investment decision without first conducting your own research with due diligence and consulting with a financial professional to determine what may be best for your individual needs. While the publisher and author have made their best efforts in preparing this book, they do not make any guarantee or other promise as to the results that may be obtained from using the contents of this book. To the maximum extent permitted by the law, the publisher and the author disclaim any and all liability in the event any information, commentary, analysis, opinions, advice, and/or recommendations contained in this book should prove to be inaccurate, incomplete, or unreliable, or result in any investment or other losses. Your use of the information in this book is at your own risk.

To my parents

... who will be able to read this book
when the French translation is ready

Contents

List of Figures   xi
List of Tables   xiii
Preface   xv
Acknowledgements   xvii
Note to the Reader   xix

Introduction   1

1 Why Invest   7
    1.1 Your motivations   8
    1.2 SMART goals   9
    1.3 Costs   10
    1.4 Practice cases   12
    1.5 Moving forward   13

2 How to Invest   15
    2.1 Your time value   15
    2.2 Your assets and liabilities   17
    2.3 Your income and expenses   19
    2.4 Priorities   22
    2.5 Details   26
    2.6 Savings rates   31
    2.7 Moving forward   34

3 What to Invest   39
    3.1 Why it is important to invest   40
    3.2 Portfolios   42
    3.3 How to build a portfolio   43
    3.4 Types of portfolios   46
    3.5 Moving forward   47

4	**Career**		**49**
	4.1	Defining your career	50
	4.2	How to get a job	59
	4.3	Salary and promotion negotiation	69
	4.4.	Key takeaways	73
5	**Business**		**75**
	5.1	Establishing a company	75
	5.2	Operation and management	77
	5.3	Marketing	82
	5.4	Finance	88
	5.5	Other useful theories	95
	5.6	Key takeaways	98
6	**Financial Assets**		**99**
	6.1	The basics	101
	6.2	Index funds and exchange-traded funds	107
	6.3	Mutual funds	115
	6.4	Stocks	120
	6.5	Bonds	133
	6.6	Resources	137
	6.7	Going further	139
7	**Real Estate**		**141**
	7.1	Why invest in real estate	142
	7.2	Why not to invest in real estate	142
	7.3	What to buy	143
	7.4	Strategies	147
	7.5	Where to buy	155
	7.6	Your team	157
	7.7	How to find the best real estate	159
	7.8	Finance	162
	7.9	Comparing real estate	168
	7.10	Tenants	170
	7.11	Going further	173

8	**Gold and Other Precious Metals**	175
8.1	The basics	175
8.2	What brings value to gold	176
8.3	What form of gold to invest in	178
8.4	Where and how to get your gold	183
8.5	Gold collections	184
8.6	Going further	186

9	**Collectibles**	189
9.1	What brings value to a collection	189
9.2	What collection to start	193
9.3	Evaluating, buying, and selling a collection	194
9.4	The rise and fall of famous collections	195
9.5	Going further	197

10	**Wine and Other Alcohol**	199
10.1	What brings value to wine and other alcohol	199
10.2	Factors to consider when investing	201
10.3	How to invest in wine	203
10.4	Going further	204

11	**Art**	207
11.1	What brings value to art	207
11.2	Where to buy and sell	209
11.3	How to invest in art	210
11.4	What to buy	212
11.5	Going further	212

12	**Cryptocurrency and Non-fungible Tokens**	213
12.1	What is cryptocurrency?	213
12.2	Types of cryptos	214
12.3	Why invest in cryptos	216
12.4	How to benefit from crypto investment	217
12.5	How to invest in crypto	218
12.6	Scams	219

	12.7	Non-fungible tokens	220
	12.8	What gives value to an NFT	221
	12.9	How to invest in NFTs	222
	12.10	Going further	223
13	**Investment Plan**		**225**
	13.1	Framework for an investment plan	225
	13.2	Case study 1	228
	13.3	Case study 2	233
	13.4	Alterations to your plan	240
	13.5	Moving forward	240
14	**Conclusion**		**243**

Glossary 245
References 249
Further Reading 251

Figures

2.1 Comparing savings rates 33
6.1 Percentage of all domestic equity funds underperforming the S&P Composite 1500 on an absolute basis 110
8.1 Gold price, 1974–2021 178

Tables

2.1	Assessment of assets and liabilities	17
2.2	Identifying major assets and liabilities	18
2.3	Model budget: income and expenses	20
2.4	Self-assessment of assets and liabilities	34
2.5	Self-assessment budget: income and expenses	35
3.1	Two families: income and assets	41
5.1	Marketing: internal strengths and weaknesses	85
5.2	Marketing: external opportunities and threats	85
5.3	SWOT analysis: fruit juice company	86
5.4	Balance sheet: assets and liabilities	90
5.5	Balance sheet: fruit juice company	91
5.6	Income statement	92
5.7	Income statement: fruit juice company	93
5.8	Cash flow statement	94
5.9	Cash flow statement: fruit juice company	94
6.1	Historic performance of selected indexes, 2018–2022	109
6.2	Comparative stock price and earnings per share of companies	131
6.3	Comparative price–earnings (P/E) ratio of companies	132
7.1	Property finances	166
7.2	Fact sheet: real estate analysis	169
13.1	Investment plan: assessment of assets and liabilities	226
13.2	Investment plan: income and expenses	226
13.3	Case study 1: assessment of assets and liabilities, year 0	228
13.4	Case study 1: income and expenses, year 0	229
13.5	Case study 1: assessment of assets and liabilities, year 1	230
13.6	Case study 1: income and expenses, year 1	230
13.7	Case study 1: assessment of assets and liabilities, year 5	232
13.8	Case study 1: income and expenses, year 5	232
13.9	Case study 2: assessment of assets and liabilities, year 0	234

13.10 Case study 2: income and expenses, year 0   234
13.11 Case study 2: assessment of assets and liabilities, year 1   236
13.12 Case study 2: income and expenses, year 1   236
13.13 Case study 2: assessment of assets and liabilities, year 5   238
13.14 Case study 2: income and expenses, year 10   238
13.15 Case study 2: assessment of assets and liabilities, year 15 239

Preface

When I wanted to start my investment journey, I was overwhelmed by the task ahead. I had no idea where to start, what to read, or which information to trust. This is a common problem many people face as we are not taught adequately how to invest. Generally speaking, people have to learn to invest on their own. That's why it is so difficult and can be overwhelming—it's not an innate skill we are born with. Everyone starts with a blank canvas and must learn from scratch.

I have read many investment books and found a common problem with most of them. General books have little practical application to investing; they motivated me to invest but did not give me the necessary insights. In contrast, when I read more specific and technical books, they generally consider only one type of asset to invest in without looking at the bigger picture or my personal needs and goals. It was only after reading many different books, following classes, watching videos, and talking to other investors that I was confident enough to start investing.

I believe many people face the same issue and don't have the time to gather information from different sources and create a comprehensive investment plan. In addition, there is not a single type of investment strategy that can be copied nor one that works for everyone. People have different needs, come from different backgrounds, and have different goals. This is why I decided to write this book, to create a comprehensive guide and help people define an investment strategy that takes into account their objectives, needs, and current situation. Put simply, *The Complete Investment Guide* is the book I wish I had in my hands when I started investing and learning the way forward. I have created this book for people who are beginning their investor journey and for advanced investors looking for other investment opportunities that they aren't familiar with.

My genuine wish is that people who pick up this book get really interested in investing and that it can help in your journey.

Acknowledgements

Writing a book is not a solo journey. I have met and worked with many passionate people who have influenced this journey and the contents of this book.

I want to express my gratitude to my beta readers who offered valuable feedback on earlier drafts—François Fadeux, Gaël François, Kaleigh Nelson, Line Daco, Margot Henneaux, Michael Neidhardt, Philippe Singleton, Olivier Lambert, and Xavier Gonzalez. They corrected many mistakes and gave me invaluable insights to improve my work.

A good book doesn't get made without a great team. I would especially like to thank Gareth Richards and Eryn Tan for their fantastic editorial work; Janice Cheong for her skillful typesetting and layout; and Patsy Yap who was able to create the cover design of my dreams.

And, of course, my partner Dayana Wong who helped me believe in myself and convinced me that my ideas are worth sharing.

I can't thank you enough for your contributions.

Kévin Poncelet
Penang, April 2023

Note to the Reader

I intend this book to be a practical guide, so I have written it as if I am talking directly to you the reader, and have included many hands-on exercises to enhance the learning process. Although I am European by origin, I have lived in various countries and have a very cosmopolitan outlook. This is reflected in the examples drawn from different countries. However, for most analyses and calculations, I have written this book from an American perspective and have used the US dollar as the reference currency. The main reason is that many people who read investment books are used to this writing style. Most English-language books and other resources on business, finance, accounting, and entrepreneurship are published in the United States and inevitably reflect those realities.

This book is meant to guide you and offer an investing method. Much of the material covered in a particular chapter is then used in subsequent ones and should be considered as known facts. I would therefore advise beginner investors to read the book from beginning to end in order to enhance your understanding in a coherent manner. However, more advanced investors are at liberty to forgo this method and move from one chapter to another, depending on the investment topic you're interested in. While reading, you might come across some technical terms that are generally defined within the text. If need be, you can always refer to those definitions in the glossary at the end of the book.

Finally, this book is designed to be a stepping stone, and I really encourage you to seek more knowledge and refer to other books and resources to gain the necessary experience before investing.

Introduction

Throughout our lives, we are taught the importance of having a job and earning money. But we are often left unaware of what to do with that money or how to allocate our resources to work and create lasting wealth for us. Imagine a world where everyone knows how to manage their money effectively, use a budget, start a profitable business following their passion, invest in something they love, and get rewarded for it. Wouldn't people be more in control of their own lives, more likely to do what they want, and simply happier? Wouldn't the world feel like a better place?

Many people have mixed views regarding investing, often confusing it with speculating or gambling. So I would like to define what I mean by investing in the context of this book as well as clear up some common misconceptions. This will enable you to approach the subject with an open and creative mind.

Investing is about allocating resources—money, land, raw materials, time, physical and mental skills, and so on—to generate a profit and achieve a specific goal. While speculating and gambling are shortsighted and more akin to games of chance, investing is about having a long-term strategy to achieve something significant. The general perception of investing may not be too positive as the media constantly remind people that companies are destroying the environment, exploiting child labor, manufacturing weapons, and worse. Despite these very real concerns, we can't deny that some individuals, companies, and countries have made significant investments that benefit society as a whole. Thanks to investments in medicine we can now cure fatal diseases; because states have invested in infrastructure people can use efficient public transport systems; due to investments in renewable energy we can harness wind and solar power.

Though many people like to see everything in black-and-white oppositions, this simply isn't an accurate assessment of a world that is actually complex and offers a range of choices and opportunities. Insisting on a blinkered worldview only prevents you from considering different perspectives and from seeing the bigger picture clearly. Likewise, dismissing investments because you believe they are somehow morally wrong isn't a valid argument and can cause you real harm over time.

In addition to these general—and largely unfounded—concerns about investing, there are also many false assumptions and misconceptions. It is therefore useful to go through some of the misunderstandings I often hear about investing and offer my own reflections, which I hope will strengthen your resolve to take investing seriously.

Misconception #1. I am too young to invest. Contrary to this claim, I see two main reasons for starting to invest as young as possible. First, investing is a skill, and like any skill the more and the longer you practice it the better you get. By starting young, you will gain more knowledge and experience to help you in your investment journey. Second, any good investment will bring you great returns if you give it time, thanks to a concept called the compound effect. The idea is to reinvest your earnings into your invested capital, which increases your total capital and makes more significant profits over time that you can reinvest. This creates a wealth snowball effect.

Misconception #2. I am too old to invest. Although you might face time restrictions in your investment strategy, it is never too late to start your investor path, broaden your portfolio, or have more secure investments. There are lots of different investment solutions that can fit your needs.

Misconception #3. Investing is dangerous, and I don't want to put my capital at risk. There are risks involved in every type of investment, but there are also potential rewards. Your goal as an investor is to minimize risk and maximize the potential reward. Even if you don't invest, there is a certainty of losing your purchasing power over time due to inflation.

Misconception #4. I'm not good with numbers or I can't invest. You will do away with this assumption by reading this book, which explains various possible investment strategies. You can have a very active approach to investing by being analytical and taking regular actions, or you can also have a more passive approach that doesn't necessarily require you to be good with numbers. Your investment strategy is entirely up to you.

Misconception #5. I don't know anything about investing. Your investment journey starts with learning and gathering knowledge. You don't need a postgraduate degree in economics or to work in a bank in order to invest successfully. There are many free online resources, affordable books, or people who have excellent knowledge in a specific investment and would be happy to share information with you. All you need is to learn in a way that suits you best.

Misconception #6. I'm not interested in investing. Investing doesn't have to be boring. It can be something you are interested in or excited about, and your goal as an investor is to find a way to make a profit from it. For example, if you love a particular product, why not own some company shares? If you are a fine wine enthusiast, why not age some bottles and sell them for a profit? If you like to bake cakes, why not open a bakery and sell delicious pastries? Everyone has interests and knowledge in a particular field. The key is to transform this passion into an investment you can profit from.

Misconception #7. I don't need to invest. There are multiple reasons for investing other than getting wealthier: having a passive revenue for your retirement to compensate for the loss of your salary; building an emergency net; creating an inheritance for your family; affording the best education for your children; being able to donate to a non-profit you believe in; and so on. Although money doesn't solve every problem it definitely helps.

Misconception #8. I don't have enough money to invest. This book mainly looks at means to create or increase income, but we also explore ways to minimize or reduce expenses to help you have more savings to invest. So you don't necessarily need much money to begin investing as you can start with minimal capital and compound your earnings over time.

Misconception #9. I don't have time to invest. When someone says they don't have time to do something, it's more often the case that they don't make or take the time to do it. What they are referring to is not an issue of time but of priorities. When something doesn't feel necessary or urgent, people procrastinate and prioritize things they think are more important or enjoyable. Realistically, investing is not necessarily time-consuming nor a great burden, and it can significantly change your life over time.

As I have already stated, your watchword should be to approach investment with an open mind and use this book as a guide—you will see new vistas opening up.

***

I believe that there is not one type of investment strategy that fits everyone. People have different needs, come from different backgrounds, and have different goals. This book accounts for all that and shows you many possibilities to choose from, thus giving you the freedom to define your path moving forward. The book is organized into fourteen chapters, each clearly subdivided to maximize flow and coherence.

Chapter 1—Why Invest—is designed to determine your investment goals. Before starting any journey, you must know why you are traveling and where you want to go. I believe it is the same with investing. You must be aware of why you want to invest, what drives you, and the goals you want to achieve. Those goals will help you define your investment strategy.

Chapter 2—How to Invest—is meant to assess your current situation. When creating a plan, you must determine the resources you have and the ones you will most likely obtain in the future. Here we evaluate your assets, liabilities, income, and expenses to assess your current situation and optimize the resources you have on hand. This will help you start to invest with a solid foundation and allocate your available capital and time responsibly.

Chapters 3–12 tackle the types of investments you can make. It is the heart of the book, where, after a general introduction to building a portfolio, I dig deeper into nine categories of investment.

- Career: how to invest in your career
- Business: how to launch or improve your business
- Financial assets: how to invest in stocks, bonds, exchange-traded funds (ETFs), and mutual funds
- Real estate: how to select and invest in real estate
- Gold and other precious metals: how to invest in gold and other precious metals
- Collectibles: how to invest in a collection you are passionate about
- Wine and other alcohol: how to invest and finance your passion in wine
- Art: how to understand its value and invest in art
- Cryptocurrency and non-fungible tokens (NFTs): how to understand the blockchain and invest in cryptocurrencies and non-fungible tokens

Chapter 13—Investment Plan—gathers all the elements we have dealt with in the book and structures them into a coherent plan to achieve your goals. The idea is to create a one- or two-page document that states your objective, your current situation, and what you are going to do during the year to get closer to reaching your goal. Once you have created this plan, you will have to update it every year, assess your progress, and implement the necessary changes.

Chapter 14—Conclusion—offers a reinforcement of some of the most important takeaways the book offers, helping you focus on what's really important.

Investing is a journey and I hope this book will guide you, help you reflect on what you want to accomplish, teach you how to achieve those goals, and give you the necessary insights to start or go further on your investment journey. But a guide only shows you the path. Your responsibility is to take the first step. And the first step of your journey starts on the next page.

Chapter 1

Why Invest

Investors are always interested in their return on investment, but they don't often consider the bigger picture and precisely what they will do with that money. And yet investing to pursue wealth will not make someone happy. Money is only a means to achieve something concrete, build a legacy, have additional income when retiring, grow a business, and so on.

That's why, before investing, you must have goals that will guide you and give you an edge that average investors don't have. Here are some of the key differences.

- Where average investors have a short-term vision that only extends to the next couple of months, you will have a vision for the next couple of years. You will have a bigger picture to consider, something more important to look forward to.
- When average investors get overly excited about a new investment opportunity, you can take the necessary step back to determine if this will help achieve your long-term goal, or if it's a distraction that could potentially harm your plans.
- When average investors panic and sell their long-term investments in times of crisis, having a vision for the future will help you keep your cool and make wiser choices.
- Where average investors don't have an investment plan, you will have an effective strategy to save money every month, invest regularly, get returns, and review your plans to reach your goal.

In this chapter, we determine the reasons that motivate you to invest and how to create effective goals to help you develop an investment plan. Later, with the goals you have created, you will build an investment plan that you can pursue.

1.1 Your motivations

Before setting an objective, you must determine what motivates you and what you are looking for. Would you like to build a family, grow your wealth, and create an inheritance for your children? Are you looking for financial security? Do you want to change the world? Do you want to be out of debt? Those are only some examples of motivations that could drive you. One reason isn't better than another. They are all relative to your situation, age, culture, family, location, and many more factors that relate to you personally.

You need to reflect on what motivates you in life. Once you have a better idea of your inspirations, you can start formulating them into goals you can pursue and achieve. For example, if you say that you're looking for financial freedom, then your goal could be to become wealthier. If you say that you want to be free and do whatever you want, then your goal could be to retire early. If you say that you want to have a stable situation and build a family, then your goal could be to get out of debt and buy a house. Those are great goals that translate from your motivations, but they share a common shortcoming—they are not precise and lack essential information. To come back to the previous examples, if you say that you want to be wealthier, what does becoming wealthier mean? Being out of debt? Having a million dollars in your bank account? If you say that you want to retire earlier, when exactly? How are your costs of living going to be impacted? How are you going to support your daily expenses? You say you want to get out of debt and buy a house. But what type of house? Where? What's your budget? When do you want it?

As you can see, these goals could reflect your motivations, but they lack essential information and are not too helpful in constructing an investment plan. That's why we next look at how you can structure those goals to help you create your investment plan.

1.2 SMART goals

To help create effective goals, you can use the well-known SMART framework, first published by George T. Doran (1981). In his paper, Doran argues that effective goals have specific characteristics summarized by the acronym SMART. Although this framework has unsurprisingly evolved a bit since then, the core principles are very similar. Today the acronym SMART stands for: specific, measurable, achievable, realistic, and time-bound.

A goal is *specific* when it is clearly defined, and you know exactly what you want to achieve. For example, "I want to be wealthy" is a vague goal. A more specific goal would define the type of wealth, such as real estate, gold, stocks, or cash.

A goal is *measurable* when it has criteria that can be quantified in order to assess progress and accomplishments. To return to the previous example, "I want to be wealthy" does not fix a threshold for achieving this goal. However, saying "I want to have one million dollars in my bank account" clearly defines the threshold to achieve your target.

A goal must be *achievable*, meaning that you can attain this goal with your capacity. For example, saying "I want to be a military jet pilot" may not be an achievable goal if you don't have good eyesight or are too old as you might not qualify for enrollment in an aviation training school.

A goal must be *realistic* given the time and resources you have now or in the future. For example, "I want to be a millionaire by next week by trading stocks" may be an unrealistic goal if your starting capital is $100. It is irrational to think that you can become a millionaire that quickly.

Finally, having a *time-bound* goal with a deadline creates a sense of urgency. It pushes you to take action. Further, it helps you create a plan and set milestones to achieve it. Simply saying "I want to retire earlier" doesn't help you create a plan or milestones. However, saying "I want to have enough passive income by the age of 50 in order to retire from my day job" is a time-bound goal that sets a deadline and the type of revenue you need to achieve it.

Applying the SMART framework to our previous examples may look something like this. You will assess that "I want to be wealthier" is not a specific, measurable, or time-bound goal. Instead, you can say, "I want to own an apartment worth $400,000 that creates passive revenue and a portfolio worth $1 million of stocks within 20 years." Alternatively, if your goal is "I want to retire earlier," you may convert it into a SMART goal by saying, "I want to quit my current day-to-day job before the age of 50 and live from my new business revenue." Or if your goal is "I want to get a house," you may clarify that goal by saying, "I want to buy a $600,000 condo in California within 10 years." These new goals give you much more information and can help you define what you need to do next.

1.3 Costs

Once you have defined a SMART goal, you must determine what you need to get there. To help you define its actual cost, you can break down your SMART goal into individual statements. Let's take a concrete example. Your goal is to own an apartment building in Belgium that will create passive revenue to sustain your lifestyle within 10 years. When breaking down this goal into different pieces, you can start to see what each individual part entails.

- *Sustain my lifestyle within 10 years.* Let's imagine you currently spend $2,000 per month. Your objective is that this investment will bring you $2,000 worth of net revenue. If you want to be more precise, you can account for inflation in your calculation, but you will have to do it for your future income and expenditure as well.

- *Create passive revenue.* When evaluating an investment opportunity, one apartment in a five-unit apartment building in the area you target can be rented for about $1,200 per month. Therefore, a five-unit building can bring in $6,000 per month and $72,000 per year. However, you need to consider the monthly costs: at least $3,000 for the mortgage payments and $500 that you put aside for maintenance, insurance, taxes, vacancy, repairs, and so on. In total, the average monthly costs are $3,500 and $42,000 per year. The potential net revenue is therefore $2,500 per month and $30,000 per year, which is above your current objective.

- *Own a building in Belgium.* If you analyze the Belgian market and look at the price of an apartment building, you can find some structures with five units that cost about $800,000 (including taxes and renovation). To acquire this building you need at least a 10% down payment of $80,000.

By evaluating the cost of your SMART goal, you can clearly define a path forward. In this example, you know that to achieve this goal, you will have to save $80,000 to acquire a five-unit apartment building to create enough passive revenue to sustain your lifestyle.

Keep in mind that the monetary cost is one thing, but you often need to acquire specific skills, knowledge, or even a diploma to achieve certain goals. Let's take another example. Your goal is to establish and run a carpentry company in a new workshop within five years. When breaking down this goal, you can identify these elements.

- *Establish a carpentry company.* You need legal authorization to establish a company. If you don't have the necessary diploma you might need to take night classes targeted at professionals.

- *Run the company.* You need the proper tools and machinery to run a business. Although you can start small and rent some machinery, there is always a minimum material cost you should account for. In this example, you evaluate the minimum capital at $30,000.

- *In a new workshop.* New companies often need to rent first before having enough capital to acquire a new place. In this case, you will need to find a workshop available for leasing that can accommodate machinery.

Now you have a path forward: you have determined that you need to take classes, have a minimum capital of $30,000, and find a suitable place to rent.

1.4 Practice cases

To really grasp the process, here are two practical applications of SMART goals.

It's January 1998. Michael is 25 years old and freshly graduated. He sets himself the goal of having $400,000 in his bank account before the age of 50 so that he can retire earlier if he wishes to. Michael sees the stock market as a great investment opportunity to reach his goal. However, he doesn't want to do much research and decides to invest in a cheap exchange-traded fund (ETF) that follows Standard and Poor's 500 share index (S&P 500, see Chapter 6). Michael has a job that pays well and gives him the opportunity to save $500 every month that he automatically invests in the stock market. Some years he gets great returns, while other years his holdings lose some value, but he never takes his money out and he compounds interest over time. After 25 years, his holding grows yearly by an average of 8.5% and is worth close to $450,000.[1] It's not a bad outcome if you compare it to saving $500 every month for 25 years, which would have yielded only $150,000.

Now let's take the example of Michael's neighbor Jeanne, who is similarly 25 years old and freshly graduated. Her goal is also to have at least $400,000 in her bank account when she is 50, but she wants to do better than the average S&P 500 and to select the companies she will invest in. She analyzes and handpicks every stock she invests in. Like Michael, she puts aside $500 each month, but she only invests when the price is right and in specific stocks where she sees great potential. Sometimes she is right and gets a tremendous return; sometimes she is wrong and loses money. She has been investing for 25 years, beating the market, and getting an average

---

[1] You can check this calculation by using an S&P 500 calculator such as: https://dqydj.com/sp-500-periodic-reinvestment-calculator-dividends/.

return of 12% per year. After 25 years, her holding is worth close to $850,000.[2]

So who do you think had the better strategy?

The answer is both of them—because they both achieved what they wanted. Michael increased his wealth over time while not putting much effort into his investment strategy. Jeanne drastically increased her wealth, beating the stock market, but she had to work hard for it and do a lot of research.

These examples represent very different investment paths, yet both achieved their goals. As I stated earlier, there isn't one path to wealth; one is not better than the other. As an investor you must choose the path that is convenient for you and can help you achieve your goals.

1.5 Moving forward

It is now time to determine your reasons for investing. On this page, write what motivates and drives you every morning, convert those motivations into one or more SMART goals, and consider the resources needed to achieve those goals.

My motivation(s):

....
....
....

My SMART goal(s):

....
....
....

---

[2] You can use the following calculator to check the results: https://www.calculator.net/investment-calculator.html.

Resources needed to achieve my goal(s) (cost, skills, certification, and so on):

....

....

....

Don't rush. Take your time to create your goals. Remember that they must be something to challenge you, a reflection of your motivations in life, something that you want to wake up to every morning thinking about, and something you will strive to get closer to every day. These goals will determine your investment strategy, and you will work for years or even decades to achieve them. So make sure that your goals are meaningful and worthwhile to you. These goals are crucial because we will build a plan to reach them.

Chapter 2

How to Invest

Every active person invests in and trades two assets: time and resources such as intellectual and physical skills, money, land, and raw materials. For example, employees invest their time by working to earn a salary; business owners invest time and resources to create a product or a service and get revenue from their customers; investors buy financial assets in the stock market to get a return on their capital over time. In all these examples, we are trading and investing time and resources.

This chapter aims to evaluate and optimize the time and resources you have on hand. In order to do so, we first set a monetary value for your time and then we evaluate and optimize your assets, liabilities, income, and expenses.

2.1 Your time value

We all have a limited time on Earth, and however wealthy we are we all run out of time at some point. It is this scarcity that should encourage you to fix a monetary value to your time, which in turn will help you make the best use of it when considering an investment opportunity. In other words, setting a value to your time helps you determine if an investment is worth the effort you will put into it.

The monetary value you fix for your time is very subjective. You could take your current hourly salary, consider your home country's average wage, or decide to arbitrarily set a value like $5 per hour, $20 per hour, or $50 per hour. Alternatively, you could fix different values based on the nature of the task: if it is repetitive it's $30 per hour, if it requires active thinking it's $80 per hour, if it is something you hate doing it's $40 per hour. These are, of course, only examples. The value you choose depends on your own unique situation.

This technique is beneficial when you hesitate between two ways to invest in an asset. For example, if you value your time at $50 per hour and have acquired and furnished a $300,000 apartment within a tourist area, there are two possible ways you could rent this place.

- You could rent it long term and get an average 5% yearly return of $15,000.

- You could rent it short term via Airbnb or another platform and get an average 10% yearly return of $30,000 (see Chapter 7 for more details).

The time you spend on the long-term rental is minimal. By contrast, you have a much more active role in the short-term rental as you regularly change tenants. If you decide to do it yourself and actively manage your rental to save costs, you have to consider the additional time you spend on this investment. In this case, let's say you spend an average of four hours per week, which is about 208 hours per year. If you divide the extra revenue you get from the short-term rental of $15,000 by the additional 208 hours of work your average income will be $72 per hour, which is above your minimum target salary of $50 per hour. This could therefore constitute a good use of your time. There are, of course, many other factors that you must consider before choosing this type of investment, but your time value is already a good indicator to assess an investment opportunity.

It is also beneficial to keep this principle in mind when performing mundane tasks. Imagine you have just bought a piece of furniture from Ikea. Unfortunately, it's too big for your car. You consider having it delivered to your home for $60 or renting a van from Ikea for $30 to transport the furniture yourself. Let's say you value your time at $20 per hour and the drive from your home to Ikea is one hour. It would be a four-hour drive with the van (from your house to Ikea, back to your house with the loaded van, returning the van, and going home), plus an extra hour for loading, unloading, and queuing. So it would take you five hours or $100 worth of your time plus the fuel and $30 rental. Accounting only for your time value you can already conclude that a direct delivery to your home might be a better use of your time.

2.2 Your assets and liabilities

Now that you have established a price for your time, let's evaluate your financial situation by looking at your assets—tangible or intangible resources that have economic value, such as a house or a car—and liabilities—debts that an individual or an institution owes.

In a simple a table, evaluate the market value of the assets you own, the income they generate per year (if any), the liabilities you owe, their interest rate, and your yearly reimbursement. Table 2.1 provides a good example.

Table 2.1 Assessment of assets and liabilities

	Assets ($)			Liabilities ($)			
Assets	Market value	Cash in	Debts	Interest (%)	Remaining debt	Cash out
House	200,000		House	5	80,000	10,800
Real estate investment	200,000	10,000	Real estate	5	120,000	6,000
Cars	20,000		Cars	5	5,000	4,800
Stocks	30,000	500	Student loan	4	40,000	12,000
Emergency fund	5,000		Credit card	15	3,000	400
Cash and savings	5,000					
Total assets	460,000	10,500	Total liabilities		248,000	34,050

By writing down your assets and liabilities you are creating the starting point from which you can evaluate your situation. This exercise is relatively simple and it should only take a couple minutes to gather all the necessary information. To do so, you should only consider the main assets and liabilities that will likely impact your future financial plans. If you own playing cards or owe $50 to your best friend, those items will likely not affect your financial situation and shouldn't be accounted for.

I have included a blank model at Table 2.4 at the end of the chapter to help you evaluate your situation. When filling this out you will most likely find the items noted in Table 2.2.

Table 2.2 Identifying major assets and liabilities

Assets	Liabilities
• Houses and real estate investments	• Mortgage debt on real estate
• Cars and other means of transportation	• Car loans
• Stocks and other financial assets	• Student loans
• Cash, savings, and emergency funds	• Credit card debt
• Cryptocurrency, NFTs, precious metals, arts, collectibles, and other assets of significant value	• Other types of credit

Once your table is complete you can evaluate at a glance your financial situation by asking yourself the following questions.

- Do you own assets? Do those assets increase in value over time, like real estate and stocks? Or do they decrease in value over time and need to be replaced, like a car?
- Do your assets create cash flow, like real estate or stocks that pay dividends?
- Do you have enough cash, savings, and emergency funds?
- Are you overly exposed to one particular asset? Would you lose everything if that specific asset's market crashed?

- Do you owe much debt? Is the interest rate high? Is your monthly payment appropriate?

All these questions help you determine if you have a stable situation and can hint at possible next steps. For example, if you don't have any assets that create passive income you should consider investing in assets that generate income. If you have high-interest debts you should try to refinance them. If you don't have an emergency fund you should create one before investing.

2.3 Your income and expenses

You can find many articles, books, and websites that claim to have cracked the secret to wealth and promise you a pathway to get rich quickly. Although those sources might work for some people, they are often clickbait or purely schemes to sell you something you never thought you needed.

If you want to know the secret about wealth, it's actually quite simple. There are only two ways to get wealthier. You can either increase your income by increasing your revenue and/or finding new sources of income. Or you can decrease your expenses by reducing and/or by avoiding current and future costs.

You can look at it whichever way you want, but ultimately the secret to wealth is to increase your income and/or decrease your expenses. So the real question is not: what is the secret to becoming wealthy? The more interesting question is: how do you decrease your costs and increase your revenue? Although it is a simple question, it doesn't necessarily have an easy answer.

Before investing your money and increasing your income, we will try to optimize and reduce your living costs by establishing and evaluating your budget. It's a tedious task and it will probably take you a couple of hours to gather all the information, but the more you know about what you earn and spend the better results you will get.

This chapter is not meant to be critical about every expense you have or make you feel bad about them. Instead, the idea is to gain awareness of your living costs to determine which are necessary and which can be optimized, reduced, or eliminated. If you think you have already minimized all your expenses then that's great. However, I suggest you review them again and see if there are any possible ways to further optimize your cost reduction. Table 2.3 is an example of a budget with all the sources of income on the left and all the expenses on the right.

Table 2.3 Model budget: income and expenses

Income ($)			Expenses ($)		
Employee salary	Month	Year	**Home**	Month	Year
Salary	4,500.00	54,000.00	Loan	900.00	10,800.00
Subtotal	**4,500.00**	**54,000.00**	Taxes	333.33	4,000.00
Business revenue	Month	Year	Insurance	166.67	2,000.00
Revenue	4,000.00	48,000.00	Maintenance and repairs	100.00	1,200.00
Subtotal	**4,000.00**	**48,000.00**	Garbage	10.00	120.00
Real estate investment	Month	Year	Electricity	110.00	1,320.00
Rent	1,500.00	18,000.00	Water	105.00	1,260.00
Additional fees	50.00	600.00	Gas	80.00	960.00
Subtotal	**1,550.00**	**18,600.00**	Other	50.00	600.00
Stocks	Month	Year	**Subtotal**	**1,855.00**	**22,260.00**
Dividends	41.67	500.00	**Real estate investment**	Month	Year
Subtotal	**41.67**	**500.00**	Loan	500.00	6,000.00
Other	Month	Year	Taxes	250.00	3,000.00
Other	50.00	600.00	Maintenance and repairs	100.00	1,200.00
Subtotal	**50.00**	**600.00**	Insurance	83.33	1,000.00
			Other	50.00	600.00
			Subtotal	**983.33**	**11,800.00**

Income ($)	Expenses ($)		
	Transport	*Month*	*Year*
	Car loan	400.00	4,800.00
	Taxes	50.00	600.00
	Maintenance and repair	50.00	600.00
	Petrol	150.00	1,800.00
	Insurance	80.00	960.00
	Saving replacement	200.00	2,400.00
	Bus, trains, taxis	50.00	600.00
	Other	—	—
	Subtotal	**980.00**	**11,760.00**
	Subscriptions	*Month*	*Year*
	Magazines	10.00	120.00
	Internet	30.00	360.00
	Network (TV, platforms)	20.00	240.00
	Phone	50.00	600.00
	Sports and other clubs	50.00	600.00
	Other	—	—
	Subtotal	**160.00**	**1,920.00**
	Living	*Month*	*Year*
	Groceries	416.67	5,000.00
	Healthcare	100.00	1,200.00
	Alcohol and tobacco	75.00	900.00
	Clothes	100.00	1,200.00
	Restaurants	166.67	2,000.00
	Vacations	200.00	2,400.00
	Credit card debt	37.50	450.00
	Electronics	41.67	500.00
	Education	100.00	1,200.00

Income ($)			Expenses ($)		
			Charity donations	100.00	1,200.00
			Entertainment	200.00	2,400.00
			Other	200.00	2,400.00
			Subtotal	**1,737.50**	**20,850.00**
			Finance	*Month*	*Year*
			Student loan	1,000.00	12,000.00
			Taxes	100.00	1,200.00
			Health insurance	250.00	3,000.00
			Life insurance	100.00	1,200.00
			Personal insurance	200.00	2,400.00
			Retirement fund	200.00	2,400.00
			Other	100.00	1,200.00
			Subtotal	**1,950.00**	**23,400.00**
Total income	10,141.67	121,700.00	**Total expenses**	**7,665.83**	**91,990.00**

At the end of the chapter you will create your own budget using this model.

2.4 Priorities

Once you have gathered all the information and created your budget you will have an enhanced grasp of where your money comes from and where it goes. The discussion here aims to optimize your financial situation by giving you a list of priorities to help minimize expenses and improve your financial foundation. Although minor cuts in your budget don't mean a lot when you make them individually, they can quickly add up as you reinvest the capital over a long period.

The priorities identified here are only suggestions and you don't need to finish one stage before starting another. They are simply classified in a logical order to help you start optimizing your financial situation. Be aware that this is a summary, and we will go into more detail on how to save costs on individual items in the next chapter.

The *first* priority is to refinance all your loans. This is an effective way to cut costs in a low interest rate environment. When refinancing a loan you are paying off an existing debt with a new one that has superior terms and conditions.

Unless you can immediately pay off your highest interest rate debt you should focus on refinancing all your loans: mortgage, credit card, or student loan. Do some research about credit card companies, look around at all the banks and see if they can offer you improved conditions with a lower interest rate on your loans. It is especially easy in a low interest rate environment, but remember that you might not find an improved rate in a high interest rate environment.

Once you have done your research, and if you have found a superior offer from one of your credit provider's competitors, you can ask your current provider to do better or else change to the alternative. As credit providers do a lot of marketing to find new customers, they might consider it advantageous to give you a discount rather than finding a new client. It may take a couple hours, but the potential results are worth your time. Even a 0.5% difference on your mortgage loan could save you tens of thousands of dollars over time. For a 20-year mortgage loan of $200,000 at a 3% interest rate you would pay a total of $66,206.85 in interest. If you can renegotiate your credit conditions with the bank and only pay 2.5% interest, the total interest paid would be $54,353.39. The difference is $11,853.46, which isn't bad for a couple of hours' work. I strongly recommend you see for yourself by using a free loan calculator online to find out how much money you could save by reducing your interest rate by 0.5%.[1] There is no point paying too much interest on a loan. Your money would be put to better use in your pocket rather than paying a higher interest rate to a bank or any other credit provider.

---

[1] You can use the following website to make the calculations yourself: https://www.calculator.net/loan-calculator.html.

Your *second* priority is to pay off your highest interest rate debts. Debts are not bad; they are a form of leverage that help you get what you want. Keeping your debt level under control is an excellent way to enable you to achieve your goals. But if your debt level gets out of control then this leverage could threaten your financial dream.

That being said, not all debts are the same. In his book *Rich Dad Poor Dad*, Robert T. Kiyosaki (2018) describes the concept of good and bad debts. Essentially, good debts give you leverage to buy assets that create cash flow, like businesses or rental properties. Conversely, bad debts give you leverage to buy assets that don't produce cash flow, like credit cards, cars, or personal debt. Ideally, you should maximize the good debts that create revenue for you and minimize bad debts taking cash from you.

To illustrate, I would like to share a story from an article reporting Warren Buffet's conversation with a friend who wanted to invest some money and was seeking investment advice. His first question to her was whether she had credit card debt. She did and was paying an interest rate of about 18%. "If I owed any money at 18%, the first thing I'd do with any money I had would be to pay it off," Buffett told her. "It will be way better than any investment idea I've got." (Elkins 2020). What is interesting about this story is that even one of the leading investors in the world would prefer to pay off an 18% interest rate rather than investing it.

If you have several debts, I suggest you start to pay back the one with the highest interest rate. Once this debt is settled, go to the next one, the next one, and so on. I am not suggesting that you shouldn't invest before paying off all your debts, but credit card debts and personal loans should be a priority as their interest rates are generally high. High interest rate debts will be a massive burden in the future so they should be avoided and reduced as much as possible.

The *third* priority is to create an emergency fund. If you haven't got an emergency fund you should create one as soon as possible before investing. According to a Bankrate survey from 2023, only

43% of Americans would be able to pay for an emergency from their savings (Gillespie 2023; Green 2023). When unexpected expenses or emergencies occur people are forced to take on personal loans or credit card debts with high interest or sell some excellent investments at an unfortunate time. Life is full of surprises—some good and some bad. Although money doesn't solve every problem, it can help you in hard times. That's why you should build an emergency fund worth at least three or four months of your expenses and place it in a high-interest savings account that doesn't cost you any fees. This emergency fund is reserved for crises, like an essential medical bill or an unexpected layoff from work. Buying the latest iPhone or a fancy dress doesn't constitute an emergency.

The *fourth* priority is stopping or minimizing the expenses that don't change your habits. These are the most effortless changes to make as they won't affect your lifestyle and will save you money. You can change your internet or phone provider to get a good rate, cancel a TV cable subscription you barely watch, or cancel a gym membership you are not using. You won't make better use of the internet or your phone with another provider, and you won't miss the TV cable or gym membership you're not using. As you will see in the next chapter, there are many ways to reduce your living costs or find alternatives without changing your habits.

When optimizing costs that don't change your life, the key is to stop paying for things you don't use and to check the competition's price and contact your current supplier with the best offer from one of their competitors for the things you use. As you are a profitable customer and it costs them a lot in marketing to get a new one, they might bend and lower their current price to keep you as a loyal customer. If not, you can always take the best offer from the competition.

Although those changes might represent little initially, they will quickly add up over time. Besides, they won't affect your lifestyle in any way. Imagine you had saved $200 per month over the last 10 years without changing your habits. Those savings equal $24,000 over that period, which isn't bad for something that didn't require you to change your lifestyle. If you had constantly invested these savings in a cheap ETF that followed the S&P 500 over 10 years you would have almost doubled this money and earned $41,104.91 (see Chapter 6). In this example, you need to account for taxes and fees, but making more than $40,000 in 10 years by saving and reinvesting your capital without changing your lifestyle seems like a good deal.

The *fifth* priority is to reduce the expenses that will change your habits. These are the changes that impact your lifestyle. The reason why it's important for you to create a budget that reflects your actual spending is that you will realize that some of your expenses are too high and that it might be a good time to change those habits and reduce some of your living costs. For example, if you feel that you pay too much for restaurants, expensive clothing, or high-tech gadgets, it might be opportune to set up boundaries and create a tighter budget for those expenses. These changes can even be good for your health and well-being if you decide to reduce or stop smoking, drinking alcohol, eating fast food, or gambling. These are not easy changes to make, but every sacrifice will help you reach your goal.

2.5 Details

Now that you have a list of priorities to work with, we can also look at your budget in more detail and determine if we can optimize or reduce some of your expenses. This chapter goes into more detail about specific expenses; therefore, you might see some repetition with the elements we have outlined earlier as the cost reduction strategy often follows the same pattern.

2.5.1 Housing and real estate investment

There are many costs involved in housing and real estate investment (see Chapter 7). Below you can find some suggestions to optimize your housing expenses.

First, as noted earlier, I would suggest that you check all the banks around you to see if they can refinance your loan with a better interest rate. Even a slight reduction of 0.5% interest rate on a mortgage loan could result in tens of thousands of dollars in savings over the years.

There might be many ways to minimize maintenance and repair costs by taking cheaper materials or postponing repairs. However, you will save much more money by properly maintaining and fixing a house as soon as a problem occurs rather than by neglecting and paying significant consequences in the aftermath. A small leak in a roof can quickly transform into a big hole and create flooding issues that will be more costly than reasonable maintenance expenses. So you should always allocate a budget for the maintenance and repairs of your real estate.

In some countries, insurance on real estate is not mandatory. Nonetheless, it is really advisable to have good insurance coverage by a reliable insurer on all the real estate you own. Risking all your hard-earned money by not taking insurance is not worth it. You can still optimize your costs by checking your insurer's competition and seeing if someone can offer you a better deal at the same or even improved terms and conditions.

Utility suppliers of water, gas, and electricity often provide the same services but at different prices. If you are not living in an area with a monopolistic hold on utilities you should check the competition and see whether they can provide the same services at the same conditions but at a more affordable price. If you own a house you might also be interested in placing solar panels and heat pump systems, or installing superior thermal insulation to save costs on energy and positively impact the environment. Although those projects represent a substantial installation cost, they pay off over the long term. However, be very careful if you rely on government subventions to make your project viable. There are many tragic stories of people investing everything in those types of installations, where economic viability depended entirely on subsidies to make a significant profit. The issue with relying on government grants is that policies and laws change, and when they do you can be the one who suffers the consequences.

2.5.2 Subscriptions

If you haven't checked it already, an internet and phone subscription might be an easy way to cut costs without changing your habits. If the speed and reception are the same you will not do more effective internet research or have better phone conversations with a different provider. Internet and phone line suppliers often cut their prices, giving out promotions and packaging solutions that could be advantageous over the long term. Even a $10 reduction per month on your phone subscription represents $120 per year, which isn't bad for changing something that has no impact on your life.

There has been a shift from traditional cable media and satellite TV to streaming platforms. There was a time when there was only one possible provider, but those days are long gone and you now have many choices. You should therefore determine which one(s) fit your needs, if they are helpful or should be canceled.

It is not a secret that more people sign up for a gym subscription in January than any other month because of their new year's resolutions. However, for many people those resolutions last only a short time and they stop going to the gym or their new club after a couple weeks or months. People often use the excuse that they need this subscription to motivate them to exercise. But statistics don't lie, and many will quickly give up. If this description fits you, don't worry, you are like hundreds of thousands of other people. I would encourage you to cancel useless memberships and put that money to better use, or to find an activity you actually care about.

If you have subscribed to newspapers, magazines, or other types of printed matter you need to ensure that you are using them. If you are still receiving the paper version of your subscription you might want to check if an online version is available. The content stays the same, it is generally cheaper, you can enjoy it wherever you are, and it reduces your impact on the environment.

2.5.3 Living expenses

Regarding living expenses, such as groceries, clothing, restaurants, and entertainment, it is up to you to decide if you want to reduce those costs to save more and get closer to your financial goal. By recording your living costs you will gain awareness of your living standards and decide if you can or should reduce them. If you are eating out every night, buying designer clothes, and going on holiday every month, it's absolutely fine as long as you are aware of the total cost they represent and you are comfortable with the benefits you get from them.

When taken individually, tobacco and alcohol consumption might not look like a high cost. But those expenses can rapidly add up to a substantial amount at the end of the year. Suppose you smoke, on average, a pack of 20 cigarettes a day at $6.65 per pack. That represents 7,300 cigarettes per year for a total cost of $2,427.25. In addition, those costs don't account for your health issues or increased insurance premiums. This example is also valid for alcohol consumption. Although a small amount from time to time might not be a big deal, alcohol can become a health problem if consumed in large quantities every day. Writing down your annual consumption might help you realize the monetary cost it represents and you should consider the long-term health implications of such a cost.

If you do have gambling habits, you should also consider their long-term implications. People often make the mistake of comparing investing to gambling. There is a fundamental difference between the two. When investing, you can research and put the odds in your favor. In contrast, when gambling, chances are purposely set against you. Otherwise casinos and other gambling organizations would never be profitable. So don't think that you have exceptionally good luck or that gambling is the only way to be rich and get out of financial trouble as actually the opposite is true. The gambling industry is a very profitable sector that uses third-party companies' data to target people with low incomes and credit card debts, and individuals who stopped gambling. These people are often in a bad situation and see gambling as their only way out. Unfortunately, the media often promote stories of those rare lucky winners but seldom tell the many stories of those who lost everything. If you have a gambling addiction, there are many free services and professionals that can help you. Many casinos and other gambling websites even allow you to ban yourself from their platforms so that you don't get tempted.

2.5.4 Finance

Depending on your wealth level, another high cost to consider are the taxes you pay. As each country has different legislation and tax aid you can take advantage of, I am not able to write a complete strategy about it here. But it might be in your best interest to spend an hour with a competent tax expert who can advise you on your country's tax system and what is the best solution given your financial plan.

Depending on the country you live in, a credit card might be an unfortunate necessity. If you are a US citizen and don't use a credit card because you pay everything in cash, the bank will have little account of your credit score history and might charge a more significant interest rate on a mortgage loan. But if you use a credit card and constantly pay your bill on time, that helps you get a good credit score which can, in turn, get you a lower interest rate on your mortgage.

According to Federal Reserve data, the average credit card interest rate in the United States was 20.40% in 2022. Very few financial investments could reliably bring a 20% interest rate per year. However, that's what Americans have to pay on average when they were charged for the interest on their credit cards. If you have an unpaid credit card bill I suggest paying it back as soon as possible.

There is no denying that credit card institutions can give you great incentives, such as credit miles or various discounts in some shops, which can help you save money. They can even apply a 0% credit card rate for a specific period. But if you plan to use those benefits you should know all their conditions and carefully read what you are signing up for.

If you live in a country where using a credit card does not negatively impact your credit score I suggest not using them. Credit card institutions lure you with gifts, special discounts, and other marketing traps, encouraging you to consume and use their services. However, those companies are very profitable and don't give away gifts for no reason. If they are doing it, they benefit from it, and you don't want to be the one paying that bill.

As for interest rates on personal, student, or other kinds of loans, these can vary a lot. They could be small, but they can also represent a significant burden that will follow you for the rest of your life. There are many examples of people carrying student loans into retirement. Although many have refunded loans multiple times, the interest they paid was higher than the amount refunded. So their loans kept growing over time. Some credit institutions don't even allow you to pay off those debts at once or refinance your credit. When taking on these loans you must know the terms and conditions you sign up for and exactly how much you will pay back and for how long. In addition, you must always take a loan that allows you to refinance with another bank offering more profitable conditions. And finally, you must always have an exit door that will enable you to get out of these loans.

Many traditional banks charge you fees just to open a bank account with them. But there are many alternatives with reliable banks charging zero fees to handle your money. Even if your current bank fees are only $5 per month this still represents $60 per year and $600 over 10 years. If you change bank accounts it's money you save by doing nothing.

2.6   Savings rates

Once you have optimized your expenses and are satisfied with the cost reduction, it is time to save and invest money. Usually, people receive their salary, pay all their bills, and save whatever they have left at the end of the month. This is an inefficient and inconsistent way of saving. Most people can't live with a fixed budget as different expenses or unexpected costs will come up every month.

To help you improve your savings rate, I would like to share some insights from George S. Clason's (1989) *The Richest Man in Babylon*, originally published in 1926 and still in print almost a century later. The book is a collection of short fictional stories of Arkad, the richest man in Babylon, who shared his wisdom about gold and wealth management. Among those lessons, he stated that people often confuse necessary expenses with desired ones, which is why many end up with no savings. His advice was that people need to learn to live on less than they earn. To do so, before paying any other expenses, people should pay themselves first and save at least 10% of their earnings. They will then learn to live from whatever they have left. In my opinion that's great advice. If you pay yourself first by putting money on the side when you receive your salary you will ensure that your savings are constant. Then, even if it is difficult to follow a budget, you will automatically adjust your living standards by reducing your expenses to whatever money you have left.

To follow this advice, I suggest you open a new bank account dedicated to investment where you can automatically transfer a portion of your income on the day you receive it. The important part is that you only withdraw that money if it is for an investment.

How much you should save is a more difficult question. There are no absolute rules about the percentage you need to save up. It depends on your situation: if you have children, if both you and your partner are working, if one person in your family has high medical bills, your location, and many other aspects you need to consider. Keep in mind that the more you can save, the closer you will get to your financial goal as your savings and investment will compound over time.

Let's take a practical example and compare four families, each earning $100,000 and reinvesting their earnings in the same investment vehicle that brings them a 10% yearly return for ten years. The only difference between these families is their savings rate.

- The first family saves 5% of their earnings.
- The second family follows the advice from *The Richest Man in Babylon* and saves 10% of their earnings.

- The third family is like the average millionaire in the United States, as Thomas J. Stanley and William D. Danko (1996) state in *The Millionaire Next Door*, and saves 20% of their earnings.
- The fourth family saves 50% of their earnings, like some people in the Financial Independence, Retire Early (FIRE) community.

Here is what happens with their savings over 10 years, presented in Figure 2.1.

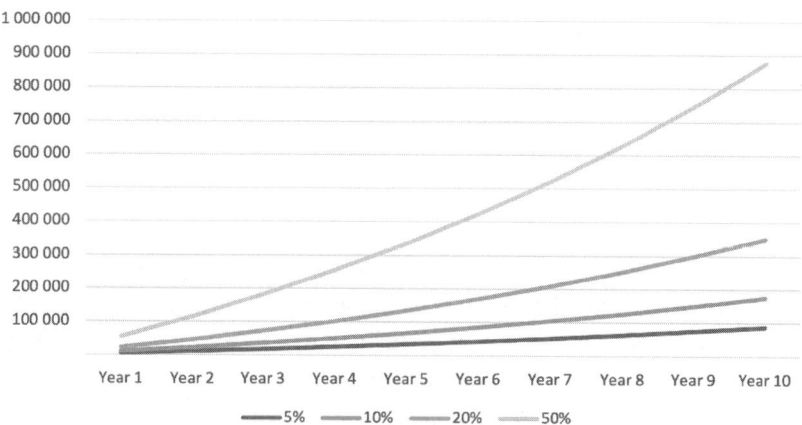

Figure 2.1 Comparing savings rates

Although the return on investment for each family is the same percentage, their total capital after 10 years is quite different. As you can see, the more you save and reinvest, the more exponential the return is. However, I don't suggest that it is possible for everyone to save 50% of their earnings. Once again, there is no absolute rule about saving a specific percentage of your earnings. But remember, the more you save the faster you will reach your final goal. To determine which savings rate is most suitable you can start with a high savings rate and decide whether it is sustainable over the long term. If not, you can lower it.

2.7 Moving forward

Let's summarize the most important points in this chapter and put them into practice. First, let's evaluate the monetary value of your time. As it will be helpful to assess your future investment prospects, I suggest writing down how much you value one hour of your time. As discussed earlier, you can also define different monetary value according to the nature of the task.

....
....
....
....
....

Then you must evaluate your financial situation. You can use the model in Table 2.4 to assess your situation or create your own. (The Excel version of the table is also available on my website www.kevinponcelet.com if you would prefer an electronic version of the table you can work on.) On the left side of the table you list all your main assets, their current market value, and the cash flow they produce per year (if any). On the right side you list your debts, the remaining money you owe, the interest rate, and the amount you pay every year.

Table 2.4 Self-assessment of assets and liabilities

Assets ($)			Liabilities ($)			
Assets	Market value	Cash in	Debts	Interest	Remaining debt	Cash out
Total assets			Total liabilities			

Now you have to reflect on those assets and liabilities. What could you do to improve your financial situation in terms of assets you have and liabilities you owe?

....
....
....
....
....

After that you can complete your budget. You can use the model in Table 2.5 or create your own if you prefer. (The Excel version of the table is also available on my website www.kevinponcelet.com if you would prefer an electronic version of the table you can work on.)

Table 2.5 Self-assessment budget: income and expenses

Income ($)			Expenses ($)		
Employee salary	Month	Year	Home	Month	Year
Salary			Loan		
Subtotal			Taxes		
Business revenue	Month	Year	Insurance		
Revenue			Maintenance and repairs		
Subtotal			Garbage		
Real estate investment	Month	Year	Electricity		
Rent			Water		
Additional fees			Gas		
Subtotal			Other		
Stocks	Month	Year	**Subtotal**		
Dividends			**Real estate investment**	Month	Year
Subtotal			Loan		
Other	Month	Year	Taxes		
Other			Maintenance and repairs		
Subtotal			Insurance		
			Other		
			Subtotal		

Income ($)	Expenses ($)		
	Transport	Month	Year
	Car loan		
	Taxes		
	Maintenance and repair		
	Petrol		
	Insurance		
	Saving replacement		
	Bus, trains, taxis		
	Other		
	Subtotal		
	Subscriptions	Month	Year
	Magazines		
	Internet		
	Network (TV, platforms)		
	Phone		
	Sports and other clubs		
	Other		
	Subtotal		
	Living	Month	Year
	Groceries		
	Healthcare		
	Alcohol and tobacco		
	Clothes		
	Restaurants		
	Vacations		
	Credit card debt		
	Electronics		
	Education		
	Charity donations		
	Entertainment		
	Other		
	Subtotal		

Income ($)	Expenses ($)		
	Finance	Month	Year
	Student loan		
	Taxes		
	Health insurance		
	Life insurance		
	Personal insurance		
	Retirement fund		
	Other		
	Subtotal		
Total income	**Total expenses**		

Once you gain awareness of your holding and living expenses you can put your finances in order by reducing and optimizing your expenses. I suggest that you start with the five priorities we have seen in the previous chapter.

- Refinancing your loans
- Paying off your highest interest rate debts
- Creating an emergency fund
- Canceling or minimizing the expenses that don't change your habits
- Reducing expenses that will change your habits

Finally, you can open a separate dedicated investment account where you will save a constant percentage of your earnings by paying yourself the first day you receive your monthly income. Now you should write down what percentage of your earnings you will save every month.

....
....
....
....
....

Once you have done all those steps you are in a more comfortable position to invest and are now ready to take the next step in your investment journey.

Chapter 3

What to Invest

So far I have been helping to define your goals and improve your financial situation by reducing and optimizing your living expenses. Although there is a limit to what you can save by lowering your expenses, there is in theory no ceiling to what you can gain from investing. This is why we now focus on finding ways to increase your revenue. In the following chapters, we will go through nine categories of investment.

- *Career*: how to invest in your career
- *Business*: how to launch or improve your business
- *Financial assets*: how to invest in stocks, bonds, exchange-traded funds, and mutual funds
- *Real estate*: how to select and invest in real estate
- *Gold and other precious metals*: how to invest in gold and other precious metals
- *Collectibles*: how to invest in a collection you are passionate about
- *Wine and other alcohol*: how to invest and finance your passion for wine
- *Art*: how to understand its value and invest in art
- *Cryptocurrencies and non-fungible tokens*: how to understand the blockchain and invest in cryptocurrencies and non-fungible tokens

Some of you might wonder why I talk about career and business development in an investment book. The reason is quite simple. As

I highlighted earlier, I believe we invest and trade two assets: time and resources, such as intellectual and physical skills, money, land, raw materials, and so on. People spend a lot of their time working on their careers and business. For most, it's their only source of income, which is why the chapters about your career and business development are relevant since they can help people make the most of them. Although it might be difficult to quantify a career and business in an investment portfolio, it is nevertheless important to integrate them into your investment plan.

There is something for everyone in the following chapters. Even if you don't intend to invest in a particular type of asset it may still be interesting to learn more about it. You don't need to create your own company to be intrigued by techniques or management practices that have shaped how companies work and people consume. Likewise, just because you don't want to invest in wine and art this doesn't mean it won't be interesting to learn how they are valued.

Before going through each investment category we need to discuss the importance of investing, having diversified investments, and how to create a portfolio that helps you reach your goals. Keep in mind that in this chapter I briefly talk about specific investment vehicles that are then discussed in more detail later.

3.1 Why it is important to invest

In the words of Warren Buffet, "If you don't find a way to make money while you sleep, you will work until you die." Many people think investing is dangerous because you put your capital at risk. The general wisdom is to get a job that pays well, buy a house, build a family, and you will live a happy life. The problem is that this approach might not be as safe as everyone thinks. Let's take an example and compare the sources of revenue from two different families.

- The first family comprises two people. One works as an employee and has a $50,000 annual salary; the other is a business owner who earns $60,000 per year. In addition, this family has $10,000 in savings, owns a $250,000 apartment that they rent, and regularly invests in the stock market.

- The second family also comprises two people. One is a pilot and has a $100,000 annual salary; the other is a flight attendant who earns $50,000 per year. They own a house, live an expensive lifestyle, have no savings, and don't invest (Table 3.1).

Table 3.1 Two families: income and assets

First family	Second family
• Employee salary: $50,000	• Employee salary: $100,000 + $50,000
• Business revenue: $60,000	• Real estate: $500,000 house
• Financial assets: $50,000 stocks that pay $2,500 yearly dividends	
• Real estate: $250,000 apartment that pays $12,500 annual rent	
• Savings: $10,000	

As you can see, the first family has revenue from four different sources. If a problem occurs, such as the business owner falling ill and not being able to work for a while, this family can still rely on their other sources of revenue and assets. In contrast, the second family depends entirely on their salaries and both incomes are from the aeronautical sector. If an industry crisis were to happen, such as a new global pandemic, they risk losing their jobs.

Based on their current status, which family do you think is in a safer position and will most likely have more revenue in the future? The answer is obvious. Although the first couple earn less money, their revenues are spread, and they regularly save and invest money that they can use in case of emergency. They are therefore in a much better position than the second family, who did nothing wrong but followed the widespread norms to have fulfilling jobs that pay well, own a house, and live a happy life.

From this simple example, you can see the advantages of diversified investments and revenue sources. Although I took an extreme case to prove my point, the fact remains that relying entirely on one source of revenue while not investing is very risky. There are indeed risks involved in every type of investment, but people often overlook the fact that there are also significant risks to not investing at all.

3.2 Portfolios

As with having only one source of revenue, there are also risks in having only one type of investment. The best way to mitigate this risk is to diversify the assets in your investment portfolio.

An investment portfolio is an ensemble of assets such as stocks, bonds, real estate, cash, gold, art, or collectibles. It was the economist Harry Markowitz (1952) who first advanced the concept of portfolio theory in an article titled "Portfolio Selection." His main thesis was that investors could reduce risk and maximize returns by diversifying their investments across various assets. If you own only one asset your wealth will increase and fall based on the ups and down of the market price of this asset. By contrast, if you own several assets that are not directly related, even if the market price of one asset crashes, the rest of your portfolio will compensate for it. In other words, only one portion of your wealth will be at risk from this crash. With this theory, Markowitz showed that investing is not only about picking the right assets, but also about allocating your resources to create the best portfolio that minimizes risk and maximizes returns.

So should you have a diversified portfolio? The short answer is yes! Most leading investors advise retail investors to have a diversified portfolio. However, many legendary investors such as Peter Lynch, Charlie Munger, and Warren Buffet are famous for only owning a handful of assets and being extremely successful. So why should retail investors have diversified portfolios instead of following the example of those great investors?

To answer this question, you have to understand that two main things happen when you have a diversified portfolio. First, you spread the risk and volatility related to one specific asset by having several that are not directly related. If you own only one stock of a company and that company goes bankrupt you might lose all your investment. On the other hand, if you invest equally in 10 stocks, and one of those companies goes bust, you will only lose 10% of the overall value of your portfolio. Second, the returns from your best-performing assets are diluted by the returns from your worst-performing ones. If you invest equally in 10 stocks, and one of your stocks doubles in value while the others stay at the same level, your overall portfolio will only grow by 10%.

The legendary investors only invest in the best long-term performing companies as they don't want to dilute their returns. They would rather have one excellent company than 10 average ones. In addition, those investors are exceptional individuals who are highly specialized, have their own investment teams, and possess knowledge, skills, time, capital, information, and many more advantages you don't have access to. Without those privileges, it would be hazardous to only invest in a handful of assets. The safer and more effective strategy that accounts for your circumstances and capabilities is to have a diversified portfolio.

3.3 How to build a portfolio

There are many factors to consider when building a portfolio.

First and foremost, you should consider your investment objectives as they directly determine the types of assets you invest in. Are you looking for assets that create regular income or assets that have a high potential to grow in the future? Are you looking to buy undervalued assets? You must design a type of portfolio that helps you achieve your long-term objectives. Suppose your objective is to create an income-generating portfolio, then in that case you should allocate a significant part of your portfolio in income-generating assets.

Next you must review your personal situation and investment horizon. Everyone has different goals and faces different situations. There isn't one type of portfolio that suits everyone. Even if your portfolio is adequate for your current situation, you may need to adapt and rebalance it in the future as personal circumstances change over time. For example, when you are young and have a great deal of your life ahead of you, it might be best to build a growth portfolio to maximize returns over time. However, this type of portfolio fluctuates a lot and may no longer be appropriate when you are close to retirement as you will want to ensure you conserve your capital or have a steady source of income from your assets to replace your salary. Your situation can also change. If you decide to stop your day-to-day job to become an entrepreneur, you might need to compensate for your early loss of revenue with a portfolio focusing on creating additional income. So it's good to review your portfolio from time to time and determine if you need to rebalance it or reallocate some resources to ensure that it suits your purpose.

There is also your risk tolerance. The correlation between risk and reward when investing means that the riskier an investment is the higher the potential reward tends to be. Conversely, low-risk investments usually offer lower potential returns. For example, a stock in a small high-tech company that created a new product that may revolutionize an industry offers excellent potential returns. However, there are many risks to consider: the technology could become outdated, the company's success might not last, or the company could go bankrupt. In contrast, sovereign bonds from a country like the United States are considered safe, but generally offer lower returns.

When building your portfolio you must understand your risk tolerance and determine if you are an aggressive, moderate, or conservative investor. Your risk tolerance can be determined by your age, investment horizon, available capital, objectives, and how you personally react to risk. For example, if you are young and have a lot of time ahead of you, you can afford to lose some money on riskier investments that might be more lucrative, as you should have a lot of time to recoup your potential loss. On the other hand, if you are close to retirement, you might need to have a more conservative approach and invest in safer assets that keep their value over time to preserve your capital.

Another factor to consider is your expertise. Everyone has different ideas about portfolio allocation. If you talk to a banker, they will usually advise you to have most of your portfolio in mutual funds adapted to your risk tolerance. If you talk to a real estate agent, they will say that most of your portfolio should be in property. If you talk to a real estate investment trust expert, they will suggest you allocate about 30–40% of your portfolio to REIT investments. Experts will advise you to buy what they sell because that's their job. However, it's important to remember that your portfolio should also reflect your expertise as well. Many investors, myself included, believe that you shouldn't allocate more than 5–10% of your portfolio to other assets such as precious metals, collectibles, art, wine, or cryptocurrencies. There are of course exceptions if you have knowledge and expertise in one of those particular assets. For example, if you are an art gallerist, you almost certainly know much more about art investment than most people and can probably get a better return on your investment. Art can therefore represent a more important part of your portfolio if that fits your objective.

Finally, the core principle of every portfolio is to ensure that you have a good allocation of your investments and diversify them properly. Having a lot of assets doesn't necessarily mean that you have a diversified portfolio. If you have invested in 50 stocks from different oil companies your portfolio is still only focused on one industry. If that sector is in trouble your entire portfolio will be impacted. Conversely, if you own 10 stocks from different industries and countries, your portfolio will be much more varied. To diversify your portfolio you can

- Invest in various asset classes such as stocks, gold, art, or real estate.
- Invest in diverse industries such as technology, mining, or banking.
- Invest in different countries by having stocks from companies in the United States, China, or Europe.

When allocating your portfolio, also keep in mind that because of their very nature, some assets automatically represent a significant part of someone's portfolio. For example, real estate investments are significant and likely represent an important part of a portfolio.

3.4 Types of portfolios

The perfect portfolio doesn't exist. There isn't one that suits everyone's needs, objectives, or risk tolerance. Instead, there are many types, each having a particular focus and answering specific needs and goals. The choice of the type of portfolio you create is crucial as it determines the kinds of assets you invest in.

- *Growth portfolio*. This portfolio focuses on assets that have good growth potential. It's very aggressive, with high-risk, high-reward types of assets. It typically contains stocks in small-cap companies, technology companies, ETFs, and mutual funds focused on growing capital.
- *Income portfolio*. This portfolio focuses on assets that generate recurrent income, such as bonds, dividends stocks, rental properties, or REITs.
- *Conservative portfolio*. This portfolio focuses on defensive assets that conserve their value over time, such as bonds, gold, mutual funds, or ETFs focused on conservative assets.
- *Value portfolio*. This portfolio focuses on undervalued assets, such as companies with great fundamentals that are currently underpriced. The objective is to buy excellent assets and stocks of companies at a low price.
- *Balanced portfolio*. This portfolio aims to achieve a balance between capital appreciation and generating a steady income.

Keep in mind that the type of portfolio you decide to create depends on your investment strategy, personal situation, expertise, risk tolerance, and objectives.

3.5 Moving forward

Now it's time to reflect on your own situation and determine the type of portfolio that will help you reach your goal. To do so, you should write down the type of assets that could help you reach your long-term objectives.

....
....
....
....

You must then review your personal situation, investment horizon, and risk tolerance. How much time can you leave your investment? Are you risk-averse in your investment strategy or are you a risk-taker? Can you afford to lose a significant part of your portfolio or are you living paycheck to paycheck?

....
....
....
....

What about your expertise? Do you have deep knowledge or experience in a particular area that can be helpful in your investment selection?

....
....
....
....

Now that you have answered those questions, you are a bit closer to the type of portfolio that will be appropriate for you. So what kind of portfolio is suitable for you? Growth portfolio, income portfolio, conservative portfolio, value portfolio, or balance portfolio.

....
....
....
....

If you are still uncertain about the type of portfolio that would suit your needs, there are many free tests you can easily find online that can help you select the type of portfolio that suits your needs.

Chapter 4

Career

Many people don't instinctively think that an investment book would have an employment chapter. But investing in a career is what relates to most people as there are more employees than entrepreneurs across the globe. More than this, many people rely on employment as their only source of revenue. So if you are an employee, devoting time and effort to your career might be one of the most profitable investments you ever make in the long term.

Unfortunately, a lot of people feel their job is a burden and do it merely because they have no other choice. In a perfect world, employees would feel proud of their work accomplishments and not only do it for the money. Employment should be a symbiosis—a relationship between a company and its employees where both parties accommodate each other and grow this bond over time to get the best out of it.

When working as an employee, you exchange your time and physical and mental skills to perform a task and get a salary. But those conditions are not set in stone, and as you evolve in your career and get better at your job, you should also earn more or have better working conditions. If you only have one source of revenue you must do everything possible to make the most of it. This chapter's goal is to guide you in choosing or changing a career path, to help you with the research process, job application, interview, and negotiation of better salaries and working conditions over time.

4.1 Defining your career

If you hesitate between a career or an entrepreneurial vocation you must consider the pros and cons of pursuing each path. As an employee, you enjoy many advantages.

- The salary you get is generally constant and paid at a set date (unless you are working on commission).
- You have a short- or long-term employment contract, and therefore you know the end date of your employment and can plan accordingly.
- You get many benefits such as healthcare plans, pension schemes, social security benefits, or company cars.
- You have career development opportunities.

The main advantage you get as an employee over an entrepreneur is the security and predictability that come with your job as they can help you plan an investment strategy accordingly.

On the other hand, there are also disadvantages to consider.

- Your salary is limited and does not necessarily represent what your company gains from your work.
- You are generally working to a fixed schedule that may or may not always be convenient for you.
- Your tasks are often assigned to you and might differ from what you want.
- You work in an setting you don't choose, such as colleagues, work culture, and workplace environment.

The main disadvantages as an employee are that you have less control over your work and don't get the full benefits from what you do, unlike an entrepreneur. If you hesitate between an employee or an entrepreneurial path, you must consider every advantage and disadvantage to make a choice.

4.1.1 Self-assessment

In order to define or change a career path, you must first understand who you are: your passions, skills, personality, and values. This part of the book contains a lot of questions that can help guide your self-assessment journey. Writing down your answers helps you define who you are and what you are looking for in a career, which in turn assists you in narrowing down your career choices. Although you know yourself better than anyone else, gathering all this information and writing it down helps create a clear image of what you are looking for and determine a career path that suits you.

First, let's have a look at your enthusiasms and interests. You will work harder if you are genuinely interested in something. If you can define a career path based on your passion, you can achieve more and have a fulfilling life. Consider the following questions.

What are your passions and interests?

....
....
....
....
....

What would you like to do every day?

....
....
....
....
....

Answering these questions helps you define what you like to do and lead you toward a fulfilling career path. If you can find a way to make money from something you are passionate about and get a job that allows you to work on something you love every day, you will have made the best career move of your life.

Now that you have written about your passions and what you like to do in general, it is time to write about your skills and what you can do.

What are your hard skills? These are the technical skills that help complete specific tasks, such as accounting skills, fluency in a language, or computer programming.

....
....
....
....
....

What are your soft skills? These skills help you interact with people and your environment to perform tasks. For example, problem-solving, time management, communication, or leadership.

....
....
....
....
....

What are your main working and life accomplishments?

....
....
....
....
....

Writing all these skills and achievements helps you define your specialties and what you can do.

Determining your personality and who you are is also an essential part of defining a career. You cannot be a good teacher if you are not patient or an effective computer programmer if you aren't detail oriented. However, you can be a good marketer if you are creative or a successful salesperson if you are good at dealing with people. Knowing your personality guides you to professions that you naturally excel at.

What's your personality like? Creative, helpful, independent, honest, patient, outgoing, confident, aggressive, or loyal? Write five of your best and worst traits.

....
....
....
....
....

What natural position do you occupy when interacting in a work environment? Are you a leader, follower, problem-solver, mediator, motivator, or organizer?

....
....
....
....
....

What are your fundamental values? Being socially responsible? Filial piety? Honesty?

....
....
....
....
....

What motivates you when you work? What are you looking for? Do you want to have a stable family situation? Are you looking to have the highest-paying job? Are you an overachiever who doesn't count the hours?

....
....
....
....
....

Next you must consider how you like to work. You generally don't control your work environment, such as the customers and colleagues you deal with, but you can decide what environment you like or refuse to work in.

What type of work environment helps you thrive? Do you want to work in a competitive environment, in a team, or do you prefer to work on a project alone?

....
....
....
....
....

What type of work environment negatively affects your quality of work, mental health, and general well-being?

....
....
....
....
....

What type of people do you like to work with? Although you will likely not have a choice with the colleagues or customers you deal with, some professions attract specific personality types. As you will spend a sizeable portion of your life with these people, it can help to know the typical colleagues or customers you would like to have.

....
....
....
....
....

Conversely, what type of customers and colleagues don't you want to work with?

....
....
....
....
....

Where would you like to work? Where would you like to live? Do you already have a home and don't want to be too far from it?

....
....
....
....
....

Finally, it's time to determine your salary expectations and the level of responsibility you would like. Your salary is based on your work and what the market offers, so it is difficult to determine a salary range without having a specific job in mind. However, the goal here is to define a salary range you would be comfortable living with.

What is your current salary range expectation? What salary range would you like to have in the future?

....
....
....
....
....

What level of responsibility would you like to have? Does this align with your long-term goals?

....
....
....
....
....

These questions play a key role in the following pages, where we narrow down your career choice. If you are looking for additional resources you can find many free personality or career tests online to help you define your career, such as the 16 Personalities test (www.16personalities.com). Alternatively, I recommend reading *What Color Is Your Parachute* by Richard N. Bolles (2021) which goes into much more detail about self-assessment for a career choice.

4.1.2 Filter your career choices

Once you have completed your self-assessment you will have a better idea of the kind of career you want to pursue. But you might still have hundreds of options that you must narrow down. You can start eliminating some choices by going through sectors of activities and determining which industry you are interested in. Economists suggest that there are five sectors of activity.

- *Primary sector*. This focuses on extracting and creating raw materials such as agriculture, fishing, or mining operations.
- *Secondary sector*. This transforms raw materials into finished goods like manufacturing, clothes design, and construction.
- *Tertiary sector*. This is about services, focusing on performing tasks for people or selling finished goods to customers like retail, insurance, or hospitality.
- *Quaternary sector*. This deals with information and knowledge such as libraries, schools, or laboratories.
- *Quinary sector*. This aims at human services such as the police, government, or housekeeping.

Once you have determined a sector you can narrow it down by choosing a specific industry: agriculture, mining, fishing, construction, energy, food and beverage, fashion, manufacturing, computer and technology, education, finance and economics, health care and pharmaceuticals, hospitality, marketing, news and entertainment, publishing, telecommunication, transport (air, water, road, and rail), and so on.

You can also narrow down your choices by determining the types of organization you would like to work for.

- *Non-profit.* People generally work for non-profit organizations because of their values rather than salary expectations and personal ambitions. If you want to impact something you deeply care about, such as creating new habitats for wildlife by planting trees, fundraising for cancer research, or supporting those who can't afford hospital bills, there are countless non-profit organizations that are changing the world and could use your help.
- *Public.* People who work in schools, in government, or in public hospitals often choose this sector to have a direct impact on people or their local community. They may also be led by patriotism, work security, or other social advantages that often come with these types of jobs.
- *Private.* People often work in the private sector because of salary expectations, personal ambition, and the social values a company espouses. The private sector generally offers more career choices and development than other sectors.

Defining a sector of activity and a type of organization helps you choose a career path. Keep in mind that just because you have worked in one sector doesn't mean you can't work in another one later.

Once you have defined your industry, sector of activity, and type of organization you would like to work with, it's time to list and explore possible occupations that interest you. Once you have a complete list, try to get it down to fewer than five using your self-assessment criteria: what you love, what you can do, your personality, how you like to work, as well as salary and responsibility expectations.

Finally, when you hesitate between those last few career options, consider the reality of the job market and determine if the work is in demand or oversubscribed by applicants. You can also use your networks for advice or talk to other professionals within that industry to get input and help you make your final decision. Alternatively, you can seek professional help to guide your choices.

If you need additional resources, you can find much information on this website: https://www.onetonline.org/. You can look at sectors or specific professions that could inspire your career choice. This web page even details the tasks that are generally performed for each job and the skills and experience required.

4.1.3 Reaching your career goals

Once you have selected your dream job you must determine what you need to reach it. To do so, you can first consider the legal requirements for a profession. Does this profession require a particular diploma or certificate? Once you define what is legally required, it's up to you to take the necessary steps: take some classes, go back to school, or follow seminars that give you the legal right to perform this job. Another factor to consider is the knowledge and skills you need. You can buy books, research, and follow courses online. You can also take classes or seminars that give you the necessary theoretical knowledge for your profession. The last aspect to think about is the experience and connection you need to get the job you want. Again, you can figure out the type of experience necessary for a specific role by searching or looking at job requirements online.

4.2 How to get a job

Now that you have a better idea of what you want, you have to go through the frustrating and tedious process of applying for a job. It is not easy, and applicants are often met with closed doors rather than wide open arms. This section gives you tips on the research, application, and interview process to help you in this journey. There is no guarantee you will get your dream job, even if you are doing everything right, but this gives you a much better chance.

4.2.1 Research

There is no one correct path when job hunting. There are many different tools and people that can help you in your research process. My advice is to not discriminate and to utilize them all.

One reliable way to search for a job is via your own network and the connections you have. If you know people in your industry, they might be aware of openings and even recommend you to the recruiting manager. Many jobs are not advertised and sometimes managers only discuss hiring without putting the process in motion. Meeting the right person at the right time might give you a chance for an interview before anyone else. Hiring someone is time-consuming and costly for companies as they have to create job offers, place ads, reach out to recruiters, conduct interviews, and meet several candidates. If a company can save on costs and time by meeting person with the right qualifications, they might not look for anyone else.

You can broaden your network by participating in networking events or reunions related to your industry. You are likely to meet people in your industry who might refer you to an opening they're aware of. So use your network, talk to everyone you know, participate in networking events, and advertise that you are available and looking for a position. Of course, searching for a job by randomly talking to people is a game of luck, but the more you roll the dice the higher your chances of getting the prize.

Multiple social media platforms are now advertising job openings online, and people in your network might even share those ads themselves. However, the ease of applying for jobs on social media also means that companies might receive hundreds of applications every day. You therefore need to stand out to land an interview. But don't dismiss this opportunity because of the competition as you can still find some great jobs through social media.

Specialized platforms like LinkedIn that focus on professional networks are good tools to advertise yourself. Some companies consider this online network presence a must-have, so be aware of your social media presence. Try to write and share articles relevant to your industry. And don't hesitate to advertise that you are looking for a job on social media as your network might come to help you. On another note, always assume that companies scrutinize your social media because they often do. Applicants have been rejected because of what companies found on their Facebook, LinkedIn, and other social media.

Going through agencies, headhunters, and recruiters is an excellent way to find employment. Companies typically pay agencies a commission to find applicants and fill a position, so those agents are incentivized to find a suitable candidate. When contacting an agency, share your curriculum vitae or resume, experiences, skills, education, and career goals. The main advantage of going through an agency is that they do the research for you by leveraging their database and connections to find you opportunities. You can find recruitment agencies and headhunters everywhere. Some specialize in short-term contracts in specific sectors while others focus on long-term contracts. It is generally free to ask an agency to find you opportunities as they are paid by companies that want to find applicants. However, some might charge you a fee or bind you with a contract, so be aware of anything you sign with them. Remember that you are generally not the customer of those agencies and headhunters because it's the companies paying them. If anything, you are more the product they propose. As such, they don't necessarily have your best interest in mind. They are more focused on filling a position for a company than finding the best possible job for you.

Other than that, companies often participate in job fairs to fill positions. At those fairs you have the chance to meet dozens of companies, but keep in mind that the recruiters might see hundreds of candidates a day, so you have to be very convincing to make a good first impression. Although there is a lot of competition, you should still participate in these events as a networking opportunity that helps you meet important representatives. This is an excellent way to ask them questions about the companies you are interested in. Then, later on, you can contact those prospects to see if an opening might interest you.

A job search engine is also an effective way to go through dozens of adverts in a couple of clicks and filter out the best ones in a few minutes. There are hundreds of job platforms. The best-known ones are Indeed, Glassdoor, Monster, Ladders, and ZipRecruiter. These platforms have the advantage of being prominent all over the world and advertise all kinds of jobs.

You can even try a different approach and look at specialized platforms that only advertise the type of job you are looking for. If you want to work for a start-up, you can use AngelList or WorkinStartups. If you want to work remotely you can use Flexjob or JustRemote. These are only examples; there are many specialized platforms you can research to find your dream position.

Alternatively, depending on your location, you can visit job centers that organize training and openings for applicants. These places are often run by people who know your area's employment market and can advise you.

If you are looking for a job in specific companies, you might simply want to look at their websites first as many organizations publish job openings that way. Or else you can connect directly with a company and present yourself by phone, email, or in person. They might have an opening they have yet to advertise and could be interested in your application.

4.2.2 Curriculum vitae or resume

Whenever you apply for a position, you must present a curriculum vitae. This is a document that highlights your professional and academic journey—a one- or two-page autobiography of your professional life that serves as a self-introduction for the company you are applying for.

When writing your CV, you must think that the person reading it will most likely spend less than a minute on it. Most human resource managers in big corporations receive dozens or even hundreds of CVs per opening, meaning they have to analyze many of them in a short time. For this reason, you must make your CV as straightforward as possible, using short sentences or bullet points to highlight the essential information they are looking for.

You must have a well-structured CV that managers can go through by section, such as work experience, education, and achievements. You should also list everything chronologically, starting with the most recent experience. Your CV ought to contain the following.

- *Contact details*. To ensure employers can contact you, include your name, home address, phone number, and email address. You can also add your LinkedIn profile and website link if you have them.

- *Profile*. Write two to three sentences that quickly explain who you are, why you are a good candidate for this position, and what you are looking for. Through this statement, recruiters should know you are qualified for the job. You should adapt your introduction to every job application. For example, "I am an experienced content creator specialized in business writing and looking to create long-term freelance contracts."

- *Picture*. Many European, South American, African, and Asian countries prefer to include profile pictures. However, some countries like Britain and the United States have implemented strict antidiscrimination laws whereby organizations must prove their hiring process isn't discriminatory. So they don't want to see a picture on your CV; they might even automatically reject your application if you have one. Of course, there are exceptions, such as modeling or acting, where people can be hired based on appearance.

- *Work experience*. This is the most crucial part of your CV. Managers check if you have the appropriate experience and skills required. You must write about your latest work experience and highlight your significant skills and projects. If you are applying for a different sector requiring other qualifications, you should highlight the transferable skills.

- *Education.* Your education is an essential factor that managers take into consideration. Add your highest degree and other education or extracurricular courses or activities you took. You should also include any significant and related experience: grades, competitions you won, clubs you led, and activities you took part in. This part of your CV is not restricted to school education. You should insert any professional training and certification you acquired.
- *Relevant experience.* Include any relevant hobbies and interests. The fact that you own and rent real estate might not be important if you apply for an accountant's role, but it makes sense to mention it if you apply for a real estate position.
- *Skills.* In this section you should use bullet points to highlight your significant hard and soft skills, and any languages you speak.

Many people try to make their CV as beautiful as possible. And though a CV has to be appealing to the eye, keep in mind that unless you are a designer you are not competing to have the best-looking CV. Most importantly, it has to be efficient. In a few seconds, the person looking at your CV must understand your background and feel like you are the right fit for this position.

Use countable figures whenever possible to give a measure of what you have accomplished. For example, you can state that you have led a team of 10 people, successfully brought in $1 million in sales, or contributed to a project impacting the lives of 100,000 people. With these figures, the reader has a better grasp of your contribution and your potential.

Although many parts of your CV will stay the same, you should still adapt some sections to be more relevant for the job you are applying for. You can use keywords found in the job advert. As the person assessing the applications will reread the advert before skimming through CVs, those keywords will attract their eye and give you more of a chance to go forward to the next stage.

4.2.3 Cover letter

You generally have to provide a cover letter alongside your CV when applying for an opening. This letter is an introduction that details your interests and the reasons why you are a good candidate for this position. The cover letter is a supplement to your CV that allows you to provide additional information.

All your cover letters can have the same structure, but you must adapt their content for every application. It should not be longer than one page and must be written in a professional format with a letterhead, date, your contact details, name and position, and the company address of the recipient. Your cover letter should be structured as follows.

- An introduction to who you are.
- The reasons you are applying for this position.
- Details of why you are a good match for the company.
- The relevant skills, experiences, and qualities that make you an excellent candidate for this position; it's even better if you can add figures and examples to strengthen your arguments.
- A conclusion and call for them to contact you.

Before writing this letter, you should contact the company to gather as much information as possible regarding the position you are applying for, the necessary skills, what it is like to work in that company, and any other essential details. If possible, try to contact the person who reads your application directly. It is a helpful way to introduce yourself, show additional interest in the position, and put your application on the radar of the manager who reads it.

You should write a different cover letter for each application. You must know and address the person who reads your application: "Dear Mr. Wilson" or "Dear Ms. Johnson." In addition, you should customize your cover letter with the information you have gathered from this company to match what they are looking for. In this vein, it is preferable to use some keywords in the job description or the company's values to stand out from other applicants.

When designing your letter, try to attract attention with a design that matches your CV's style. If you use a template for your CV with a blue background you should use a similar pattern for your cover letter.

Keep in mind that a cover letter is only a supplement to your CV. You mustn't repeat everything, but highlight and go into more detail about the relevant elements for this position.

4.2.4 Getting an interview

Once you have sent your CV and cover letter you can still improve your chances of getting an interview by following up with the hiring managers about a week after your application. Following up helps set you apart from the competition and shows your enthusiasm and eagerness for the position. You can contact them by phone or email, reiterating your interest in the position and encouraging them to pay particular attention to your application. You can also let them know that you are happy to clarify or expand on any information in your application.

4.2.5 The interview process

If everything goes well, you will be invited to one or several job interviews that could lead you to getting the job you want. As preparation is critical to any interview, we now go through the steps you should take beforehand.

Before the interview you should research the company, its competitors, and the industry. You should know the company's values and any noteworthy news related to its industry. You must also research the position and knows precisely what it entails.

The interviewer will ask you questions about the position and any concerns they might have with your application. You should predict these questions and prepare your answers in advance. Suppose you lack experience or have a blank in your CV, these would be valid concerns for an employer to bring up during the interview. You must develop good arguments to state your case and convince them to hire you.

Other than that, there is a series of common questions in interviews. As a candidate you should have your answers prepared and rehearsed. Below are some typical questions you may face and advice on how you could answer them.

Tell me about yourself. Your answer to this question should subtly convince the interviewer to hire you. Tell them what makes you better than other candidates, demonstrate the most important quality they are looking for, and show what you can do for the company without being too obvious about it.

What are your strengths and weaknesses? When responding to this question you want to highlight strengths relevant to the position and weaknesses unrelated to it. For example, if you apply for a programmer position you can say that you are not great at dealing with big groups of people, don't mix around too much, and prefer to stay hyper-focused on your task. These might be considered weaknesses for a salesperson, but are not too damaging for a programmer. Furthermore, these carefully curated "weaknesses" indirectly inform the interviewer that you are less likely to waste time at work and are task-driven. Keep in mind that you must talk about strengths and weaknesses in a work environment. So the manager won't care that you are gluttonous or greedy.

What do you know about this company? When replying this you should talk about the company, but also about market trends and how the company is positioned in relation to its competitors. This shows interest and knowledge about the company and the overall industry.

What do you know about this position? To answer this question you should discuss the details of the role and why you applied for it. This shows the interviewer that you understand and are prepared for the responsibilities that come with the job.

Where do you see yourself in five years? Here you can discuss your personal and professional goals. It's even better if you can note how they align with this position and potential career development within the company.

Why have you left your previous position? It is always better to be an ambassador of your previous company rather than to shame and badmouth it. For a diplomatic answer you could say that your personal and professional interests no longer align with your previous company. For an extra touch you could provide examples or explain how this new position fits you better.

These are only examples of the most common interview questions and recommendations for answers. You can find many more online.

You should also prepare questions for the interview. If you don't have any questions about the position you are applying for this can be interpreted as a lack of interest. Don't forget that you are also looking for a good fit for yourself. If you get the job and it ends up not being what you are looking for, you might have to start the job research process all over again.

Finally, you can practice mock interviews beforehand. Ideally, you would do this with a hiring manager friend who conducts those interviews regularly and can help you improve.

Next, here's some advice on what to do just before the interview.

- Be appropriately dressed for the job you are applying for. An interview isn't the time to make a fashion statement, so don't overdo it and stay professional.

- Reread the job description. This helps you remember what they are looking for when you answer questions.

- Be polite and friendly with everyone in the company. There are many stories of people who didn't get a position because they were rude or had inappropriate conduct with the receptionist or another company employee while waiting for their interview.

- Bring a book or a magazine related to your industry. If you have to wait for the interview, it is better to show interest in your industry rather than play Candy Crush on your phone.

- Print a copy of your CV and have it ready just in case the interviewer has forgotten it.

Once the interview has started, remember that it is a conversation not an interrogation. So be sure to contribute with the questions you prepared in advance. Although the interviewer should stay in charge of the conversation flow, it is better if both parties speak and listen. The interviewer should walk out knowing why they should hire you and not someone else. You must therefore find an opportunity to share your unique selling point. Don't leave the interview without mentioning it.

At the end of the interview, you can also ask what the next steps of the application process are. If it is the last interview, ask when you can expect an answer from them. Don't forget to thank the interviewer for their time as well.

Right after the interview, it's important to follow up with the interviewer by email or even a handwritten note to thank them for their time and this opportunity. Personalize your letter based on your conversation and reiterate your interest in the company. As some interviewers expect to receive a thank-you note it is vital that you follow up.

4.2.6 Job offer

After all this effort you might finally receive a job offer. If you have the chance to receive more than one you have an opportunity to compare and determine which suits you best. Consider what is more advantageous for you over the long term: salary, future career development, health insurance package, company benefits. Remember that although money is crucial your happiness and fulfillment are more important in the long run.

4.3 Salary and promotion negotiation

Your salary shows how the market and your company value your work and skills. As such, salary negotiation is a normal part of the employment process when you advance in your career. A salary increase is one possible outcome you can negotiate, but you could also bargain for other company benefits such as a car, phone line, or better retirement plan.

In this section, we go through the essential parts of salary negotiation: the preparation, negotiation, and follow-up. Keep this information in mind during the interview process while you are negotiating.

4.3.1 Preparation

The key to any negotiation is good preparation. It can be the difference between a successful outcome and a disappointing result. You must therefore come to the negotiation knowing what you are worth and have a clear idea of what you want from this meeting.

The first step in your preparation is to know the current market conditions and your worth. Is there much competition for your position? Are your skills scarce? Are there many companies recruiting for this particular position? Knowing the market conditions helps determine if you have leverage for the negotiation.

To understand if you are being sufficiently paid for your skills you must know your salary range on the market. You can find this information in a number of ways.

- Talking to people with similar jobs in your area.
- Researching rough salary figures online on websites like Glassdoor or PayScale.
- Contacting headhunters as they are likely to know the current market price of your salary.
- Researching government websites. Although they generally give you national averages that could be quite different from your area, especially if you live in a large country, they can still be informative. If you are in the United States, you can use the following website to find the average wage of more than 800 professions: https://www.bls.gov/oes/current/oes_nat.htm#00-0000.

After this you must determine what you want. When negotiating a raise, try to set a salary range you would likely accept rather than a fixed figure. If you have a couple of years' experience and know that the salary range for your job in your area is between $60,000 per year at a junior level and $100,000 per year at a senior level, then you can expect a salary within a range of $70,000 to $80,000. Keep in mind what your company usually offers to other employees and determine if you deserve the same benefits. If you request more than one benefit, try to make it a package deal and state your desires clearly and their relative importance.

Another aspect to consider is the timing of your negotiation. Large corporations tend to have rules and set dates for assessing and negotiating their employees' salaries. In contrast, smaller corporations don't necessarily have a set date and employees can influence when the meeting takes place, which can significantly increase the chances of a successful negotiation. When the time of your negotiation is not set in stone and you can influence the date, you should make it when conditions are favorable for you. For example, if the company has just lost one of its three biggest customers because of a contracted job you worked on that's probably not the best time to ask for a raise. A timely moment to negotiate would be when the company is making good sales and you have just negotiated a new record contract with a customer. On the other hand, if you don't have a choice of date, but you know in advance when it will take place, you should double your efforts to finish essential projects just before that time.

You are often at a disadvantage when negotiating for the first time, and the solution to that issue is to practice. Ideally you could ask a colleague in the same company or a friend who manages salary negotiation to help you do this exercise. Negotiation is a skill—the more you practice the better you will get and the more confident you will be during the negotiation.

During this negotiation you will be asked several questions regarding your performance, role in the company, and key projects you have worked on. You can ask other employees how the negotiation process is typically conducted and the type of questions you will answer. Try to predict the questions they will ask you and be ready with an answer. Keep in mind the main reasons your employer should give you a raise and prepare a response with your main arguments.

4.3.2 The negotiation

To begin the negotiation, explain your case and why you believe you deserve a promotion. If you haven't worked in the company yet, state your skills, experiences, previous successes, and what you can bring to the company. If you have worked in that company, provide them with concrete figures and examples of your success. For instance, as a salesperson you can note how much money the company has made thanks to you. As an engineer you can talk about the technical progress you contributed to. As a chief financial officer you can point out the savings you delivered. Depending on your profession, bring proof and concrete evidence of what you have accomplished and what you plan to do in the future. At the end of the meeting, it should be clear to interviewer why you deserve this promotion.

During the negotiation you must show confidence and stay positive, even if the person is not receptive to your argumentation and the conversation is not going the way you want. If you don't show professionalism and confidence in your argument the company will not believe in you.

If you are interviewing for the job and not yet part of the company, you must keep in mind that you are competing with other candidates and that your salary could be a significant factor in their decision. However, this doesn't necessarily mean that you have to accept this position with the first figure they put on the table—your future employer should still pay what you are worth.

Be aware that the most critical salary you will negotiate is the first one you get in your company. After that, all your wage increases will be based on the current one. For example, if your company's competitors are paying 50% higher for the same position it won't be easy to ask for that kind of a raise after signing your contract.

A negotiation process is often a compromise from both parties rather than an outright demand for better salary and working conditions. It might be more advantageous for you to accept company benefits and lower your salary expectations. As your company purchases benefits in bulk, they have cost reductions you don't have. You could reduce your salary expectations in exchange for a smartphone and phone line worth $1,000 or a company car and fuel card worth $10,000 per year. It is generally much cheaper for the company to purchase these advantages rather than to give you the same amount in a salary increase. So such cases are a win-win situation for both parties. If you disagree with the offer you receive you should explain why you believe you are worth more. You could point out what a person in a similar position is earning, the key projects you took part in, the money you saved or brought to the company, and the positive changes you have implemented. In other words, all the positive ways you have impacted the company.

Not getting what you want in the first negotiation doesn't mean you can't get it in the next one. Keep in mind that you play the long game. Be sure to end the meeting positively and ask how you can improve in the future, what type of projects you can work on, and how you will be assessed for your next salary negotiation. If you know the criteria you are judged on you can work on those areas. It will be hard for the company to refuse you a raise if you fulfill and go beyond what is required of you.

It is always better to keep positive relationships by sending a thank-you note afterward. In this note, include the points you have discussed, the results, and future objectives you have set. Finally, thank them again for their time and show that you appreciate the opportunity to talk with them.

4.4 Key takeaways

To return to this chapter's essential points, you must remember that working as an employee shouldn't be a burden. You should be proud and like doing your job, which is why you must choose your career path carefully. There are multiple factors you must take into consideration: your personality and what you like to do, your skills and experience, your salary expectations, and the type of environment and responsibilities you like to take. You must always keep in mind your career objectives and what you want to achieve in the future as well.

Getting a job is always challenging. There isn't one perfect way that will always get you the dream job you feel you deserve. It requires hard work, and you need to find interesting opportunities by networking, going through agencies, job fairs, search platforms, or companies' websites.

When you get an interview for a position or negotiate a promotion, the key is preparation. You must know exactly what you want from this meeting and prepare in advance for the type of questions you will answer, and find countable data that puts you in the spotlight.

There isn't only one smooth path to career success and, as we have emphasized, it requires a lot of hard work. But the benefits you receive can be tremendous.

Chapter 5

Business

Starting and growing a business is not an easy task; it requires a lot of hard work. This chapter is intended for small business owners or people considering launching their own companies. It aims to inspire entrepreneurs to identify and apply economic theories to solve issues they face and take their business ideas or existing businesses to the next level. To do this, I explain the basics of establishing a company and some economic concepts in operations, marketing, and finance, and other useful theories that large organizations use on a daily basis, and then showcase those concepts by applying them to a small fruit juice business.

5.1 Establishing a company

Becoming an entrepreneur can be a tremendously rewarding experience. Unfortunately, many people establish their businesses without proper planning and thus face issues they aren't prepared for. Those entrepreneurs are following a project dear to their hearts and are driven by passion rather than reason. Don't get me wrong—an entrepreneur must be passionate to succeed. But they must also plan carefully to ensure the odds are on their side. Whatever your passion, it's not worth jeopardizing your future by not planning for success.

You can consider the following steps to help you establish your business.

1. *The idea*. It's an obvious step, but every business starts with an idea you are passionate about, whether it's to create a restaurant, an architect's office, or a new product that solves

a particular issue or revolutionizes the way we live. Whatever your project is you must start your business journey with an idea of what you want to do.

2. *Feasibility and viability.* One crucial measure many entrepreneurs fail to take is to determine the feasibility and profitability of their idea. This should be obvious, yet many people don't even take this basic step. To check the profitability of a project you simply need to create a budget with the expected income and expenditure. You should research the market and your competitors to determine your expected profit margins. If you realize that you can't make a profit on paper, you need to research other solutions to make the business viable, otherwise you won't be able to move forward with your business idea. Another factor to consider is the authorizations and legal requirements you must fulfill to create and execute the business. You must determine if you have permission to start this specific business. If you don't, you need to check how you can get them.

3. *Create a business plan.* This step is not mandatory, but highly advisable. If you are looking for external funding from angel investors, venture capitalists, or even banks you need to create a business plan. This is a formal document that outlines your objective, strategy, and financial projection. There is no unique format to business plans, but they often share a common structure with the following elements.

- *Executive summary.* A one-page description of the business plan; this is the only page potential investors read, and from this they decide if they will go further and invest in your project.

- *Business idea, product, and service.* Your vision and the product or service you want to create.

- *Operation.* How you plan to create and sell your product or service.

- *Marketing.* Your marketing strategy and targeted customers.
- *Finance.* Your cost and sales projections.
- *Exit door.* The first thing investors look for when investing in a business is a way out; you must outline how they will get their money back.

This document is not only useful to get funding, but it also helps you reflect and plan on your business idea.

4. *Formalize the business.* Once you have planned everything and are confident with the execution moving forward you must formalize your business by legally establishing it. Consider which legal form your business should have based on its activity and your capacity. You also need to check with the local authority about the steps and requirements necessary to establish your business.
5. *Get to work.* Once you have been through all these steps you must roll up your sleeves and get to work.

There is, of course, no such thing as a complete list of steps to follow that ensures your business's success. But the more prepared you are the higher your chances of succeeding.

5.2 Operation and management

This section explores some management principles that revolutionized the twentieth century by changing how companies produce goods. Taylorism, Fordism, and lean management: these techniques are considered the classics of management and focus entirely on maximizing the production process. I have selected these three principles because they build directly on one another. Frederick Taylor introduced task-based specialization, Henry Ford improved this system by creating the assembly line, and the Toyota company brought it to the next level by developing lean management and continuously improving its production process.

My goal is not to convince you to copy these management methods exactly, but encourage you to take inspiration from them or find other management theories that can help improve your business. As an entrepreneur you constantly face issues, so you need to learn from those who have already faced the same problems before. I hope this discussion can motivate you to find solutions and theories to help you. As Henry Ford put it: "I invented nothing new. I simply assembled ... the discoveries of other men behind whom were centuries of work."

5.2.1 Taylorism

At the end of the nineteenth century, Frederick Taylor was a consultant who visited companies to improve their production processes. He realized early on that workers were undertaking jobs their own way and customized them for each buyer. Taylor saw this manufacturing process as wasteful and decided to improve it.

One of Taylor's methods to improve productivity was by dividing a job into specialized tasks. He timed each task and calculated how many motions were necessary to perform them. He then determined the most efficient way that minimized the time and movements required to complete each task. For example, when visiting a brick company, Taylor saw workers bending down to pick up and place five-pound bricks, which was a significant waste of time and effort as each worker would have to perform that motion a thousand times a day. So Taylor decided that lower-paid workers should place those bricks on a shelf at hand level to reduce the time and motion necessary for the higher-paid workers to pick them up and place them. Although individual changes did not account for much at the beginning, they quickly added up over time, and the final results were staggering. Before, workers placed about 120 bricks per hour. After Taylor's training, they placed 350 bricks per hour. In other words, one person could now do the same amount of work as three workers.

Taylor also emphasized the creation of specialized tools to achieve the best results. For example, one day he asked workers to dig a pile of dirt. He then measured how much time it took them to shovel it away. The next day he slightly changed the shovel's head size to see how much time it took them. He repeated this experiment until he was confident he found the perfectly sized shovel to perform the task most effectively.

Finally, Taylor proposed that workers be paid based on their daily production and not working time. This encouraged workers to be more efficient as they would be paid more if they produced more units. He also emphasized workers' training on a specific task to specialize and improve their productivity. As a result, his system rewarded and trained only the best performers. The idea was to increase the production level by motivation and getting specialized employees to do specific tasks.

Now let's take a concrete example of an orange juice company about to set up a new production factory. This company can apply Taylor's methods to improve productivity in a number of ways.

- Dividing the production process into small, specialized tasks to study and develop a more efficient way to perform them and improve the production process over time.

- Creating specialized tools, such as juice pressers, that are adapted to the company's fruit size.

- Offering special training to improve their employees' productivity.

5.2.2 Fordism

In the early twentieth century, inspired by Taylor's methods, Henry Ford revolutionized the automobile and manufacturing industries worldwide. His idea was to create a car that was affordable for everyone. It was a big challenge at the time as every car was handmade and only the wealthiest could purchase them.

To accomplish his goal, Ford completely changed the production methods of the time by creating the assembly line, where workers stayed at the same place, always making the same motions while products moved toward them. The assembly line determined the working pace, everyone in the factory moved at the same speed, and no one could stop the production process. Everything was standardized and mass-produced, which drastically reduced production costs. In 1908, before the assembly line and standardization revolution, it took 12 hours to produce a car that cost about $825. By 1924 it only took a bit more than an hour and a half and cost $290 per car. Ford became the father of standardization and is famous for saying, "Any customer can have a car painted any color that he wants, so long as it is black."

Working conditions were hard because the operating speed was much more intense than in other factories, so Ford almost doubled the hourly wages of his workers to ensure he didn't lack a workforce. These higher wages, along with his cheaper prices, incentivized Ford's workers to buy his mass-produced cars. He was giving money out of one hand and receiving a portion back in the other, simultaneously creating mass production and consumption.

Fordism had a major impact on manufacturing and is still very much alive today, as you can see the application of his principles in factories worldwide. Although robots now often replace humans, Ford's company is still employing people on their assembly lines.

To come back to the juice factory example, they can improve their production process in the following ways.

- Creating an assembly line where the fruits and bottles are moving without any human input to ensure a constant production speed.
- Modernizing the assembly line with machinery whenever possible.
- Offering employees stocks options or bonuses to incentivize them to stay in the company for a longer period of time and doing everything they can to improve their productivity, as they directly benefit from the company's success.

5.2.3 Lean management

The next management revolution also came from the automobile industry. In 1937 Kiichiro Toyoda established the Toyota company after a visit to the United States, where he witnessed the genius application of Ford on assembly lines. Toyoda wanted to introduce this industrial revolution to Japan. However, the system could only be partially replicated as there were many differences between the two countries. The United States was resource-rich and had much space, so it could mass-produce material and easily store years of supplies in advance. Japan, by contrast, had limited space and few natural resources. So instead of copying Ford's model, Toyoda adapted and improved it by creating the just-in-time model where production followed demand.

Toyoda's principles evolved over the years to create what is known today as lean management. This model is not set in stone and it is still in constant evolution. What Toyota, as a manufacturer, brought to the world is an approach to continuous improvement by implementing small changes that enhance the quality and efficiency of the production process. This approach is not only used in automobile manufacturing but in all kinds of sectors: Boeing uses it for its assembly line; it is applied in hospitals to reduce waiting time in operating rooms; and Intel employs it to improve the production process of its components.

One of the core principles of lean management is to reduce wasteful activities that don't add value to the product: transportation, unnecessary waste, movement, inventory, overproduction, waiting time, or defective goods. You can drastically improve productivity and profitability by continuously reducing those wasteful activities.

The juice company can apply those principles in its new factory as follows.

- Implementing a culture that promotes continuous improvement in the production process by rewarding employees that find new solutions and improve productivity.

- Finding ways to reduce time wasted in transporting the goods, finding alternative use for the fruit pulp and seeds that are usually discarded in the production process, create a more efficient production line that reduces waiting time, and so on.

5.3 Marketing

Even if you have the best product or service in the world your business may fail if you can't market it correctly. That's why it's crucial to have a marketing team that defines a strategy to help your company sell its goods. In this section, we go through three well-known analytical tools to help you build a marketing strategy.

5.3.1 Marketing mix

The marketing mix is a framework initially developed by E. Jerome McCarthy (1960). This tool helps companies develop marketing strategies by considering essential factors. Originally there were only four elements: products, price, place, and promotion. Over the years, three new elements were introduced to the framework: people, process, and physical evidence. The marketing mix is often referred to as the 7Ps.

Product. The first P refers to the product or service, its features, customer benefits, and so on. Before launching a new product, you must consider what your customers need and want from this specific item. You must then look at what you sell, its quality, design, technology, warranty, and accessories. Is your product precisely what your customers are looking for? How does your product differ from the competition?

Price. The second P indicates the price of your product or service. Once you understand the product you offer it's easier to put a price tag on it. There are various ways you can fix the price. You can look at your competitors' prices and align with them, fix a premium price with additional services, or offer a discounted price for large quantities. Consider what your customers are willing to pay for your product and how they perceive its value and react to its price. A cheap product might be seen as low quality. In contrast, an expensive product might be viewed as luxurious. The price therefore directly impacts what people think of your product and brand.

Place. The third P concerns where you sell your product and how your customers purchase it. In marketing, location is where your customers can find and purchase your product: in a shop, at wholesalers, at pop-up events, or on your website. Whatever means you choose, you must ensure that your target customers can easily find and access it. If you target elderly people for a product, advertising your website on TikTok is not a good idea. On the other hand, if you target teenagers and young adults, then that might be a suitable platform. Your selling strategy is strongly impacted by your location as you must consider local customers' tastes, preferences, beliefs, and what your competitors offer.

Promotion. The fourth P is all about your sales techniques and tactics used to sell your product. When developing a sales strategy, you must consider how you communicate with and reach your target customers. Should you create adverts in newspapers, radio slots, or television? Should you send sales representatives to meet your customers? Should you create promotional activities? Should you communicate via social media? The type of promotional strategy very much depends on your target customers and how you can effectively reach them to achieve a sale.

People. The fifth P has to do with all the people who are part of or represent your company, those who create the product, sell it, or deal with customer service. Your employees are the face of your company. How they interact with customers, explain your product, and answer problems plays a crucial role in building your brand.

Process. The sixth P includes all the actions and processes your company develops to create and deliver the product to the customer. Having an efficient process in place improves your sales, customer's overall experience, but also your productivity.

Physical evidence. The seventh P is the proof that your company is a legitimate business. Pieces of evidence can take various forms: the office, the factory, the brand (logo, social media, advertising), or transaction documentation (receipts, order confirmations, invoices). These elements reassure your customers that you are a legitimate business and that they are safe to purchase your products.

Let's apply these principles to the juice producer that is developing its marketing strategy.

- *Product.* Our product is a premium orange juice sold in a stylized bottle. We only use organic oranges without additives in the juice.
- *Place.* Our juice can be bought online on a subscription base. The company has also partnered with high-brand supermarkets and bespoke restaurants. Our factory benefits from its proximity to a popular harbor for cruise liners where hundreds of tourists visit the factory and buy juice each day.
- *Price.* Our juice is sold at a premium price compared to other brands, but it is still not the highest price tag on the market. It is possible to buy it at a discount directly from the factory.
- *Promotion.* A lot of our advertising targets local and international tourists. The company has deals with local tourist agencies that promote their products directly to tourists coming to the region.
- *People.* Our workers are all local and passionate about the long-standing tradition in the area of producing fruit juices.
- *Process.* People can easily buy our products online and customers on subscriptions don't have to do anything as the products are immediately delivered to their door.
- *Physical evidence.* The factory is a tourist attraction—there is a restaurant, a bar, and a beautiful orchard people can visit.

Having applied the 7P framework, you now have a much better idea of where your company stands, the type of customer it targets, and what it should focus on. In this case, the company should continue to focus on local tourists with its partnership with tourist agencies and propose a guided tour of the factory and special offers with hotels. For local people, the company can promote the benefit of the subscription program by sending ads by physical mail or social media campaigns.

5.3.2 SWOT

SWOT is an acronym for strengths, weaknesses, opportunities, and threats. The SWOT framework is one of the most popular marketing tools used to help organizations analyze their position in a specific market and visualize the internal and external factors that affect their business model.

Internal factors are the elements inherent to the company itself—its strengths and weaknesses (Table 5.1).

Table 5.1 Marketing: internal strengths and weaknesses

Strengths	Weaknesses
• Company's unique qualities that give it a competitive advantage	• Areas where the company is not performing well
• *Examples*: market share, efficiency, brand recognition	• *Examples*: profitability, key performance indicators, lack of resources, outdated technology, bad reputation

External factors are the aspects outside of the company's control—its opportunities and threats (Table 5.2).

Table 5.2 Marketing: external opportunities and threats

Opportunities	Threats
• Chances the company can seize	• Risks that can potentially harm the company
• *Examples*: positive market trends, new technology that helps reduce costs, high demand for the product, lack of competitors	• *Examples*: new legislation, new competitors penetrating the market, climate change, inflation

When performing a SWOT analysis, you should only include the most critical elements that affect your business model. For example, a giant asteroid coming to Earth is a significant threat to your organization. But it is also highly unlikely and there is not much you can do to avoid it anyway. On the other hand, a competitor setting up a new shop near yours is a threat that you have to appropriately take into consideration in your marketing strategy. The idea is to visualize the market conditions that your business evolves in to help you develop a strategy. For that purpose, you must keep your SWOT analysis simple and relevant. When examining these factors, a company can develop a strategy to seize opportunities, address threats, build on its strengths, and manage its weaknesses.

Now let's apply the SWOT framework to the juice producer as summarized in Table 5.3.

Table 5.3 SWOT analysis: fruit juice company

	Strengths	Weaknesses
Internal factors	• The juice is well recognized and appreciated by every customer	• Understaffed
	• Good location appealing to local tourists	• Only one product
External factors	Opportunities	Threats
	• Possibility to create more revenue from local tourism	• A new competitor nearby is selling apple juice
	• Possibility to export juice thanks to proximity to the harbor	• Local government might impose a new tax on beverages

From this SWOT, we can conclude that the company has a great product but has not reached its full potential, as it can still export and expand its activity with local tourism. In addition, it is currently understaffed and only has one product.

Thanks to this SWOT, we have spotted some threats and opportunities that we can try to take advantage of. In this case, the company could acquire the apple juice producer and not only eliminate a competitor but also extend its offer by selling a new product.

5.3.3 PESTLE

PESTLE is a framework used to assess political, economic, social, technological, environmental, and legal factors that can impact a company. It can help an organization to prepare for external dynamics that affect the company's business and develop a strategy to take advantage of those opportunities and shield against those threats.

- *Political.* Factors related to politics, such as government, laws, grants, conflict, free trade agreements between countries and regional blocs, industry regulation, corruption, and political instability.
- *Economic.* Considerations associated with the economy, such as interest rates, consumer spending, exchange rates, inflation, and unemployment rates.
- *Social.* Elements related to society, such as demographic change, religion, consumer taste, culture, and beliefs.
- *Technological.* Technical features related to innovation, such as production process or a new technology that can disturb the market.
- *Legal.* Points concerning the law and regulation, such as health laws, environmental regulations, safety laws, and minimum wage legislation.
- *Environmental.* Aspects related to the environment, such as sustainability requirements, pollution, recycling necessity, waste management, and energy efficiency.

The PESTLE framework for the juice company is as follows.

- *Political.* The company is in Spain, the government is stable, and there is no corruption that directly impacts its activity. However, the local authority might create a new tax on beverages.
- *Economic.* There is a high unemployment rate in the region and many companies are facing solvency issues.

- *Social.* Local people take great pride in the juice brand.
- *Technological.* There is no new technological revolution that would impact the sector.
- *Legal.* There are no new, stricter legal regulations that would impact the company's activity. It's an easy environment to acquire other companies.
- *Environmental.* The company received an award because it helps promote sustainable agriculture.

It is, of course, a condensed version of a PESTLE analysis, but you must have realized that some of its elements are also present in the SWOT framework. We concluded earlier that it would be a good opportunity to acquire a competitor; from this PESTLE, we can also see that the tough economic situation and the permissive legal environment might make it easier to do so. Furthermore, due to the high unemployment rate and the fact that the brand is appreciated by local people, it should be straightforward for the company to hire new staff.

5.4 Finance

Many people shut down when discussing finance, scared by the prospect of complicated calculations and endless spreadsheets. However, the basics of finance and accounting are simple if you look at each element individually. It's like opening a car hood to look inside. At first everything seems complicated, but it all makes sense when you start to understand each component and how they relate to each other.

This section guides you through the basics of accounting. Keep in mind that it is crucial to understand these principles in order to invest in the stock market.

5.4.1 Financial statements

Financial statements are comprehensive reports of the business activity and performance of a company. When reading them, you can understand what a company has been through and get hints about its strategy moving forward.

Although the law differs from country to country, generally speaking public companies are required to publish their financial statements every quarter while private companies don't have to disclose their results publicly and need only submit their results once a year to the local authority. When reporting to the local authority, both public and private companies must provide a financial statement, which consists of three reports: the balance sheet, income statement, and cash flow statement.

What I am about to explain usually takes up entire books, so this is a very condensed and simplified version of accounting; it is in no way an exhaustive explanation. My goal is to give you a very basic understanding of financial reports. That won't give you the necessary knowledge to write them yourself, but simply to read and understand them.

5.4.2 Balance sheet

A *balance sheet* is a statement of a company's assets, liabilities, and shareholders' equities at a specific date. In other words, it's a report that shows what a company owns and owes. The balance sheet has two sections.

- *Assets*. Everything the company owns, such as land, equipment, pattern, or raw materials.
- *Liabilities and shareholders' equity*. Everything the company owes, such as debt and the ownership stake shareholders have in the company.

The balance sheet is classified from the most liquid to the least liquid. Liquidity in finance refers to how rapidly you can transform an asset or a liability into cash. For example, stocks can easily be exchanged for cash, but it would take much more time to sell a car for cash. The balance sheet is generally represented in a table and contains the following elements (Table 5.4).

Table 5.4 Balance sheet: assets and liabilities

Assets All the resources a company owns	Liabilities All the debts a company owes
Cash and cash equivalents The cash a company has on hand—includes petty cash and also money in the bank account; any cash that is immediately available to the company	**Accounts payable** All the invoices received but not yet paid **Accrued liabilities** Products and services the company has used, but that the supplier has not yet invoiced
Marketable securities Investments in stocks, bonds, ETFs, and mutual funds that can be quickly sold off for cash	**Customer prepayments** Payments and deposits made by customers for products and services not yet provided
Prepaid expenses Invoices from suppliers that have already been paid but the products or services haven't yet been delivered	**Taxes payable** Taxes the company must pay **Short-term debt** Debts that must be paid within a year
Accounts receivables Invoices that the company issued to its customers but haven't yet been paid	**Long-term debt** Debts that must be paid in more than a year
Inventories Stock of raw materials, works in progress, and products ready to be sold	**Shareholders' equity** Shareholders' ownership in the company **Stocks** Value of all shares the company has sold
Long-term investments Land, plant, vehicles, equipment, big machinery—any tangible assets of significant value that are not immediately transformable into cash	**Retained earnings** Amount of profit or loss the company has generated
Intangible assets Assets that don't have a physical form—patents, royalties, trademarks, and any others that have a significant value	**Treasury stocks** Amount of money the company has paid to buy back its shares

When calculating the total value of your assets and liabilities, both sides of the tables must be equal. In other words, they must balance, which is why this report is called a balance sheet.

Now let's have a closer look the balance sheet of the fruit juice producer (Table 5.5).

Table 5.5 Balance sheet: fruit juice company

Assets	Amount ($)	Liabilities	Amount ($)
Cash and cash equivalents	50,000	Accounts payable	10,000
Marketable securities	10,000	Accrued liabilities	10,000
Prepaid expenses	15,000	Customer prepayments	5,000
Accounts receivables	10,000	Taxes payable	10,000
Inventories	30,000	Short-term debt	35,000
Long-term investments	300,000	Long-term debt	205,000
Intangible assets	10,000	Shareholders' equity	110,000
		Stocks	0
		Retained earnings	140,000
		Treasury stocks	0
Total assets	525,000	Total liabilities	525,000

From the balance sheet, you can see that the juice company has a lot of cash on hand and a relatively low level of debt compared to the value of its assets. The company has a solid financial foundation and could take a loan if it decided to acquire a competitor, as we have seen in the marketing section earlier.

5.4.3 Income statement

An *income statement* shows the company's income and expenses during a specific period. It is used to determine if a company has made a profit or loss. The income statement is generally represented in a table and contains the following elements (Table 5.6). This is then applied to the fruit juice company (Table 5.7).

Table 5.6 Income statement

Total revenue or sales
All the sales and revenue from the company

Cost of goods sold (COGS)
All the direct costs necessary to produce the product or service sold, including raw materials and direct labor

Gross profit
The total revenue minus the cost of goods sold

Selling, general, and administration (SG&A)
All the indirect costs necessary to run the business—marketing expenses, office employee salaries, insurance costs

Earnings before interest, taxes, depreciation, and amortization (EBITDA)
This is calculated by subtracting the SG&A from the company's gross profit

Depreciation and amortization
Long-term assets are used and need to be replaced over time—this category represents the loss of value of long-term assets over time

Earnings before interest and taxes (EBIT) or operating income
Calculated by subtracting depreciation and amortization from EBITDA

Interest expenses
Interest the company pays on its loans

Tax expenses
Taxes the company pays

Net revenue or loss
The company's results are calculated by subtracting the interest and expenses from the operating income
If the result is positive the company makes a profit; if the result is negative the company makes a loss

Table 5.7 Income statement: fruit juice company

Income statement	Amount ($)
Total revenues	**500,000.00**
Cost of goods sold	240,000.00
Gross profit	**260,000.00**
Selling, general, and administration	95,000.00
Research and development	—
Total operating expenses	**95,000.00**
EBITDA	165,000.00
Depreciation and amortization	10,000.00
EBIT	**155,000.00**
Interest expenses	5,000.00
EBT	**150,000.00**
Tax expenses	10,000.00
Net income	**140,000.00**

From this income statement, we can see that the company sold $500,000 worth of juice. It paid $240,000 in oranges, water, and direct labor costs. Therefore, the total gross profit is $500,000 minus the COGS of $240,000 which equals $260,000. Regarding expenses, the company paid $95,000 in rent, employee salaries and marketing expenses. When deducting all those operating expenses from the gross profit, we get an EBITDA of $165,000. All the materials and equipment must lose value over time and be amortized, which is evaluated at $10,000. Finally, any successful business has to pay taxes which amount to $10,000. We can see that the business had a net revenue of $140,000 after taxes.

5.4.4 Cash flow statement

A *cash flow statement* is a report showing the movement of cash in and out of the company during a specific period. This statement shows you where the money comes from and where it goes. With this statement you can understand how the company earns and uses its money. The three components of the cash flow statement are as follows in Table 5.8. This is then applied to the cash flow statement of the fruit juice company (Table 5.9).

Table 5.8 Cash flow statement

Cash flow from operating activities
Cash generated and used from the company's main operation, the most important source of cash—includes income from goods and services sold, salary payments, and so on

Cash flow from investing activities
Cash generated and used from the company's investing activity—includes stocks, bonds, land

Cash from financing activities
Cash generated and used from funding the company—includes debt issues, interest paid, selling shares of the company, dividend payments

Table 5.9 Cash flow statement: fruit juice company

Item	Amount ($)
Cash flow from operating activities	
Net income	140,000.00
Depreciation	10,000.00
Increase in accounts receivable	−5,000.00
Decrease in prepaid expenses	−5,000.00
Decrease in accounts payable	−10,000.00
Cash provided (used) in operating activities	**130,000.00**
Cash flow from investing activities	
Purchase of marketable securities	−10,000.00
Purchase of property	−70,000.00
Cash provided (used) by investing activities	**−80,000.00**
Cash flow from financing activities	
Proceeds from issuing debt	10,000.00
Dividend payment	−20,000.00
Cash provided (used) by financing activities	**−10,000.00**
Net increase in cash	**40,000.00**
Cash at the beginning of the year	10,000.00
Cash at the end of the year	**50,000.00**

From the company's cash flow statement, we can see that it used most of its cash by investing in properties and marketable securities. It's a sign that the company invests heavily in expanding its activities.

5.5 Other useful theories

5.5.1 Vertical and horizontal integration

There are different ways large corporations get even bigger, create economies of scale, and increase their profits. One of these processes is called vertical and horizontal integration. In *vertical integration*, a company acquires a supplier or a distributor in the same production chain and takes over one production process. The company is therefore cutting out the middleman, integrating its margin, reducing duplicate costs, and creating new opportunities.

Let's take the hypothetical example of the orange juice producer. To produce 1 liter of juice the producer needs 2 kilograms of whole oranges (because they need to filter the seeds, pulp, and skin). So the juice producer buys oranges at $2 per 2 kilograms from a nearby orange producer, who takes a $1 profit in the transaction. In a vertical integration situation, the juice producer acquires the orange producer and integrates its production within its own activity. This reduces the cost of raw materials from $2 to $1 as well as having the potential to further reduce expenditure (duplicate staff, redundant machinery, and so on). The juice producer could also create opportunities that wouldn't have been possible otherwise. For example, it could open its production sites and orangery to tourism and sell some of its juice directly to customers. Another way to vertically integrate is to go down the production line and cut some of the distributor sales by selling directly to customers via a website.

Another possible way to expand a corporation is via *horizontal integration*. Instead of acquiring companies down the production line, a company can acquire competitors in the same or similar industries to extend market coverage.

To carry on with our example, let's imagine that the orange juice producer now acquires an apple producer to create apple juice and diversify its production. It can now sell two products and reduce competition by integrating the apple producer that sells a complementary product.

Vertical and horizontal integration can potentially give you significant advantages.

- *Economies of scale through cost reduction.* By integrating another company, you might end up with duplicate staff costs, machinery, and programs.
- *New opportunities.* Integrating another company could bring new developments that weren't possible before.
- *Extend market coverage and grow in size.* This in turn gives you more power over your suppliers and customers.
- *Reduce competition.* This is achieved by integrating other companies instead of competing with them.

However, vertical and horizontal integration also comes with challenges.

- *Cultural.* When integrating another company, you are bringing a new work culture into an existing one, which could create tensions between workers.
- *Change.* People usually don't welcome change, especially when the company plans to lay off some staff.

In a nutshell, although vertical and horizontal integration offers challenges, it also provides excellent competitive advantages that even small businesses should consider.

5.5.2 The 80/20 principle

One fascinating framework entrepreneurs can easily apply to their companies is the 80/20 principle, also known as the law of the vital few or the principle of factor sparsity. It was initially an observation made by the Italian economist Vilfredo Pareto and has been more recently popularized by Richard Koch (1998) in his book *The 80/20 Principle*. The principle states that 20% of the inputs create

80% of the outcomes. In other words, a small number of causes produce disproportionate consequences. Koch offers many real-life examples of this principle in action: 80% of the world's carbon dioxide (CO_2) pollution comes from 20% of its sources; 80% of website traffic comes from 20% of the content; 80% of crimes are committed by 20% of the criminals.

However, this data must be taken with a pinch of salt as all these examples are observations of specific cases. It is not a great law of the universe stating that everything has a perfect 80/20 correlation. What is true is that we can often find a minority of causes that create a disproportionate amount of results. In the United States, 10% of the population owns 70% of the country's wealth; 2% of the search engines are responsible for 96% of online searches; and less than 10% of drinkers account for 50% of alcohol consumption.

As an entrepreneur, you can use this theory to your benefit. You can improve your time management and focus on the 20% effort that creates 80% of the results, optimize your benefits by focusing on the 20% of customers that account for 80% of your total margin, and find alternatives to what accounts for 80% of your costs. Keep in mind that the idea is not to have an exact 80/20 ratio but to focus on the inputs with disproportionate results.

This principle is used not only by companies to increase their profits, but also by non-profit organizations to provide solutions to our planet's biggest problems. For example, the Ocean Cleanup organization found that just one thousand rivers are responsible for roughly 80% of riverine plastic pollution. Instead of trying to clean up all the oceans and rivers in the world, their goal is to focus on the leading causes and answer these problems. They have created the interceptor, a 100% solar-powered barge that acts as a filter so that plastics and other rubbish are trapped and don't flow into the ocean. With this solution, Ocean Cleanup wants to have interceptors in each of those thousand rivers by 2025 and hopes to catch 80% of the world's water-based plastic pollution before it gets into the ocean. This is an excellent example of applying the 20/80 principle, focusing on the leading causes to create significant results.

5.6 Key takeaways

This chapter's objective has been to help you start or grow your business. By looking at operations, marketing, finance, and other useful theories, we have only scratched the surface of the possibilities open to you. You can certainly get inspiration from Taylorism, Fordism, or lean management to improve your operation. You can perform several marketing analyses like 7P, SWOT, and PESTLE to help you develop your sales strategy. And you can analyze your financial statement to help you evaluate and optimize your financial situation.

As an entrepreneur, you must learn from your predecessors and look for solutions to the problems you face, and this is why I am encouraging you to look at those theories and answers that already exist and can help you grow your business.

Chapter 6

Financial Assets

Investing in the stock market is often associated with big headlines of people earning or losing tremendous amounts of money overnight, traders in suits shouting at each other to buy or sell stocks, and companies losing the market value of a country's gross domestic product (GDP) over a trading day. In other words, investing in the stock market is correlated with excitement. Some people love it, some hate it, and there are often strong feelings about it.

Although it can be volatile, as fortunes are made and lost overnight, there is no denying that investing in the stock market has significant advantages.

- *Performance*. The annualized return over the long run is quite attractive. Historically, the S&P 500 (the 500 biggest companies in the United States) has increased annually by roughly 10%, although this growth has come with many ups and downs.[1]

---

[1] The 10% average growth I am referring to differs from a set figure, as the market fluctuates constantly. Furthermore, as the market shifts, that growth rate will depend to a great extent on the stock market's value on the day you start to invest and its value when you stop. For example:
- July 2012–July 2022: S&P 500 grew by an average of 12.9% per year
- January 2012–January 2022: S&P 500 grew by an average of 15.5% per year
- July 2002–July 2022: S&P 500 grew by an average of 9.5% per year
- July 1992–July 2022: S&P500 grew by an average of 9.7% per year

As you can see, the growth rate constantly fluctuates, which is why I prefer to give a rough estimation rather than a set figure that will change next month.

- *Accessibility and low barrier to entrance.* There are generally not many requirements to invest in the stock market. You simply need a bank account, a computer, and an internet connection to open a brokerage account and start investing online. Further, you don't need tens of thousands of dollars to start investing and can even buy stocks at $1.
- *Liquidity.* Unlike other physical assets like real estate or art, financial assets are notoriously easy to buy and sell at a moment's notice—all it takes are a couple of clicks.
- *Flexibility.* You can be active or passive when investing; you can have revenue from capitalization or dividends; you can have an aggressive or defensive strategy. In other words, you can adapt your investing strategy to your needs and plans.

For all these reasons, I believe that investing in the stock market is an excellent opportunity that many should consider in their investment plan, instead of dismissing the possibility because of personal bias.

Although some people might be afraid to invest because they lack the necessary knowledge, you don't need to be an expert and know everything about the stock market to invest wisely. It's like driving a car—you don't necessarily need to know all the mechanics to go from point A to point B. However, you need at least some minimal knowledge so you won't crash into the first wall you come cross. In this chapter, I provide you with the knowledge you need before investing in the stock market.

People often correlate investing in the stock market with assets like stocks. However, that is only one asset you can invest in. There is actually a much broader picture to consider. The type of assets you invest in depends on the time and effort you want to put into your investing strategy, risk tolerance, and plan. As such, you shouldn't buy something because someone tells you to; you should buy it because it makes sense in your investment plan and answers your needs.

In this chapter, we first cover basic information about the stock market, then we move deeper into financial assets such as exchange-traded funds (ETFs), mutual funds, stocks, and bonds.

6.1   The basics

To ensure that you start your investment journey on a solid foundation, I explain the essential information you need to know before investing in the stock market.

6.1.1   Stock market

The stock market is a collection of stock exchanges where investors can buy and sell financial assets. Today most trades are made online, and the vast majority are made by robots that can buy millions of dollars' worth of assets in a fraction of a second. The stock market has a long history and is very different today than at its origins.

- Its birth can be traced back to the fifteenth century in what is today Belgium, where merchants traded individual bonds and goods.
- The first stock trading came later, in the early seventeenth century in Amsterdam. At that time, the Dutch East India Company was the first and only publicly traded company accessible to the public.
- The New York Stock Exchange was established in 1792.
- The Dow Jones Industrial Average was created in 1896.
- An early version of the S&P 500 appeared in 1923.

As you can see, the stock market is not something new. It has evolved over the centuries and it is far from the general idea of a room crowded with people shouting "buy" or "sell" while frenetically waving papers. Today most countries have one or several stock exchanges where investors can purchase financial assets and you can invest from the comfort of your home with a computer and internet connection.

6.1.2 Definitions

Below you can find the definition of the financial assets we will discuss in the following chapters.

Stocks and *shares* are synonyms; they are a title of partial ownership in a company. By owning a stock, you are a shareholder and effectively co-owner of that company. As such, you profit from the company's growth and are entitled to voting rights and dividends.

Bonds are debt issued by governments, institutions, or corporations to finance their activity. Investors lend those institutions money for a period of time and receive it back with interest at the end of the borrowing period.

An *index* tracks the market performance of various companies. It is used as a market indicator or benchmark to compare portfolio performance. Here are some examples.

- The S&P 500 measures the performances of the 500 biggest companies in the United States.

- The Dow Jones Industrial Average measures the performances of 30 specific companies in the United States.

- The BEL20 measures the performances of the 20 biggest companies in Belgium.

If you are an investor, you can use these indexes as a benchmark and compare them with your portfolio to see how you perform.

An *exchange-traded fund* (ETF) is a financial asset that aims to replicate a specific index's performance. ETFs do this by purchasing the same assets the index includes such as stocks or bonds. By investing in an ETF you create a portfolio of diversified assets that follows a specific index. It also ensures that your investment closely follows its performance.

Mutual funds are a financial asset managed by an investment company that gathers money from many investors and uses that fund to create a diversified portfolio of various assets such as stocks, bonds, options, or commodities. Investing in mutual funds is a great way to create an investment portfolio managed by professional investors.

6.1.3 Private versus public companies

There are two types of companies. The first type are *public companies* that are publicly traded, meaning everyone can own, buy, and sell their shares and bonds on the stock market. This is how those corporations can raise their capital. Well-known examples include companies like Apple, Microsoft, Tesla, or Amazon. In contrast, *private companies* are generally owned by a handful of people or institutions, and their shares can't be freely exchanged on the stock market. Well-known examples include companies like Aldi, Huawei, or Ikea.

Most companies start private before going public on the stock market. The most common way for a company to go public is through a process called an *initial public offering* (IPO), where a company issues shares and sells them to the public. In doing so they sell ownership of the company to the public. Companies go through an IPO mainly to raise funds and use the proceeds to finance their activity. As a public company they can sell bonds directly to the stock market to raise even more funds.

In December 2020, Airbnb issued 51.5 million shares at $68 per share and sold them on the stock market to raise $3.5 billion. After this date, anyone could buy shares on the stock market and be a co-owner of the company. However, once a company sells its shares it won't receive any money from further exchanges of those shares as they don't own them anymore.

The share price on the IPO is arbitrary. However, companies tend to have a low entry IPO price to make the stock more accessible to the public because more people can buy a stock at $10 per share rather than $10,000 per share.

6.1.4 Supply and demand

The price of goods and services is determined by supply and demand. When the price of goods increases, if all other factors remain the same, demand for these goods decreases as people won't be able to afford as much and could buy a substitute product at a lower price. Let's say the cost of an apple is $1. If the next day the price doubles to $2, people will buy fewer apples and might instead buy oranges or pears. If the price decreases, let's say to $0.50, people will be able to afford more apples and be willing to buy more. The demand for apples will therefore increase. In a nutshell, you can find the following relationships:

- Price of goods increases ⇨ demand for these goods decreases
- Price of goods decreases ⇨ demand for these goods increases
- Demand for goods increases ⇨ price for these goods increases
- Demand for goods decreases ⇨ price for these goods decreases

This law is pivotal in the stock market as good news about a company can trigger much interest, resulting in high demand for a particular stock and an increase in its price. By contrast, if there is bad news many people will want to sell their shares simultaneously, decreasing the stock price. The law of supply and demand is the reason why the price of stocks is constantly changing. As such, you must always keep this principle in mind when investing and don't take sudden increases or decreases in price as a reflection of a company's long-term value.

6.1.5 Market capitalization

Market capitalization represents a company's value on the stock market. It is calculated by multiplying the company's stock price by the total number of shares outstanding (the number of shares held by all its shareholders). Since it is based on the current market price, the market capitalization of companies changes every trading day. For example, a company with one million shares is trading today at $10.5 per share. It therefore has a market capitalization of $10.5 million. But tomorrow, if the stock price increases to $11 per share, the company's market capitalization will be $11 million.

When you read in a newspaper that a company lost 10% of its value overnight or that a specific company dropped $10 billion of its market capitalization, this doesn't mean that those companies have lost this money and had to pay for it. It simply means that the stock price fell and so did its market capitalization. If shareholders decide to keep their holdings everything would stay the same for them. On the other hand, if they choose to sell those shares on that day, they would receive 10% less cash than if they had sold on the previous day.

Companies have been categorized by size. This is an important concept to understand as it gives you an idea of a company's significance. But note that the market capitalization figure I am giving as an example is as of today's writing and it will therefore fluctuate over time.

- Mega caps: > $200 billion. These are the largest companies by market capitalization, such as Apple ($2,590 billion), Microsoft ($2,097 billion) Amazon ($1,091 billion), and Tesla ($514 billion). Those valuations are mind-blowing and are even more significant than the GDP of entire countries: Netherlands ($1,018 billion), Saudi Arabia ($833 billion), and Thailand ($506 billion).

- Large caps: $10 billion–$200 billion. TotalEnergies ($144 billion), Starbucks ($125 billion), and AT&T ($124 billion).

- Mid caps: $2 billion–$10 billion. Banco de Chile ($9.80 billion), The New York Times Company ($6.45 billion), and XPO Logistics ($4.95 billion).

- Small caps: $300 million–$2 billion. Jack in the Box ($1.85 billion), Nano Dimension ($605 million), and Jumia ($304 million).

- Micro caps: $50 million–$300 million. Frontier Acquisition ($299 million), Sergeferrari ($175 million), and Arlington Asset Investment Corp ($79.4 million).

- Nano caps: < $50 million. Koss ($42 million), Recon Technology ($13 million), and Nova Lifestyle ($4 million).

6.1.6 Ticker, ISIN

The same company can have different financial assets available on the stock market. To ensure that investors can adequately identify an asset they want to purchase, they can use the ticker symbol and international securities identification number (ISIN) of those financial assets.

The ticker symbol is a unique set of characters given to a particular security traded on the stock market to identify them. Ticker symbols can change and are not unique across different exchanges. The Facebook ticker symbol used to be "FB" but now it is "Meta." In addition, they are often used to refer to a specific stock or other security. Berkshire Hathaway has two types of shares with different tickers: BRK-A, which currently costs $470,000 per share, and BRK-B, which currently costs $310 per share. You can use the ticker symbol to quickly gather information on specialized websites such as Yahoo Finance or Finviz, but also when you want to purchase an asset from your trading account.

The ISIN is a unique 12-character alphanumeric code used to identify assets worldwide. Unlike ticker symbols that can change, an ISIN code is unique and never changes. Like the ticker symbol, you can use the ISIN to gather information on specialized websites but also to purchase an asset from your trading account.

6.1.7 Animals in the stock market

You might have heard of some animals from journalists who cover the stock market. A black swan is a very unlikely event. It's a one-in-a-million chance happening that could have terrible consequences, such as the terrorist attack of September 11, 2001, the dot-com crash, or the Covid-19 pandemic. All of these are considered black swan events that had terrible consequences.

Then there are the bear and bull. The famous bronze statue in front of the New York Stock Exchange is a bull and might be the trader's favorite animal. When the price of assets on the stock market is going up people talk about a bull market. On the other hand, when the market is going down people talk about a bear market. To help you remember how the market is going when journalists refer to those animals you have think about how those animals attack. The bull attacks by pushing its horn up, representing the market going up. The bear stands up on his back feet, attacking down with its front paws, meaning that the stock market is going down.

A whale is an investor with a considerable amount of money, typically an institutional investor representing a large investment company. These investors can potentially change a market mood by taking or selling huge positions. When a whale sells a large position, you can see an immediate drop in the stock price as the whale floods the stock market supply. Conversely, if a whale takes a significant position on the stock market and buys a lot of stock you will see a net increase in its price.

6.2 Index funds and exchange-traded funds

Although it would seem more logical to talk about stock investment first, I prefer to start by discussing the most straightforward path people can take to invest in financial assets: index funds and ETFs.

In this section, I demonstrate how you can beat more than 80% of fund managers by investing in index funds and ETFs. Although it might sound too good to be true, it is common knowledge on Wall Street that most actively managed funds lag behind ETFs and other index funds that are passively managed and simply track the performance of an index.

As mentioned earlier, an index in the stock market tracks the market performance of various companies or a sector of activity. It is used as a market indicator or benchmark to compare portfolio performance. Indexes are established by selecting a group of securities following specific rules, such as stocks or bonds from a particular market or sector activities. There are many different indexes such as the S&P 500, the Dow Jones 30, the BEL 20, and so on.

Although you can't directly invest in an index, you can invest in an index fund or an ETF designed to replicate its performance. An index fund is a financial asset that aims to replicate a specific index's performance. It does this by purchasing the same assets the index includes, such as stocks or bonds. For example, an index fund following the S&P 500 buys all the shares of the companies in the S&P 500 in the proportions they are represented. So if Apple represents 5% of the S&P 500, 5% of the index fund portfolio are Apple stocks.

An ETF is similar to an index fund and serves the same purpose: replicating an index performance. The main difference between an index fund and an ETF is how you acquire those assets. Like stocks, you can buy and sell ETFs by unit on an exchange as often as you want during the trading day. You can buy 10 units of the iShares Core S&P 500 ETF (IVV) at around $400 per unit for a total of $4,000. For an index fund you usually need to buy them through a fund manager at a set price at the end of the trading day. For example, you can buy $5,000 worth of the Vanguard 500 Index Fund Admiral Shares (VFIAX).

6.2.1 Performance

As stated earlier, the performance of your investment in an index fund or ETF is directly correlated to the performance of the underlying index. Here I present the historical performance of some of the most popular indexes you might have heard of (Table 6.1).

Table 6.1 Historic performance of selected indexes, 2018–2022 (%)

Index	2022	2021	2020	2019	2018
S&P 500	−19.44	+26.89	+16.26	+28.88	−6.24
Dow Jones	−8.78	+18.73	+7.25	+22.34	−5.63
Nasdaq	−33.10	+21.39	+43.64	+35.23	−3.88
Nikkei 225	−9.37	+4.91	+16.01	+18.20	−12.08
Dax 30	−12.35	+15.79	+3.55	+25.48	−18.26

So if you had invested in an index fund or ETF that tracked those indexes, your performance would not have been exactly the same, but very similar.

Bear in mind that index funds and ETFs are provided by investment companies and several different funds from various companies can follow the same index. This is especially true for popular indexes such as the S&P 500 or the Dow Jones. For example, indexes such as the Vanguard 500 Index Fund Admiral Shares (VFIAX), State Street S&P 500 Index Fund Class N (SVSPX), and the Fidelity 500 Index Fund (FXAIX) follow the S&P 500 and they therefore have a very similar performance.

Although you would expect that actively managed funds should mostly outperform passively managed index funds and ETFs, the opposite is actually true. According to the S&P Dow Jones Indices' annual SPIVA report in 2021, about 80% of fund managers across the United States underperformed against a similar index. This means that only one in five actively managed funds outperformed a comparable benchmark. What's worse is that it wasn't a particularly bad year for mutual funds, as they had often underperformed mutual funds over the last decade (Figure 6.1)

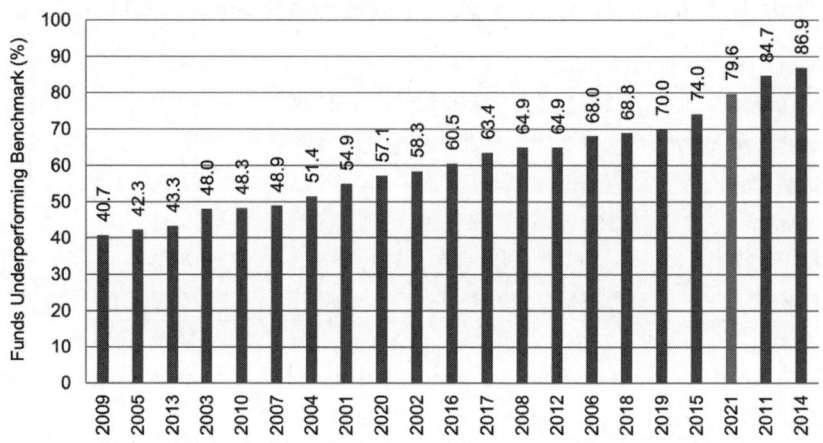

Figure 6.1 Percentage of all domestic equity funds underperforming the S&P Composite 1500 on an absolute basis

Source: S&P Dow Jones Indices LLC. Data as of December 31, 2021. Past performance is no guarantee of future results. The figure is provided for illustrative purposes.

In addition, just because a mutual fund beats the market one year this doesn't mean it will continue to beat it the following year and the next 10 years. Statistically, mutual funds cannot reliably beat similar indexes over an extended period. Therefore, if you want to beat those managers you must perform similarly or better than those indexes. Although you can be confident in your investment capability, trying to beat professional investors at their game is not the smartest move. You most likely do not have as much knowledge, tools, information, or resources as them. Instead, you can play it safe by investing in an index fund or ETF that follows the performances of the S&P 500 or another index you prefer.

This investing strategy is well known and backed by many of the greatest investors of all time, among them Warren Buffett himself: "By periodically investing in an index fund, for example, the know-nothing investor can outperform most investment professionals" (cited in Tuchman 2017).

6.2.2 Why invest in an index fund or ETF

There are many reasons to invest in an index fund or ETF.

- *Knowledge*. If you don't have any financial knowledge, you shouldn't invest in stocks, bonds, or even mutual funds as you are entirely reliant on someone else's advice for your investment strategy. In contrast, investing in an index fund or ETF automatically creates a diversified portfolio of assets that follows a specific benchmark. You don't need to understand accounting to invest in an index fund or ETF.

- *Profitability*. As noted earlier, index funds and ETFs have the potential for higher returns than mutual funds as they closely follow the performance of indexes that most mutual funds can't match.

- *Diversification*. Index funds and ETFs automatically invest in dozens, hundreds, or even thousands of different securities, depending on the type of index you follow. This diversifies the risk you invest from one company into several.

- *Low cost*. ETFs can have very low fees as they are passively managed financial vehicles. This is a very important factor for your long-term profitability.

- *Transparency*. Unlike mutual funds or hedge funds, you know at any given time what you are invested in as the index fund or ETF simply track an index.

6.2.3 Why not to invest in an index fund or ETF

While index funds and ETFs offer many benefits, they may not be suitable for everyone. Here are a few potential drawbacks that you must consider before investing.

- *Risk*. Like any financial asset, investing is risky and you might lose a significant part of your portfolio. Although this risk is mitigated as index funds and ETFs are diversified assets, you might still lose a substantial amount of your portfolio.

- *Media exposure*. One risk that not many people consider is that indexes, especially the popular ones, are constantly broadcast on TV, the internet, or radio: "The S&P 500 just lost 2.5% today," "The Dow Jones is down 35% this year," "The Nasdaq just gained 12% over the past week." If you are the kind of person who makes rash decisions or overreacts to the news, this is a significant threat you must consider as you will be constantly bombarded with information about those indexes and therefore about your investment. You must ask yourself if you can withstand the media exposure that will constantly batter you.

- *Customization*. Although thousands of index funds and ETFs are available on the market, you might not find one tailored to your needs or with the exact product you want.

- *False diversification*. We have discussed diversification being an advantage, but you must also consider false diversification. An index fund and an ETF diversify your investment into different companies or financial assets. But you must still consider the real diversification you are doing. Let's imagine you have a portfolio comprising the five biggest US companies and have 20% of your holdings in each company: Apple, Microsoft, Alphabet (Google), Amazon, and Berkshire Hathaway. You want to diversify your holding and decide to invest fresh capital in an index fund that follows the S&P 500. The problem is that those five stocks represent about 25% of the index. If your goal is to diversify your holdings from those five companies, then investing in an index that follows the S&P 500 is not efficient since 25% of your newly invested capital will be invested in those same companies through the ETF.

6.2.4 What to consider

There are various factors you should consider before investing in an index fund or ETF and I have classified them in logical order for you to follow.

The first step is determining your investment objectives and if investing in an index fund or ETF makes sense in your investment portfolio and suits your performance objectives. You must consider what you want to accomplish in the future and determine if an ETF can help you reach that goal. Are you looking for an asset that will create cash flow for you? Are you looking for an asset to diversify your portfolio?

The second factor is the risk you are willing to take and the diversification role you want this investment to play. Consider how much money you would like to invest in the stock market, if you are prepared to be aggressive in your investment, or if you have a long-term view on investing. Keep in mind that past performance doesn't ensure future performance, and having a diversified ETF is not necessarily a magic investment without risk. If you had looked at the Nikkei 225, which comprises Japan's top 225 blue-chip stocks, and invested in it at the beginning of 1991, you would only have recovered your investment in 2021.

You must then select the scope and the index. Before investing in an index fund or ETF you must select the index you will invest in. There are hundreds or even thousands of different indexes available on the market and you must choose the one that fits your need. Are you looking to invest in an index consisting of small caps? Are you looking to invest in technology? Do you want to invest in Europe? Do you want to invest in Southeast Asia? You must research and understand the index you will invest in and ask yourself several questions. What assets are in this index? What is its historical performance? How does the index select assets?

You should next ask yourself whether you prefer to invest in an index fund or an ETF. Although those are similar assets, there are some important differences to consider.

- Investing in an ETF is very similar to investing in stocks. You buy individual units on the stock market during the day when the market is open. By contrast, you can only buy or sell an index fund when the price is fixed at the end of the trading day.

- You can set up automatic purchase or sell orders in an index fund, but you can't do that with an ETF. For example, you can fix a buying order of $500 on the first day of every month to invest in VFIAX.
- ETFs often have a lower minimum investment than index funds.
- There are tax differences between index funds and ETFs that you must consider and which vary according to your situation.

After that, there is the choice of the specific index fund or ETF. Once you know which index you will invest in you must select the type of index fund or ETF that tracks its performance. As mentioned earlier, for well-known indexes such as the S&P 500, there are several companies that can offer you index funds or ETFs you can invest in. Here is a list of criteria you have to consider when selecting your index fund or ETF.

- *Fees.* You pay fees when you purchase your index fund or ETF, but you also pay an annual upkeep fee. You must be very aware of those fees as some companies charge you much higher fees than others for virtually the same asset.
- *Minimum capital.* Some index funds and ETFs might require a minimum capital for you to invest in them. It is an important criterion to consider, especially if you plan to invest every month in this asset.
- *Dividend or capitalization.* One important criterion is whether you want your investment to pay you dividends regularly or if you prefer that they reinvest earnings.
- *Historical performance.* You have to consider the ETF's past performance, but keep in mind that past results are not necessarily indicative of future performance.

6.2.5 How to invest

Whether you want to invest in ETF, index funds, mutual funds, stocks, or bonds, you generally need to follow the same steps. First, you need to select an investment platform that allows you to buy the financial asset you are interested in. You can also often buy those assets through traditional banks; however, they generally charge higher fees than online platforms.

Second, you have to ensure that you compare the fees of each platform and that you select a reputable platform from the country you are from. Answer all the security questions and ensure you understand all the risks related to your investment. Do not invest unless you understand the risks you take.

Third, once you have sent funds to your account, you simply need to place an order to invest in the financial asset you are interested in. You'll need to specify the ticker symbol or the ISIN number from the asset you want to invest in.

Fourth, once you have invested, it's important that you regularly monitor the situation to ensure that your investment follows your objectives.

Keep in mind that stock exchanges have working hours. For example, the New York Stock Exchange is open from 9 a.m. to 4 p.m. As mentioned earlier, you can purchase your ETF during those hours, but your order of an index fund will only be acted on at market close.

6.3 Mutual Funds

A mutual fund is a financial asset managed by an investment company that gathers money from many investors and uses it to create a diversified portfolio of various assets such as stocks, bonds, options, or commodities. When investing in a mutual fund you entrust your money to a professional fund manager who makes investments on your behalf.

There are many kinds of mutual funds, each having different objectives, such as generating a consistent return on investment, paying a yearly dividend, or creating a diversified portfolio of securities specialized in tech companies. As an investor you have no choice in how the fund operates, but you can select the fund that suits your investment strategy.

In this section, we determine why you should or shouldn't invest in a mutual fund. We also discuss the different factors to consider when investing and how you can invest in a mutual fund.

6.3.1 Why invest in mutual funds

Investing in a mutual fund can be very beneficial for a retail investor. Here are some advantages to consider if you plan to invest in a mutual fund.

- *Diversification.* When investing in mutual funds, you instantly diversify your portfolio as those funds are generally invested in dozens or hundreds of securities to diversify their holdings and spread investment risks to several assets.

- *Management.* Mutual funds are actively managed by professionals with broad knowledge, expertise, specialized tools, and millions of dollars backing them up. They are experts with years of experience and resources you can't possibly match as a retail investor. This prospect can be very appealing to someone lacking investing knowledge.

- *Flexibility.* Depending on the fund you invest in, you can automatically reinvest or withdraw money from it and reinvest any dividend you get. You can also set up automatic regular buying or selling orders.

- *Cost-efficiency.* It is much more cost-efficient to invest in a mutual fund and pay one transaction fee rather than the hundreds you would have to pay to replicate their portfolio.

- *Specialization.* You can invest in specialized funds in a specific field you believe in, such as 3D printing, technology, gold, or sovereign debts. Those mutual funds employ experts in their field who should know their industry and make the best decisions for your investment portfolio.

6.3.2 Why not to invest in mutual funds

Although there are many benefits to investing in mutual funds there are also significant drawbacks to consider.

- *Performance*. If you invest your money with professionals who dedicate their careers to investing and actively managing your funds then you expect that they should beat passively managed securities such as ETFs. Unfortunately, as we have seen earlier, in 2021 about 20% of fund managers beat the performance of a comparable index, and fewer than that can consistently surpass it year on year.

- *Fees*. Investing in a mutual fund can be costly. You have to pay an entry fee to invest in the mutual fund, but the mutual fund can also charge you annual upkeep fees, which is one of the reasons why their performances lag behind index funds and ETFs. Mutual funds pay themselves first before their investors.

- *Influence*. When investing in a mutual fund you have no power to influence their investment decision. If you don't like the fact that 20% of your fund is invested in the oil industry there is virtually nothing you can do about it except withdraw your investment.

- *Lack of transparency*. Unlike ETFs that follow specific rules when tracking an index, you generally don't know at any time what securities your mutual fund is invested in. When you invest in a mutual fund, you might receive a brochure detailing their current holding, but once you have invested, many funds don't openly share all the information regarding the securities they have invested in and prefer to maintain secrecy.

- *Restrictions*. Some mutual funds have many restrictions on the financial securities they invest in. For example, if you invest in a defensive mutual fund, it generally contains a lot of safe bonds and might not be much invested in stocks, which could make you miss a bull market opportunity.

- *Customization*. Mutual funds offer diversification but may not be tailored to your needs and objectives as an individual investor.

- *Risk.* Investors might not be willing to take the risk to invest their capital in the stock market, and therefore mutual funds might not constitute a good investment opportunity.

6.3.3 What to consider when investing in mutual funds

Although the process of investing in a mutual fund is fairly similar to an ETF, there are some differences you need to consider because of the financial asset's nature. Here is a non-exhaustive list of factors to ponder before investing in a mutual fund.

First, reflect on your investment objectives. Like for index funds and ETFs, you should determine if investing in a mutual fund makes sense in your investment portfolio and suits your performance objectives.

The second aspect to weigh up is the risk you are prepared to take and the investment scope you want. Knowing your goal helps define the type of mutual fund that suits you: an income-generating mutual fund, a defensive mutual fund, a bond fund, and so on. You must also think about the financial impact of such investments on your situation and if it creates fiscal advantages or disadvantages.

The third consideration is selecting the mutual fund. Here are things to keep in mind when selecting your mutual fund.

- *Research.* Start by researching different mutual funds to find one that aligns with your investment goals and risk tolerance. You can do this online through investment firms, or by talking to bankers and financial advisors.
- *Minimum amount.* Mutual funds usually have a minimum amount of money you must invest. You should therefore ensure that you have enough capital.
- *Historical performance.* Whenever a broker proposes you invest in a mutual fund, they show you historical figures and compare their fund's performance to the market benchmark. If they show you the last six months or even five-year charts where they beat the S&P 500 index this is insufficient. Ask

for a comparison of at least 10 years to determine whether the fund consistently outperformed its respective benchmark. Brokers often show data that puts them in a positive light, and you should know the complete story before investing.

- *Strategy*. You must know what is the fund strategy, what are their objectives, what type of assets they invest in, and so on.
- *Fees*. You should know the transaction fees you pay and the upkeep fees as these drastically impact your long-term return on investment.

6.3.4 How to invest in mutual funds

When investing in a mutual fund, you are basically putting your savings in the hands of someone else, and you have to trust that person to earn you money. Let's imagine you have worked for six months to save $5,000. If you invest all this money in a mutual fund, you are entrusting someone else with six months' worth of your hard work. So you shouldn't just trust the first person in a fancy suit from a reputable bank—you should trust the right person.

You can buy mutual funds through a broker like a traditional bank (although if that's the case, be very wary of the additional fees you pay for their services), from a trading platform, or from the fund itself. When opening your account, you need to provide personal information and ensure that you understand all the risks related to this investment.

When investing in a mutual fund, you receive a number of shares representing a portion of the total investment portfolio from all the investors in that fund. If a mutual fund has $100 million capital that is divided into 10,000 shares, then each share would cost $10,000. In this case, if someone invested $50,000, they would get five shares.

Once you have invested, just like any other investment, you must regularly monitor the situation and ensure that it follows your investment objectives.

6.4 Stocks

As mentioned earlier, a stock or a share is a title of partial ownership in a company. Stocks are traded, meaning you can buy and sell shares on the stock market. As they are exchanged their price fluctuates constantly. If the stock increases by 5%, this means that the value of your stock increases by 5%. But you only get that money if you decide to sell. Imagine you just bought an Apple share for $140. The next day the value increases to $150. You will get a profit of $10 only if you sell the stock.

In this section, I explain why and why not to invest in stocks, what to consider when investing, and how to invest in the stock market. Before that, I need to share an important disclaimer and explain how you can beat the market as a retail investor.

6.4.1 Disclaimer

Picking up individual stocks is not for everyone; it is a hazardous process that requires hard work and skills. Furthermore, you need to keep your head cool when market volatility hits and can wipe out much of your gains in one trading day. As noted earlier, many of the greatest investors in the world think that most people shouldn't pick individual stocks themselves. If you want to participate in stock market growth, you should instead invest in a cheap index fund or ETF that follows the general growth of the market and you will do better than most fund managers.

This section is meant for people who intend to beat the market and gain more than most mutual fund managers and indexes over the long term. I insist on this point because if you don't intend to beat the market, there is no point investing so much of your time, hard work, and money to pick up stocks and have less return than a simple index fund or ETF. To reinforce the point: there is absolutely nothing wrong with investing in those assets. As a matter of fact, I believe most people should invest in index funds and ETFs instead of picking up individual stocks.

However, stock investment might be for you if you are not afraid of hard work, active management, analyzing financial statements, and are willing to take some risks. Picking up individual stock is a great way to learn in-depth about a company you love or a sector of activity you have expertise in. In addition, you can learn to benefit from market discrepancy where many other financial tools can't, and I explain precisely how.

6.4.2 How to beat the market

You might be thinking, how can you beat professionals who dedicate their entire career and are full-time investors? Fund managers have better skills, knowledge, expertise, millions of dollars of leverage, sophisticated tools, and many other advantages you don't have. So how can you possibly be better than professionals with so many advantages?

It seems like an unfair fight, but the truth is that as a retail investor you also have significant advantages. In my opinion, you have five important advantages over fund managers that you can leverage.

- *Time frame*. Unlike fund managers, individual investors don't have a specific benefits target to reach every quarter or every year. A fund manager might have to make less profitable short-term investments to reach those targets. As an individual investor, you can focus on your long-term goal and only get the fruits of your investment when the time is right.

- *Limitation in investment vehicles*. Fund managers, ETFs, and index funds follow specific rules. There are investments they can and cannot make. For example, a mutual fund might have rules prohibiting it from investing in small-cap companies or only investing a limited percentage of its portfolio in stocks. You don't have to follow such rules as an individual investor.

- *Fees*. Managers must pay their team to run the funds and charge high upkeep fees for that purpose. Those fees are what make many funds lag behind indexes. As an individual investor, you only need pay transaction fees and eventual holding fees that are generally much lower than the upkeep fees a mutual fund would charge you annually.

- *Activity*. Mutual funds have to be active. If you pay someone 5% of your investment portfolio as an upkeep fee, you expect them to work hard, to buy and sell assets all the time to make a profit. This is actually a very bad strategy. Buying and selling all the time shows that you constantly change or adapt your long-term strategy. As an individual investor, you can wait for years to buy and sell assets at the right time.

- *Expertise*. Everyone has their own expertise. You most likely have extensive knowledge in a particular area because of your profession or your passion. As an investor, you must leverage that expertise because you know something that the overall market doesn't realize yet. If you work in construction and you realize that there is a new tool in your business that is much better than anything else available on the market, it can be interesting to have a closer look at that company and determine if it could be a good investment opportunity.

I would even argue that these advantages contribute to part of the success of some of the greatest investors in the world. If you consider Warren Buffett, he has been able to constantly beat the market for the last 30 years. One of the reasons is that he is notorious for having a long-term approach to investing, not often buying and sitting on a pile of cash, while not having a benefits target that needs to be met every year. If you compare his company to most of the hedge funds, he is barely doing anything in terms of buying and selling and focuses instead on his long-term strategy.

6.4.3 Why invest in stocks

There are several reasons why people choose to invest in the stock market.

- *Diversification.* Investing in several stocks is a great way to diversify your portfolio into various companies, from different sector of activity and country.
- *Liquidity.* It's very easy to buy and sell stock at a moment's notice online. Unlike other assets such as gold and real estate, you can buy and sell in a couple of clicks.
- *Potential return.* Many investors own shares for their growth potential and hope their investment will increase over time.
- *Passive income.* Many companies deliver dividends to their shareholders every year. Some companies have consistently distributed dividends for decades. Owning shares that distribute dividends is a good way to create additional passive income.
- *Learning.* Picking up individual stocks is a vital learning experience. Unlike ETFs and mutual funds, where you gain little insight into when your investment strategy works or doesn't work, you acquire a lot of knowledge by picking up individual stocks because of all the research and analysis you have to do.

6.4.4 Why not to invest in stocks

While investing in stocks is a great way to grow wealth over time, it is not for everyone. There are many factors you should consider before investing.

- *Risk.* Investing in stocks is extremely risky. If you have invested in the stock of a company that goes bankrupt, you might lose all the capital you have invested in that company.
- *Volatility.* Your stock value fluctuates significantly over time. Some stocks gain or lose more than 10% of their value in one day. As a long-term investor, you must be able to stomach this volatility and keep your head clear to focus on the bigger picture and your future plans.

- *Knowledge and time.* Picking up individual stocks requires accounting knowledge and expertise in the company's sector of activity. Furthermore, it requires much time to analyze individual stocks, keeping up with news from that company and the overall sector.
- *Time horizon.* You shouldn't invest money you will need in the foreseeable future. Some investors aren't patient during a downturn and might lose a significant amount of money because they had to sell in a hurry.

6.4.5 Technical and fundamental analysis

While reading business news or stock analysts' reports, you might encounter the term technical and fundamental analysis. A fundamental analysis focuses on the business of the company itself, its financial results, what the company wants to accomplish, and scrutiny of the product itself. On the other hand, a technical analysis focuses on the psychology of the market and what people think about the company; it studies the trajectory and historical value of the company. Whereas long-term investors focus more on the fundamental analysis of stocks to buy and sell over the years, day traders focus on technical analysis and buy and sell their positions within days, hours, minutes, or even seconds.

When performing a fundamental analysis, you have to do a lot of research on the company you examine. You look at what the company does and how it is competing, but you also analyze its quarterly and annual financial reports to determine if it's a good investment opportunity. When performing a technical analysis, you have a closer look at graphs of the stock price and technical indicators that can provide you with the overall market mood of this stock and hint at a good buying and selling price.

If you think you are a long-term investor, however, you shouldn't just discard the technical analysis. Both analyses give you tools and indicators that could be very useful over the long term to help you assess stocks and determine a buying and selling price.

Imagine I am making a fundamental analysis of a stock: I analyze the financial statements of the company, I calculate its financial ratios, I look at its competitors, its products, and its future potential. I determine that this stock could be worth $20 in the next five years. As it is currently trading at $10, I believe it is a good price and I buy 200 stocks. However, if I had made a technical analysis, I would have known that it wasn't a good time to buy this stock as it is currently overbought, far above a supporting level and just below a resistance level. The stock rapidly falls to $8 on the supporting level, which would have been a great buying point that a technical analysis could have hinted at. As it turns out, the fundamental analysis was correct and the stock eventually goes up to $20, which creates a $2,000 profit. However, if I had done a technical analysis as well, I could have bought 50 more stocks with the same budget, but at a lower price and realized a total profit of $3,000.

In a nutshell, the fundamental analysis tells you what to buy and the technical analysis is more about when to buy. You shouldn't think of one being better than another; each is a tool that complements the other.

6.4.6 What stock to pick

Wall Street is paved with stories of successes, but also failures. Your goal as an investor is to create your own path to success. As such, there are many different choices you can make to define your strategy. You can decide to invest in value or growth stocks, you can decide to have stocks that pay you a dividend or simply choose to gain from capitalization, or you can decide to not discriminate and have a mix of all types of stocks. The truth is that the choice depends on your objectives.

Value versus growth stock. A stock is considered a value stock if investors can buy it at a significantly lower price than its intrinsic value. Any stock can therefore be a value stock if there is a significant sell-off in the market. Those market crashes can be great opportunities to buy good companies at a low price. Warren Buffett is famous for investing in value stocks and keeping them over a long time. As an investor who look for value stocks, you have to do extensive research to find the diamond in the rough that everyone rejected and be able to understand the finances of companies and see if they are truly undervalued.

Growth stocks apply to companies that grow at a rate far above the market average; we are talking about growth rates of 15% and above per year. Unfortunately, those growth companies are often unprofitable at the beginning, as they reinvest their gains significantly in order to fuel their growth. These companies sometimes take several years before becoming profitable, but the payoff can be extremely attractive for patient investors who bought the companies at an early stage. Cathie Wood is a famous investor who exclusively focuses her strategy on growth stocks. As an investor who looks for growth stocks, you have to consider small companies that disrupt the market, that have launched a new product, or have found a new way to do something and can take market shares from established companies.

Dividend versus capitalization. When companies are profitable and generate positive cash flow, they can choose to keep their earnings and reinvest in their activity or reward their shareholders by giving them a share of their benefits in the form of dividends. People invest in stocks to grow their capital and get passive income from dividends.

Companies can distribute their dividends annually but also every semester or quarter. To be eligible to receive dividends, you need to own a share of a company before the ex-dividend date, which is a couple of days before the distribution date of the dividends. For example, suppose you bought 10 shares of TotalEnergies at the end of 2021 at $50 per share for a total cost of $500 (plus fees). In 2022, TotalEnergies distributed a total dividend of $3.85 per share. Since you own 10 shares you would have received a total dividend of $38.58 that year. At the beginning of 2023, you decided to sell those shares at $60 per share for a total of $600, so you made a profit of $100 + $38.58 dividend − fees.

Some established companies even hold the title of "dividend aristocrats"—those companies have distributed and increased their dividends for at least 25 consecutive years. Some companies with this title have done so for more than 60 consecutive years. You can have a look at the list of dividends aristocrats here: www.suredividend.com/dividend-aristocrats-list.

Owning stocks that constantly pay dividends is a good way to create an additional source of revenue for your retirement. However, some countries tax dividends heavily. You must determine what percentage of tax you will pay on your dividends before investing as it might drastically decrease your return on investment and therefore impact your investment strategy.

Successful companies can also decide not to distribute dividends and reinvest those earnings to finance their activity. Companies like Berkshire Hathaway have never paid any dividends and keep reinvesting their earnings to grow. When investing in those companies, you are investing to capitalize, meaning you are hoping the stock price increases over time. You make money by selling the stock at a higher price than you bought it. For example, if you bought 10 Berkshire Hathaway (BRK-B) shares at $200 per share during the Covid-19 pandemic in 2020, and decided to sell those shares in 2022 at $300 per share, you would have made a total profit of $1,000 (not accounting for tax and fees). You must be aware that you are also taxed on your capital gains. When holding a stock over five, 10, or 20 years, you maximize the chances that your stocks have a much greater value as you gave the company the chance to grow. However, be aware that a market crash could wipe out numerous years of growth in a couple of weeks or months.

6.4.7 What to consider when investing in stocks

There are, of course, multiple factors you need to consider before investing in stocks. As for any other asset, you must think about your investment objectives and determine if a particular stock makes sense in your investment strategy. This is essential as you need to create a diversified portfolio of different stocks you want to invest in.

The second factor is expertise. Many great investors like Peter Lynch or Warren Buffett recommend retail investors to only invest in what they understand. People often underestimate their own knowledge. If you are an expert and are passionate about a particular field, you most likely know more than the average investor in that field and you should take advantage of it. If you can pick up a couple of first-class companies from industries you know very well, you might be able to outperform the market.

More than investing with ETFs or mutual funds that diversify your position, you must ensure you create a diversified portfolio when selecting individual stocks. Having 10 different stocks from the automobile industry is not having a diversified position. On the other hand, having 10 stocks in various sectors of activity that are not interdependent is already a well-diversified portfolio.

You must also consider market volatility. As Baron Rothschild said in the nineteenth century, "The time to buy is when there's blood in the streets, even if it's your own" (cited in Burgess 2018). The stock market is not always rational and fluctuates a lot. Over the long term it will get the value of a stock right, but over the short term it can get overly excited or underexcited about a stock. It is not because the value of stock changes significantly that the underlying business is doing well or badly, but it could simply be an overreaction to particular news. There are times when the stocks of a company are at a high discount and you should take advantage of those times. Then there are times when companies are overpriced and you have to be even more careful if you are considering buying them. Sometimes stocks are at a sizeable discount for the simple reason that the entire market is significantly down and investors' mood is low, but this doesn't mean that the underlying business itself is bad.

The earning season is a particular time of year for companies. Every quarter, publicly traded companies have to release their financial results. For example, in the United States it is through a document called Form 10-Q. In addition to financial results, companies share information about what happened during the quarter, and discuss their future projects and predictions moving forward. As an investor, the earning season is a crucial moment as you get updates on the company you have invested in. There is a lot of volatility in the earning season as many investors make important decisions based on those company reports. The earning season can be compared to school reports for children. Basically, when your parents are expecting good grades from you and you bring back less-than-satisfactory scores, you get scolded. But if you bring back better-than-expected scores, you get rewarded. It's basically the same on the stock market. When companies report less-than-expected revenue the stock price tends to fall as investors sell their shares. In contrast, when a company reports better-than-expected results the stock price tends to go higher as many investors want to buy more stocks.

To understand a company, you need to properly understand its accounting. You shouldn't invest in a company you don't understand. Choosing a stock without understanding the basics of accounting is like trusting someone else's advice blindly. If you don't understand the stock, you don't understand why the person chose it for you. If a change in the stock occurs, you have no idea if you should keep it or sell it.

If you don't have enough capital to buy a particular share, or you don't want to spend more than a certain amount for an individual stock, you might be interested in purchasing fractional shares. Since 2019 some brokerage firms have allowed you to buy fractions of a stock for as little as $1. So, instead of paying $150 for an Apple stock, you could get a third of the share for $50 and thus not risk all your capital in one company. With fractional shares, even if you don't have much capital, you can still invest in great stocks and enjoy the same growth return percentage. In addition, you also get your dividends prorated to your percentage ownership.

Fractional shares are a valuable tool for those who want to diversify their holdings on a limited budget. Imagine you have $500 that you would like to invest equally in the GAFAM (Google: $95 per share + Apple: $150 per share + Meta: $179 per share + Amazon: $99 per share + Microsoft: $272 per share). The problem is that on this budget, you wouldn't normally be able to invest in each stock. Thankfully, with fractional share, you can buy ⅔ of Apple, ½ of Meta, and ⅓ of Microsoft to stay on budget. It's essential to notice that there might be a limit to the names you can invest in and some additional fees to consider. However, if you want to participate in the growth of big names with important share prices, fractional shares could be a great opportunity.

Finally, you should consider your investment horizon. When investing in stocks, you must have a long-term investment horizon and only invest money that you won't need for the next couple of years. Market volatility is very high and your stock investment might suffer greatly from those ups and downs. If you are able to focus on the next five to 10 years when the average investor is looking at the next five to 10 months, you will likely have a much greater result. The market rewards patience much more than any other skill.

6.4.8 How to evaluate a company

If you are interested in the stock market, you most likely have come across experts' and analysts' evaluations of stocks. When they fix a specific price target for a particular stock, this means they believe the stock will reach that price in the future. When analysts move up or down their price target, this can have a significant impact on the stock market. For example, if a particular stock is currently trading at $20, and a reputable analyst fixes its price target at $30, this suggests the analyst thinks that the stock is currently undervalued as it is trading under its target value. If many analysts have a similar target price for that particular stock, the stock price will likely increase as the overall market can see it as a buying opportunity. But how exactly do analysts value stock and determine their target price?

There are many valuation models to calculate the value of a stock, but ultimately, there are only two valuation approaches: *intrinsic* and *relative*. The intrinsic method is based on financial information from a company's financial statement and often uses discounted cash flow (DCF) analysis. Meanwhile, the relative method calculates a company's stock value relative to another by comparing their financials using multiples. The DCF method calculates a stock's present value based on its future cash flow. It is technical as it requires many assumptions and predictions on future cash flow, but it is also the most popular valuation approach analysts use. However, I personally believe that because of the number of assumptions, it is of minimal use for retail investors. Analysts who perform a DCF analysis are highly specialized in a specific sector and have access to data and knowledge retail investors can't match. In addition, because of the number of assumptions in their calculations, analysts who use the same methods can come up with very different results, which is a source of many debates between analysts on Wall Street. That's the reason why I won't go through this method in this book, as it won't bring a lot of value to the reader. But if you are interested to know more about it, I strongly recommend *The Little Book of Valuation* by Aswath Damodaran (2011).

The relative valuation, on the other hand, offers more value for the retail investor, in my opinion. This method has the advantage of being more straightforward than the DCF valuation by simply comparing the financial ratio of companies in a similar sector of activity. The first step of the multiple method is to identify similar companies and gather some financial information: their stock price and their earnings per share (Table 6.2). For example, you can compare Coke to Pepsi, but you can't compare Coke to Ford, as they have completely different businesses from different sectors of activity.

Table 6.2 Comparative stock price and earnings per share of companies

	Company A	Company B	Company C	Company D	Company E
Stock price ($)	5.10	2.30	15.00	21.00	5.00
Earnings per share ($)	0.50	0.25	1.25	2.00	1.00

Once you have gathered the information, you can quickly calculate the price–earnings (P/E) ratio of these companies by dividing their current stock price by their earnings per share. The P/E ratio is an indicator that helps you determine how expensive a stock is. For example, if a company has a P/E ratio of 5, this means that it would take five years of earnings to reach the same value you have invested in the stock. The higher the P/E ratio, therefore, the more expensive a stock is. In the example of five companies presented in Table 6.3, now that you have calculated the P/E ratio of each company, you can see that one company stands out—Company E with a PE ratio of 5. It is therefore much cheaper than the others.

Table 6.3 Comparative price–earnings (P/E) ratio of companies

	Company A	Company B	Company C	Company D	Company E
Stock price ($)	5.10	2.30	15.00	21.00	10.00
Earnings per share ($)	0.50	0.25	1.25	2.00	2.00
P/E ratio	10.2	9.2	12.0	10.5	5.0

Suppose you are interested in investing in that company and would like to know how much the stock should be worth if it had the same valuation as the others, you can calculate it by taking the average P/E ratio multiple of the other four companies and multiplying it by the earnings per share of Company E. In this case, the average P/E ratio of Companies A, B, C, and D is 10.475. So if Company E had a P/E ratio of 10.475 instead of 5, it would have a similar evaluation as the overall sector. By multiplying Company E's stock price by 2.095, it would reach the target P/E ratio of 10.475. So $10 × 2.095 = $20.95. As the stock is currently valued at $10, we can conclude that based on this valuation method the stock is undervalued by about 50%. In this example, we have used the P/E ratio, but multiple valuations are done on many other financial data, such as trailing P/E ratio, EBITDA, and so on.

Be aware that this valuation method only concludes that company E has a lower P/E ratio than the other companies and how much the stock would be worth if it was at the same level as its competitors. This valuation method doesn't tell you why this stock is cheaper than the others, and you should therefore try to figure out this information before investing.

6.4.9 How to invest

As mentioned earlier, the process to purchase stocks is very similar to other financial assets. First, you need to select an investment platform that allows you to buy the financial asset you are interested in. You can also often buy those assets through traditional banks; however, they generally charge higher fees than online platforms. You have to ensure that you compare the fees of each platform and that you select a reputable platform from the country you are from. Answer all the security questions and ensure you understand all the risks related to your investment. Do not invest unless you understand the risks you take.

Once you have sent funds to your account, you simply need to place an order to invest in the financial asset you are interested in. You'll need to specify the ticker symbol or the ISIN number from the asset you want to invest in.

Once you have invested, it's important that you regularly monitor the situation to ensure that your investment follows your objectives. Although stock exchanges have opening hours, some platforms will authorize you to buy stocks before or after market opening hours.

6.5 Bonds

Bonds are another type of asset generally considered safer to invest in. A bond is a debt that a borrower owes to an investor. When investing in a bond, you lend money to an institution such as a government or a company for a specific period. In exchange, the issuer pays you interest during the bond's life and repays the principal when the bond matures. Let's imagine that Apple issues a $10,000 bond at a 5% annual interest rate payable at maturity. If you decide to buy this bond and lend your money, Apple pay you $500 in interest every year until they pay you back your initial capital of $10,000 at the end of the lending period.

Bonds are an excellent way for corporations and governments to raise funds. They are generally considered safer to invest in because, in case of bankruptcy and when liquidation is necessary, the lender has priority to receive their funds. Bonds can also be sold before the maturity date as their value fluctuates over time. If you lend money to a company before it was in distress, there is a high chance that you would lose some of your invested capital if you sell it on the secondary market. Bonds usually have the following characteristics.

- *Issue price.* The price at which the bond is created.
- *Face value.* The amount the bond is worth at maturity.
- *Coupon rate.* The interest rate the issuer pays for the bond.
- *Coupon date.* The date when the issuer makes an interest payment.
- *Maturity date.* The date when the bond matures and the issuer has to pay the face value of the bond.
- *Credit rating.* Agencies assign a credit score to bonds which sets their creditworthiness. The higher the score, the more creditworthy the issuer is. In contrast, the lower the score, the higher the credit default risk. If an investment is riskier, the interest is higher as people want to receive more interest for the higher risk.

There are various types of bonds.

- *Municipal bonds.* These are issued by states, cities, counties, and other government entities.
- *Corporate bonds.* These are issued by public companies.
- *High-yield bonds.* These bonds are riskier and often referred to as "junk bonds" because they are issued by companies with low creditworthiness ratings.

6.5.1 Why invest in bonds

Bonds are a good option to keep your money safe and get a set return. People invest in bonds for various reasons.

- *Stable income.* Bonds provide predictable income every quarter, semester, or year. It's a great opportunity to create a recurrent passive income.
- *Preservation of capital.* A bond's principal is paid back at maturity, ensuring the capital's preservation over time.
- *Safety.* Bonds are generally considered safer than other financial assets. Even in cases of bankruptcy, the bondholder can get their money back upon liquidation. To ensure safety, people invest in very stable institutions such as the US government.
- *Diversification.* Having bonds in your portfolio is a great way to diversify holdings while ensuring a regular return.
- *Capital appreciation.* Although it's not their main purpose, bonds can increase in value on the secondary market if the interest rate falls.
- *Guarantee.* Some bonds, such as agency bonds, can be guaranteed by their respective governments.

People close to retirement prefer bonds over stocks as they guarantee a set return and avoid stock volatility.

6.5.2 Why not to invest in bonds

Although bonds are often considered a safe alternative, they are not for everyone.

- *Low return.* Bonds typically offer a lower return than other financial assets. As a bond investor, you don't take part in the market growth or success of the institution that borrows money from you. You only have a fixed predetermined income.
- *Inflation.* If inflation rises significantly, although the money you get is the amount agreed upon, its actual value is much lower than when you lent it.
- *Default risk.* If the institution you lend your money to goes bankrupt, although you have priority in getting your money

back when liquidating, it's not a certainty that you will get all your money back as there might not be enough assets to sell.

Like any investment, although it is considered safer, there are always risks when investing in bonds.

6.5.3 What to consider

There are various risks and critical factors to consider when investing in bonds.

- *Objectives.* You must consider your investment plan. Does investing in bonds make sense for you? Are you looking for a stable income or to diversify your portfolio in safer financial assets?
- *Credit quality and interest rate.* The creditworthiness and interest rate of the bond issuer are critical factors to consider. High-credit quality bonds generally offer lower interest rates but are less risky. Conversely, low-credit quality bonds generally offer higher interest rates but are riskier.
- *Default risk.* When the issuer fails to pay interest or the principal and thus defaults on its bonds, this situation can lead to litigation or even bankruptcy.
- *Maturity date.* The length of time the lender borrows your money is also an important factor as you won't have access to that money for that period. Although long-term bonds provide higher returns they are also riskier as you lend your money for a longer period.
- *Fluctuation.* If you plan to sell the bond before the maturity date, you have to consider that its face value might fluctuate based on the interest rate. Rising interest rates make new bonds more attractive as the interest rate is higher, and you might have to sell off your bond at a discounted price.
- *Inflation.* The general price increase might be a great risk for bonds. If inflation is at 5% and your interest rate is at 4%, you

are losing money on your investment. Furthermore, if you try to sell this bond, it is likely to be at a lower face value.

- *Inflation protection*. Some bonds provide protection against inflation, such as Treasury Inflation-Protected Securities (TIPS).
- *Call risk*. Issuers might decide to pay the bond at an earlier date. This is often the case when the interest rate declines. They refinance their loan with another one with better conditions.
- *Taxation*. As legislation is different from country to country, you have to consider how you are taxed on your profit and how it impacts your investment plan.
- *Diversification*. As with individual stocks, you have to diversify your holdings.
- *Liquidity*. When nobody wants to buy a bond on the secondary market because a company is in trouble, you might face a liquidity risk if you want to sell it in a hurry.
- *Timing*. Return on investment with bonds is tied closely to inflation and interest rates.

6.6 Resources

There is a famous saying that goes like this: you are the average of the five people you spend the most time with. In today's world, that is a blessing because more than ever before we have easy access to the minds of great investors all over the world and you can use many resources to help you become a better investor.

If you have limited time to read, I would suggest listening to investment podcasts. Most are free and you can listen to them while you commute to work. There are so many podcasts from great investors that are freely available online. My personal favorite is Motley Fool Money. They have new episodes every day talking about the stock market and companies' latest news (https://www.fool.com/podcasts/motley-fool-money/).

You should also read the annual and quarterly reports of public companies you want to invest in. This is a good way to learn a lot of useful information from them. Those reports are generally publicly available on the company's website, quite often under the "Investors" tab.

There are also many other useful websites for investors.

- *Yahoo Finance*. The number one platform for stock market investors. Whether you want to create an online portfolio, get information about a particular stock, look at a public company's financials, or learn about the latest business news, Yahoo Finance is your best solution, in my opinion (https://finance.yahoo.com/).

- *Investopedia*. By far the best source of information to explain complex business-related topics. There are thousands of articles and definitions of specific business terms available there. Whatever question you have on a particular type of investment, Investopedia has the answer (https://www.investopedia.com/).

- *Finfizz*. I mainly use this website for two purposes: when I am screening the market to find stocks (www.finviz.com/screener.ashx) or to find the map that gives me a visual over the latest stock market performance (http://www.finviz.com/map.ashx). Good investment books can give you an edge when investing. There are many books you can choose from to cater to any of your investment needs and questions.

- *Growth stocks*. If you are looking for a strategy to invest in growth stocks, I suggest 100 Baggers by Christopher Mayer (2018) and *The Motley Fool Investment Guide* by David and Tom Gardner (2017).

- *Value stocks*. If you are looking to invest in value stocks, I recommend *The Intelligent Investor* by the master himself, Benjamin Graham (2005); however, this book is quite advanced and it's not for beginners.

- *Investment philosophy.* If you are looking for a simple solution to invest and get wealthier, I propose *A Simple Path to Wealth* by J. L. Collins (2016) and *The Barefoot Investor* by Scott Pape (2017). These are great books that show you an easy way to invest.

Despite some controversies, I believe that YouTube is a great tool that gives you access to lots of information. You can watch videos from the best investors in the world and learn from them. Simply type names like Peter Lynch, Warren Buffett, Mohnish Pabrai, Michael Burry, Cathie Wood, or Ray Dalio and you will be able to watch legendary investors talk about stock investment strategies. I recommend you check out Aswath Damodaran. As noted earlier, he is considered the dean of valuation and has a dedicated channel that explains in great detail how to evaluate stocks. I also advise you to be very cautious when watching YouTube channels dedicated to financial investment. Some are great and focus entirely on education; however, others are more like entertainment platforms that push you to invest but won't give you the necessary insight to take the right decision for your needs.

One final resource you can use is to simply look around. Investing is all around you. To have ideas about what stocks to buy, observe your surroundings and see who is using what product.

6.7 Going further

This chapter has gone through the basic information you need to understand the stock market as well as what you need to consider before investing in index funds, ETFs, mutual funds, stocks, and bonds. What's great about the stock market is that you can easily adapt your investment strategy to your objectives and needs. You can have a very active but also a very passive strategy. You can decide to have assets that pay you dividends regularly or maximize your capital over time. You can choose to invest with professionals or make all the decisions yourself. In other words, investing in the stock market can be very flexible, and for this reason it's a significant tool that can play a central role in your investment plan.

Chapter 7

Real Estate

People are constantly looking for a place to live, whether it's their dream house, a retirement residence, a townhouse with a garden, or an apartment with a balcony. Some are willing to pay a premium to get the property they want or make the changes they desire. They are driven by feelings and emotions rather than making a profitable investment. In contrast, investors look for the best investment opportunity.

These are drastically different ways to look at real estate. Unfortunately, people often make the mistake of mixing the two. Some investors pay a premium to buy a property because they love the porch at the entrance, because they would like to invest in the garden to make it cozier, or even because they want to install designer lights inside the house. They then make the excuse that those choices are for an investment purpose. The problem is that an additional $10,000 investment in a lovely porch, garden, or designer lights won't necessarily get you a higher rent or be a dealmaker to convince a tenant to move in. Those are not choices driven by investment reasons but by emotions and feelings. When investing in real estate, you must look at it with the eyes of an investor and not a homeseeker.

Investing in real estate is different from looking for a home, and it can be overwhelming as there are so many things to consider: what to buy, what strategy to follow, which location to pick, how to finance it, how to deal with tenants, how to deal with legal issues. This chapter aims to help you go through this process and guide you to find the best investment opportunity.

7.1 Why invest in real estate

Before investing in real estate, you must think about the reasons why you want to go down this path.

- *Create passive income.* Real estate is a great way to create recurrent and reliable passive income.
- *Capital appreciation.* Many people invest in real estate for the benefit of capital appreciation over time.
- *Diversification.* Investing in real estate is a helpful way to diversify your portfolio to tangible assets.
- *Leverage.* Real estate is expensive, and it is one of the rare assets you can invest in by leveraging your capital with a specially designed bank loan.
- *Safety.* Even in a financial crisis when the value of your assets is crashing, as long as you have a tenant, you will still be able to collect the same rent.

7.2 Why not to invest in real estate

You must also consider the risks related to real estate and the reasons why you shouldn't invest in it.

- *Low liquidity.* Investing in real estate is generally a lifetime decision, and the process of purchasing or selling your investment takes time and is tedious. If you need cash in a hurry, you won't be able to sell your real estate quickly.
- *Expensive.* Real estate is notoriously expensive, and although you can leverage your position, you still need to put a significant portion of your capital into one investment.
- *Low returns.* Depending on your location, the return on real estate investment can be very low, and there is nothing much you can do about it in this market.

- *Risk*. There are many risks to take into account when investing in real estate, such as bad tenants, construction faults, or local hazards.

These are a few examples of the advantages and disadvantages of investing in real estate. You must also take account of factors relevant to your situation before making an investment decision. Investing in real estate is a clear opportunity, but you must reflect carefully on your plan and situation to determine if this kind of investment makes sense for you.

7.3 What to buy

When thinking about real estate, people often picture investing in a house or renting an apartment. Although these are the most popular types of real estate for retail investors, there are many other options.

7.3.1 Residential

There are various types of residential properties you can invest in. The first is a studio. When picturing a studio, people often think of a messy student room. However, from a real estate investment point of view, it is often the cheapest and most efficient use of space. Within one area, you generally get a bedroom, bathroom, living area, and kitchen. Although configurations differ and some studios share a common bathroom or kitchen area, the idea is to have an independent or almost independent unit in one room. When renting a studio, you primarily target students, young couples, or lower-income people. It is the cheapest type of real estate available and can get you a good return on investment. Unfortunately, you might have to change tenants often as a studio is usually a temporary situation rather than a permanent accommodation option.

A condo is a residential unit inside a building. It is physically the same as an apartment. The main difference is that an apartment is owned and managed by a property management corporation. In contrast, a condo is owned and operated by an individual investor.

Condos are generally the same from one floor to another, although they can also have slight differences due to the architectural design of the building. Each unit is independent, while there can be additional non-essential common facilities such as a swimming pool, gym, or shared garden. It is generally considered a more affordable property than a single-family home. However, as a landlord, you can't do everything you want and you have to deal with the other owners in the same building.

As for houses, there are many different types.

- A single-family home is a house that is not attached to other properties and has no common spaces with other houses.

- A multi-family home is a property with multiple units attached, each having its own entrance.

- A townhouse shares two walls with other houses. Each townhouse can have a different tenant.

There are many kinds of houses you can invest in. When you own this kind of real estate, you have more space and are generally targeting families.

7.3.2 Land

People generally only think of real estate as buildings. However, there are excellent opportunities in land ownership. It is more affordable than buying a property, there is much less maintenance, and you can benefit from capital appreciation over time or create passive income.

Be aware that you can't just do anything you want with a piece of land you own. Local legislation might forbid you having a construction or a specific plantation on this location. You must therefore know what you can and can't do on a piece of land before investing in it.

Parking rental could be an excellent passive investment; risks on your property are low, and if you are in a popular area, you can easily find a tenant for a high price, especially in big cities. In addition, there are generally minimal upkeep costs (unless it is in a guarded building).

Whether for livestock, crops, plantations, orchards, flowers, or other types of cultivation, you can benefit by renting your land to farmers or agribusinesses who can grow on them. You can also rent your land to factories for their activities.

There is a limited amount of land available to build on. If you own land in a rapidly growing area, you can simply wait for its value to appreciate over time and sell it at a higher price. However, be mindful that not all land will appreciate over time, and if it's your strategy, you must select it carefully to ensure your success.

7.3.3 Commercial

You can find excellent opportunities by renting your property to businesses. However, it's very different from residential real estate. When renting a home, tenants can live there without altering the building. In contrast, with shops, offices, and factories you might need to make significant changes to the building to adapt it to a new activity. In exchange, the leasing period is often longer; you can typically see three-, five-, or 10-year leasing periods.

When renting to a shop location is key. The success of your rental very much depends on the area where you are situated and the success of the business you are renting it to. If you acquire a shop in an unpopular shopping mall, you might have trouble finding a tenant, and even if you do, that business might struggle. That being said, the opposite is also true. If your tenant is extremely successful at your location and has loyal customers, it might be difficult for them to start from scratch elsewhere. They may thus remain as your tenant for a long time, which is every landlord's ideal.

One popular investment in commercial real estate is office space. When considering investing in an office building, you must remember that the Covid-19 pandemic has changed this industry. Businesses worldwide had to learn to work remotely and now they know that their activity doesn't require people to work full-time in a physical office. Although many employees are now working back in their offices, remote work is an easy way for companies to cut costs on their building and reduce expenses. This will dramatically impact commercial real estate over the long run. While the situation might not be as grim as I am portraying it, the pandemic certainly stained that bright future.

Industrial buildings are another possibility. Big corporations invest in factories for heavy manufacturing, warehouses, or large parking lots. This type of real estate is industry-specific and requires much expertise and capital, which is why it is generally reserved for corporations or individuals who own warehouses and extensive land in the appropriate zones.

7.3.4 Mixed use

Another alternative to choosing only one type of real estate is to mix them. You can acquire a two-level building, rent the ground floor to a business such as a pharmacy or a clothing store, and rent the first floor as a residential unit. In that case, you benefit from both residential and commercial real estate. But be conscious of the type of business you rent to. If you rent the ground floor to a popular bar, it might quickly become a noisy nuisance for your other tenants and you might have difficulty finding and keeping them.

7.3.5 Real estate investment trust (REIT)

Instead of owning real estate and dealing with the issues of being a landlord, you can invest in a real estate investment trust. An REIT is a company that owns real estate. They generally don't pay income tax, but they have to distribute more than 90% of their taxable income to shareholders. So investing in REITs is a good way to get income from real estate without any of the responsibilities. You can invest in an REIT by purchasing stocks, ETFs, or mutual funds. It's an efficient means to diversify your portfolio by having indirect exposure to real estate while having liquid assets.

7.4 Strategies

Once you have selected a type of real estate you are interested in, you must determine your strategy moving forward.

7.4.1 Long-term rental

Renting real estate over the long term is the most common way to secure a property, whether for commercial, residential, or mixed use. There are significant advantages to renting over the long term.

- The income is consistent and predictable.
- As the landlord, you can choose your tenants yourself.
- Low turnover in tenants.
- It is a passive investment that requires little work once everything is settled.

There are also some risks and disadvantages to take into consideration with long-term rentals.

- Tenants can be a burden; they can spoil your building and constantly complain.
- Local legislation can be very protective of tenants. In some cases, even if someone is damaging your property and not paying the rent, you might not be able to evict them immediately.

7.4.2 Short-term rental

Instead of focusing on long-term rental, you can join the growing number of people renting real estate over the short term on websites such as Airbnb. When choosing this strategy, you are in the hospitality business, which could be a very lucrative plan if you do it right. Although you can expect a higher daily rent when renting a building over the short term, there are many other factors to consider before choosing this option.

The first factor to think about is the location where you want to buy property. Places are not equal. Some areas are more appealing for short-term tenants than others. Some have historical sites or tourist activities, making them attractive places for short-term travelers. Other areas are surrounded by offices, which could be interesting for commercial guests. In addition, you can create partnerships with those companies to provide accommodation promptly when requested. In other words, you must figure out if this place is appealing for short-term rental and adapt your rental to the customers you will potentially have.

Another major factor to contemplate is the location of your primary residence. If you plan to take care of everything while renting over the short term, your principal residence should be relatively close by. If you have to spend hours commuting each time you change tenants, the return on your investment quickly decreases unless you plan to delegate this work to others.

Lastly, assess the competition in your area. If you spot an attractive place for short-term rental then many other people probably have too. You might need to compete with others over the price and services provided to your tenants.

On the plus side, the most appealing factor about renting a place over the short term is that the return should be more attractive than a long-term rental. Someone renting a studio over the long term in Nice could get $900 per month or $10,800 per year. However, that same studio could be rented over the short term for $86 per day and potentially $2,580 per month if fully booked. However, when considering short-term rental, you have to be realistic in your calculations. Even in a tourist area, it won't be booked 365 days a year, and you have to work with an occupancy rate that varies from place to place and the time of year. In this case, if we assume an occupancy rate of 60%, it still adds up to an average of $1,548 per month or $18,576 per year.[1]

---

[1] To evaluate the rate you can ask on a rental property, you can look at various rental websites and compare similar properties. You can also

In the example above, the potential return is almost twice the value of the long-term rental. However, there are additional costs to consider as well.

- *Fees.* As you are most likely to use a platform to rent your property, you have to pay additional fees. Those fees vary from platform to platform, but we can generally expect 15% of the rental price.
- *Taxes and license.* Depending on the location of your property, you have to pay taxes and might need a permit to rent it over the short term.
- *Repairs.* Each new tenant coming in is another potential liability who might damage your place. Sometimes you can identify damages and get a refund from the tenant, but there are some damages you won't see or that the tenant refuses to pay for. So you should allocate a small portion of your rent to repairs.
- *Housekeeping, maintenance, and supplies.* You must clean and maintain the place after each tenant, providing fresh bedding, towels, toilet paper, tea and coffee, and so on. You must keep a share of your revenue for those additional costs and ensure you are a good host.
- *Furniture.* You have to provide everything your tenant needs to spend a night, including furnishings, unlike a long-term rental where you generally don't provide furniture.
- *Time.* Unless you plan to delegate your work, renting over the short term is time-consuming, especially if you live far away from your property. You must also take into account how many times you change tenants per month.

---

look at occupancy rates on Airdna's website and evaluate how much your rental could earn you: https://www.airdna.co. It is not a guarantee, of course; it is simply a benchmark of the average rate in that area, but it can help give you a rough idea of what to expect.

These are only examples of additional costs. Each property is different and has particular costs that you must identify and evaluate before renting it over the short term. Now let's put them all together and evaluate our potential cost.

Let's say that a tenant stays on average three days in your property. At a 60% yearly occupancy rate, you have around six different tenants per month. Assuming that you live one hour away from your rental, every time you change tenants you have to drive for that time to bring them the key and introduce the place and its environs. Then you have the same drive home. The same round trip applies once the tenant leaves, when you also have to clean up the place. In this example, you can assume about four hours per tenant. Multiplied by six tenants, this is about 24 hours of work per month. Of course, it is a hypothetical example, but time management is essential when renting a place. Alternatively, you can hire people or specialized companies to manage your bookings and cleaning. But this is costly and affects your bottom line.

Considering all the factors outlined so far, let's look at our example of renting a studio in Nice. The potential long-term rental income is about $900 per month. The short-term rental is about $1,548 (at an average 60% occupancy rate). The average additional monthly costs are $232.20 for the 15% rental fee, $50 for housekeeping, maintenance, and supplies, and $50 for unexpected repairs. This leaves us with an expected return of $1,215.80 per month or $14,589.60 per year. In this example, you need to work about 30 hours per month, account for the fuel cost, and be taxed on this additional income. You therefore need to determine if the extra money is worth it compared to the $900 per month or $10,800 per year if you rented long term. Renting a place short term can be very profitable, but you should not overlook important factors like the additional cost, risk, and time spent with your rental.

You can also be more creative to make the most of your situation and the particularities of your location. In this case, you can rent a studio in France for nine months to students and the three remaining months to tourists during the summer, as long as both parties agree. It's a convenient strategy for everyone as students don't need their studio during summer break and, as a landlord, you can benefit from the high tourist season. In this example, you can rent your studio for $100 per night at a 75% occupancy rate. You can thus expect $6,750 for the three months and rent the studio for the rest of the year at $900 per month, which is $8,100 for nine months. Your total income is $14,850, which is not far from the $18,576 you would have earned working the entire year with your short-term rental because you enjoy the rent during the best season and the recurring revenue for the rest of the year. The advantage is that you have nine months less work with this mixed strategy.

There is also potential to create additional revenue while renting your place to a tenant. If you are a local person who knows a lot about your region, you might be able to offer your services as a guide. You might cook breakfast for your tenant or even prepare a welcome package with all they need for an additional fee. It's up to your imagination and the time you are willing to give to find new revenues.

7.4.3 House hacking

House hacking is a popular rental strategy in which you find ways to create income from a building while living in it. For example, acquiring a multiunit property, living in one unit, and renting the others. The main purpose of this strategy is to offset your living costs through the income generated.

Imagine you acquire a triplex and decide to live in one unit while renting the others. In this hypothetical case, your total mortgage payment is $3,000 per month and you rent each unit for $1,500. You are therefore living in a house while your tenants are paying the equivalent of your mortgage payment. Of course, you can apply this strategy to any building that can be divided into several units: shops, offices, garages. This strategy offers significant advantages.

- You get to live for free or at least significantly cover the mortgage payment.
- As you live next to your tenant, you can immediately intervene if a problem happens.
- You can get fiscal advantages since it is your primary place of residence.
- Since you are living next door, you can consider renting the unit over the short term to increase your returns.

House hacking offers many advantages, but you must be even more careful in your choice of tenants.

- You live next to your tenant, which can be very bad if they stop paying the rent, damage the property, or are noisy. This undermines your relationship with the neighbors, and a bad relationship with them can radically worsen your life.
- As your tenant is your neighbor, you might become friends and they could, unfortunately, take advantage of that. You must draw a line between a business relationship with your tenant and pure friendship.
- You often have to fix a low-priced property to make house hacking profitable. You must take into account all the repair costs and ensure you have the skills or hire good people for the work that needs to be done.

7.4.4 House flipping

Some people might run away from old buildings when they see that the walls need serious painting, the roof needs repairing, or the floor needs fixing. But where some investors see problems, others see opportunities. They imagine the house differently, not with the issues they currently observe but with the potential of what the building could become. If you are that investor, you might be interested in house flipping. This strategy is about acquiring real estate that needs renovation, fixing it, and then selling it at a profit.

It is a great way to make a sizeable profit but it requires time, effort, skills, and knowledge.

Imagine someone buys a house for $150,000, fixes the roof for $30,000, installs new windows for $20,000, decorates for $3,000, paints for $5,000, installs new lights for $5,000, and fixes the floor for $20,000. The total cost is $233,000 but the newly restored house is now worth $300,000 on the market.

This may sound like an exciting endeavor but there are many things you need to consider. You must have a clear vision of what you want to accomplish with your renovation and carefully map out every additional cost to determine if they are necessary to increase the house's value and help you sell it. When renovating a house, it can be tempting to remodel and upgrade everything, but as mentioned earlier, you must look at it with the eyes of an investor and keep the bottom line in mind. It is an investment; it's not the perfect place you have always dreamed of living in. If you are not a designer or don't have particularly subtle taste, it is advisable to stay basic. There is absolutely nothing wrong with that.

If you are flipping a condo and want to change the lights and give it a paint job, it would cost $800 to install regular lights and $800 to paint everything white, for a total of $1,600. Now let's imagine you want to upgrade your condo and have three different colors that cost $1,200 and some designer lights that cost $4,000 for a total cost of $5,200. The problem here is that taste is subjective; some people might love it, but some might hate the colors or the lights. Furthermore, when people buy a new place, they often want to choose their own colors or install lights that they like, and the first thing they might do is to change those. In addition, nobody ever tells you they didn't buy a condo because the lights are too simple or the walls are white. It is neutral and not the best, but it's not bad either.

There are various advantages when flipping a house.

- You can make a substantial profit.

- Fixing a house is a great learning experience as you deal with contractors, become aware of new building skills, evaluate repair costs, and so on.

- It is personally rewarding to see your vision take form and create something new from something old.

- You extend your network and work with people you would never have met before, such as bankers, lawyers, and contractors.

Unfortunately, there are also serious drawbacks to take into account.

- It is a risky strategy, not only for the unexpected costs that might crop up, but the selling price might be lower than expected.

- You are likely to be taxed on your profit when selling the property. In some countries, the tax might be substantial.

- The general price of construction materials may increase. Lately, prices of these have gone through the roof, and you must be very aware of this fact when estimating your construction costs.

- It is a very stressful process. Problems occur all the time when renovating a place, so you must keep your head cool under all circumstances.

- You could also make things worse if you don't have the skills or hire incompetent contractors.

If you have some building skills, have always been interested in construction, and have time to put into this kind of project, house flipping might be an excellent investment opportunity for you. Working on a house over the weekend and building it with your own hands can be a fun and rewarding experience if done correctly. However, if you don't have any building skills, I would advise against this strategy as it may become a terrible investment. You will solely rely on other people's expertise and skills, which will drastically increase your property's price.

7.5   Where to buy

It is often said that the most critical factors to consider when buying real estate are location, location, location. You might have struck the best possible deal for a good building, but if you have picked the wrong place, you could have problems attracting tenants. Unlike a building you can fix or improve, the location is something you have no power to change.

There are many factors to think about to determine if a location is good, but those factors depend very much on the type of real estate you want to rent and the type of tenants you want to attract. If you want to rent a studio to students, you are looking for universities and colleges nearby; if you want to rent a commercial building to a restaurant, you are looking for tourist attractions or offices in the environs; if you want to rent a one-family home, you are looking for a nice neighborhood. As such, a good location for one type of real estate could be a terrible location for another. If you want to rent an industrial plant, you are looking for an area with few houses, an industrial zone with proximity to a city, or good transportation and road access. This kind of location wouldn't be ideal for a family to live in.

When considering the location, you must look at the neighborhood. What is the neighborhood like? Is it safe? What's the crime rate? Are people friendly? Are the streets dirty? People want to live in a place where they feel safe and happy. So you should carefully reconsider any deal in a shady area with high criminality.

Amenities are also important. When identifying a place to live, people value proximity to shops, restaurants, good schools, public services, and so on. People are looking for convenience, for activities to do close to their homes. If you want to rent your place to a family with children, relative proximity to a good school is an essential criterion. If you want to rent a studio to a student, you are looking for a place close to universities, colleges and public transport.

Next, ask yourself if the place you rent is easily accessible by road. Can people walk in the neighborhood? Do they have quick access to public transport? Is the site far from the city center? People also often choose a place based on their current work location. Are there many factories, shops, or offices around? If you are in an urban area, do people have easy access to parking?

Be very wary of nuisance. Proximity to an airport, a popular bar with noisy clientele, the metro that shakes the building every time a train passes, or a dump with a horrible smell in summer—these are examples of factors that provide constant nuisance and could be deal-breakers. Although people can cope with a place far from their work, shops, and restaurants, it is much more difficult to find a tenant who is fine living with constant noise, shaking, or smell. You must be very careful when considering a property with various kinds of nuisance and ask yourself whether it's a decent place to live.

Some countries have legislation that is more favorable to landlords while others are more favorable to tenants. For example, Dubai requires the tenant to pay the rent one year before moving in. This ensures the landlord gets the full year's rental and encourages foreign investors to buy real estate. The same goes for taxes. Some places tax heavily while others are much less onerous.

You should also consider the return on investment. Some areas are more lucrative for renting than others. For example, a new apartment in the south of Belgium, close to the Luxembourg border, can get you a 6% return on your investment. In contrast, the same apartment 100 kilometers north only brings you 3%. You have to determine if the place you are targeting is worth the investment you make.

Some areas also appreciate more rapidly than others. If you own a building in a trendy area where more people are moving in and many projects are in development, the chances are that the price of real estate will grow rapidly and might even outpace a nearby district. In this case, you might have the chance to rent your place at a premium since the location attracts many people. Or you could sell the place at a rapidly appreciating price.

Once again, these criteria are generalities. You must think for yourself about what type of location the tenant you want to attract are looking for.

7.6 Your team

When acquiring real estate, you are in contact with many people, so it is worth taking the time to surround yourself with experts and advisors. In other words, create your own team that can help you make the best decision when investing.

7.6.1 Banker

Before selecting what you want to buy, you must check what you can afford and pay a visit to a trusty banker. This doesn't necessarily need to be the banker you take the loan with, but it has to be someone you can count on and who can advise you adequately. The first visit is to determine the amount of money you can safely borrow. At this stage, you don't even need to have a specific place you want to buy. However, it would be a good idea to talk with a banker in the area you plan to invest in, as they most likely have good knowledge of the market and can give you useful guidance.

When asking for a loan, the bank evaluates your situation and determines your creditworthiness. They look at your revenue, how much money you spend, other assets you have, other credit you have, and so on. Every bank has specific rules to determine how much you can borrow from them. In general, they apply a multiple to your income. Usually, it could range from four to six. If you earn $60,000 per year, you could borrow $240,000 from the bank. This amount varies from situation to situation, and the bank also takes into consideration any other debt you have to determine the final amount you can borrow.

Regarding the amount of money you must pay back every month, it is a certain percentage of your monthly income, generally about 40%. For example, if you earn $5,000, and you were already paying back $500 per month for a car loan, this means that you can pay back about $1,500 for a house loan. Of course, this figure varies from country to country, from bank to bank, and depends on your personal situation.

Once you have a specific project and know how much you need to borrow, it is time to shop around and get the lowest interest rate possible. The best way to do that is to be well prepared and clearly explain the project you plan, how much money you need, how much profit the project will bring you, and so on. You should visit as many banks as possible to see which offers you the best terms and conditions.

7.6.2 Notary

Another vital element of your team is the notary. Although legislation differs from country to country, you often need an impartial legal representative to witness property transfers from one person to another. This official performs various tasks in the transfer of property. They verify the loan documents, ensure everyone understands the documents they are signing, certifies all the documents are correctly signed and that the transfer of property is legalized, and confirms there is no fraud. Once again, the law varies from one country to another, but if you acquire real estate, you are most likely to deal with a notary to sanction the transfer of property.

7.6.3 Lawyer

When dealing with real estate, it is essential to be on the right side of the law and ensure everything you do is legal, which is why you should consult a lawyer who can inform you accurately of all the necessary documents and steps you need to take. One hour with a lawyer can save you a world of trouble. It is especially important when it is your first property.

Not all lawyers are the same; they each have their specialties. You should therefore deal with a lawyer in the region of the property you want to acquire to ensure that they are well aware of the real estate law from the particular area. The lawyer can help you draft the following contracts you need to rent out your property.

- *Lease agreement.* The contract that binds you and your tenant, containing all the rules, regulations, obligations, terms, and conditions of the rental. You might face lawsuits if this document is not properly written, so it is important to have it composed by a lawyer.
- *Rental inspection report.* This document generally contains pictures of your property that prove the initial state of the building when your tenant comes in.

Although you can easily find these contracts online, they are not necessarily suitable for your particular location. I strongly suggest spending a bit of money on a tailored contract that could save you trouble in the future. There are many other useful documents a lawyer can help draft, and you should ask for their legal advice for that purpose.

7.7 How to find the best real estate

Now it's time to have a look at where you can find rental properties.

7.7.1 Internet

A very effective way to start your research and filter through many options is to look online at specialized websites. As real estate is a competitive market, it is easy to find websites with several property choices in the region you are targeting. Then, with a couple of clicks, you can grasp the average market price for the type of building in the location you are looking for.

The most significant advantage of using websites is that it is a quick process that can give you a lot of information on current market prices and conditions. In a few minutes, you can screen through dozens of properties without visiting the places in person, saving you a lot of time. But you do have to assume that the pictures you see online are an idealized version of reality. It's worth remembering that, in the end, there is no substitute for visiting the site yourself, not only for the property but also the neighborhood.

Just remember that real estate websites might not project an entirely accurate version of what they're promoting.

Once you have filtered through the buildings you are interested in, you can set up virtual visits online or in-person visits. Some people buy houses online without visiting them, but I strongly advise against this. You mustn't take websites as a definitive means of choice but as a filter that helps you grasp the market. Once this is done, you only need to physically visit the best places.

7.7.2 Real estate agents

Another common way to find good properties is through real estate agents. Their job is to represent the seller, show the property, and assist in the sale process. The advantage of going through a good agent is that they represent many sellers, meaning they can show you places you didn't know or consider before. In addition, agents are generally specialized and knowledgeable in a specific area, so they can provide valuable information on the location or the type of real estate you are looking for. This includes the average market and renting price, what kind of tenants you deal with, the different issues you might face, and so on.

Beware! You might encounter some agents who are crooks. Although they might give you valuable information, they might also hide some critical data or even lie to you. You must take everything they say with a pinch of salt and constantly double-check every piece of information they provide. Even if the person you are dealing with is a good agent, you are not their customer; they get their commission from the person who sells the property and a salary from their company. Remember that they are trying to sell you something and not necessarily acting in your best interest. Whether it works out well for you or not is not their problem.

Something else you need to remember is that real estate agents very often pressurize you. They say there's another buyer for the building, that they need an answer very quickly, and that it's a once-in-a-lifetime opportunity you will lose if you don't take it now. When that happens, you must keep a cool head. People will always be betting against you on a building. I have personally come across dozens of "once-in-a-lifetime opportunities" given by real estate agents (sometimes several from the same agent).

Remember that you are making a lifetime investment and must keep calm. Whatever they say, there are always good investment opportunities, and it is better to miss a good one, to think carefully about all the facts, than to make a wrong decision that will affect you for the rest of your life.

Going through agents is a valuable experience; you will learn a lot from them during every visit. However, an agent is not your friend and you are not their direct customer either. The agent acts in the interest of their company first, their customer second, and you only last.

7.7.3 Newspapers

Although we live in a digital era, people still advertise real estate in newspapers. It remains a presence in many markets. You must think about the type of people who advertise in newspapers. These are often real estate agencies (in that case, the properties are also online), but also people who are not good with the internet and don't want to put their adverts online. Since many people don't bother to look at newspapers anymore, there is less competition for those properties and you might be able to find a suitable property that was overlooked by everyone else.

7.7.4 Person to person

Moving on, the best way to find excellent opportunities is to know someone who wants to sell. If you deal directly with this person, you avoid the fee that agents take to sell the building (which can be a fixed fee or a variable fee up to 5% or even 10% of the property's value). Not having to pay this fee makes the property cheaper and you generally have less competition as fewer people bid for the building since it is not on the open market.

Simply walking down a street might also help you find interesting opportunities. For example, many people put signboards on their property in order to sell it. Although it is not a reliable way to look for real estate, you can still find new opportunities.

There is a limit to the number of people everyone knows, but if you spread the word that you are looking to invest in real estate, people might come back to you with contact details, which can lead to an attractive opportunity.

7.7.5 Summary

All these methods to find real estate have advantages and disadvantages. My advice would be to make use of them all. When you do your research, first have a look online and in newspapers to obtain a good grasp of the market. Once you have a good idea of the price and what you are looking for, spread the word both in person and on social media that you're looking to invest in real estate. Then set up physical visits through real estate agents or directly with the owners. Make as many visits as possible, dozens or whatever it takes. During each visit, you learn something new, whether it's about the market itself, the particular area, or general building knowledge. These pieces of knowledge may be critical for you to make a good investment decision.

7.8 Finance

You can benefit from real estate investment in two ways—by capital appreciation or by renting it. However, not all properties are equal, so you must ensure that your investment is profitable. When evaluating a property, it is absolutely necessary to crunch the numbers and determine if your project is viable and worth your time, effort, and money. In this section, we go through the different costs and how you can calculate the potential return on investment from your property. You can't, under any circumstances, invest in a property if you don't calculate the feasibility of your project!

7.8.1 Building value

There are multiple costs to take into consideration when acquiring a property.

- *Building value.* It's the obvious one—the total amount you pay for the building and/or land you buy.

- *Closing costs.* When buying a property, you must pay taxes and legal fees to make the property transfer official.

- *Refurbishment costs.* Even if you buy a new property, you are most likely to have some work to do, such as installing lights or painting walls.

- *Miscellaneous.* Whatever property you buy, there are always extra costs you didn't anticipate.

7.8.2 Mortgages

Acquiring real estate requires a lot of capital and you are most likely to need to take a mortgage loan to afford it. These loans are designed to buy or renovate properties. They generally have a lower interest rate than other types of loans as they are considered safer for the banks since the property you purchase is used as collateral. This means that if you can't pay back your loan, the bank will seize the property and sell it to get its money back.

A loan has three main elements.

- *Principal.* The money you borrow.

- *Interest.* The percentage of interest you pay on the capital borrowed.

- *Fees.* The fees you need to pay the bank to create the loan.

Banks are really creative when it comes to designing complex financial assets to earn money, and they have created many different types of loans for that purpose. But for the sake of simplicity, I only highlight the two most common types.

- *Fixed interest rate.* The interest rate you pay stays constant. This gives you the advantage of knowing how much money you pay in interest every month. It's my personal favorite when investing in real estate as it is predictable, and you know exactly how much you will pay for this project.

- *Variable interest rate.* The interest rate you pay fluctuates over time based on a benchmark or an index the bank follows. The variable interest rate is generally lower than the fixed rate as it gives the bank the security that the interest rate follows this benchmark.

If you are in a period of historically low interest rates, it might be wiser to take a fixed loan as it is unlikely to stay that low over the long run. If it gets lower, you can still refinance it. If the general interest rate gets higher, you keep your loan as it is.

Let's take a concrete example to show how the interest you pay is calculated. Let's say you borrow $140,000 for 20 years at a 1.14% yearly fixed interest rate, and you pay back every month the same amount of $652.63. When paying a loan on a fixed monthly interest rate, you are paying first the interest calculated every month. In this case: $140,000 × (1.14% / 12) = $133 of interest. You then deduct this interest from the total amount you pay every month, and you know how much of the principal you are reimbursing: $652.63 − $133 = $519.63. So the next month your interest is calculated based on the remaining money you owe, which is $140,000 − $519.63 = $139,480.37 and therefore your new interest is $139,480.37 × (1.14% / 12) = $132.51. So the amount you are reimbursing on the second month is $652.63 − $132.51 = $520.12. As you can see, you pay more interest at the beginning, since the principal you borrow is more important. As time passes, the principal decreases and therefore the interest you pay as well.

Banks usually require a minimum capital called a down payment, which is a percentage of the purchase you want to make. It's the money you directly invest in buying a property. The minimum requirement depends on the country where you take the loan; it can vary from 1% to 10% or more. In some rare cases, you might not even need to bring any capital and the purchase is fully funded by the bank. Keep in mind that it's not because your bank requires a minimum down payment of 5% that you should only pay that amount. You can pay as much as you want. The more capital you bring to the table, the less you need to borrow and the less interest you pay.

7.8.3 Cash flow

Now let's calculate and evaluate a rental property's cash flow. The primary income to consider is the rent you get every month. You can take into account other income sources in your calculations if you provide additional services such as gardening, laundry, or parking.

The easiest way to evaluate the potential income you might earn from a property is to look at specialized websites for how much other similar properties in the same area are rented for. For example, look at the average rental of 10 similar properties in the same location and you will have a good idea of how much you can rent your property for.

Next there are expenses. Here is a non-exhaustive list of the expenses you will likely face and need to take into consideration.

- *Mortgage payment.* As we have seen, one of the main costs you face as a landlord is the mortgage payment.
- *Taxes.* You must calculate the taxes you pay on your property. For this you can research online or talk to a tax advisor.
- *Vacancy.* You must assume that your property is not always rented. Sometimes a tenant stays for three years, but you might need some time to find the next tenant. That's why it is important to account for vacancies and spend a bit of money every month for that purpose. It depends on your location and the type of property, but you can use 5% of your monthly rent for that purpose.

- *Repairs, maintenance, and capital expenditure.* It is always important to save money to maintain and fix the property. You also have to account for fixing big things such as replacing a roof or windows. That's why it is wise to put a bit of money on the side every month for that purpose. There isn't a specific rule, but you can allocate 5% of your monthly rent for that purpose.
- *Utilities.* Sometimes landlords include utilities in the rental price, such as water, electricity, sewage, or heating.
- Insurance. It's essential that your building is insured and covered by a reputable company. You can contact an insurance broker to have a rough estimation of how much it would cost.
- Property management fees, condominium fees. If you don't manage your property yourself or if you own a condo in an apartment building, you have to pay a fee for the management of your property.

Now that you have your income and expenses, you can assess your cash flow by simply deducting your expenses from your income. You can calculate your return on investment based on the capital you invest, but also based on the total value of the property.

All of this might seem a bit overwhelming when only writing about it. When summarized, property finances get a bit simpler to understand (Table 7.1).

Table 7.1 Property finances

Item	Amount ($)
Real estate	
Building value	200,000
Closing costs	40,000
Refurbishment costs	6,500
Miscellaneous	3,500
Total building value	**250,000**

Item	Amount ($)
Financing	
Principal	200,000
Fees	500
Down payment	45,500
Total financing	**250,000**
Yearly income	
Rent	12,000
Other income	0
Total income	**12,000**
Yearly expenses	
Mortgage principal	7,000
Mortgage interest	1,000
Taxes	500
Vacancy	500
Repairs, maintenance, and capital expenditure	500
Utilities	0
Insurance	500
Property management fees	0
Total expenses	**10,000**
Cash flow	
Income	12,000
Expenses	10,000
Total	**2,000**

7.8.4 Ratios

Once you have laid out all your income and expenses, you can determine the profitability of your investment. It is very useful when comparing several properties and selecting the best investment opportunity.

Gross rental yield. This is calculated by dividing the total yearly income by the total building value (including refurbishing and closing costs) and multiplying by 100 to get a percentage. In other words, it's the gross rate of return on your investment. In this case, it is (12,000 / 250,000) × 100 = 4.8%.

Capitalization rate. This is calculated by subtracting all the expenses (including mortgage interest but not including mortgage principal) from the total yearly income, and dividing it by the total building value (including refurbishing and closing costs) and multiplying by 100 to get a percentage. It's a more accurate version of the gross rental yield as it takes into account all your expenses. In this case, it is ((12,000 − 3,000) / 250,000) × 100 = 3.6%.

Return on capital invested. This is calculated by dividing your net income by the total capital you have personally invested. This ratio only considers the return on capital invested. In this case, it is ((12,000 − 3,000) / 50,000) × 100 = 18%.

So is this property a good investment opportunity? The answer is, it depends. When analyzing your return, you have to compare it with other local investments. If other investors in your area get an average of 10% on their capitalization rate for the same kind of property, then it's not a good investment. On the other hand, if people get an average of 2%, then it's outperforming others.

7.9 Comparing real estate

The best way to see if your real estate is a good investment is to compare it with others. Before acquiring your first property, I strongly recommend you visit many different places. In this way, you learn a lot, especially at the beginning when you don't have real estate experience. You shouldn't jump on the first opportunity because it is the most convenient for you. Take your time and compare it with others.

Something I believe is helpful when visiting multiple properties is to create a fact sheet. When looking for a place, I often ask the same questions about what is essential for me: neighborhood, potential renting price, total cost, and so on. Unfortunately, sometimes I forget to ask for essential information and have to call the agent or the owner again, which is time-consuming and unprofessional. This is why I created my own fact sheet (Table 7.2).

Table 7.2 Fact sheet: real estate analysis

Description	
Type:	
Name:	
Address:	

Location	

Building	
M²:	Utility/storage room:
Insulation:	Cellar:
Room(s):	Attic:
Hallway:	Car park:
Kitchen:	Elevator:
Living room:	Balcony:
Dining room:	Terrace:
Bathroom:	Garden/yard:
Toilet:	Roof:
Other:	

Finance	
Purchase price:	Property management fees:
Closing costs:	Taxes:
Refurbishing:	Repairs and maintenance:
Miscellaneous:	Capital expenditure:
Annual rent:	Insurance:

Additional comments

Source: https://www.kevinponcelet.com/

When I visit a property, I take this fact sheet with me and fill it up. This fact sheet reflects my own preferences—things I want to remember in the type of real estate I am looking for in the particular region I have expertise in. If you don't like this model, I would advise you to create your own real estate fact sheet for the type of real estate you want to invest in.

The only way to be truly objective is to compare real estate based on the same information. This is why it is important to complete these fact sheets once you start to visit a couple of different places. Once you have done so and you're considering investing between different properties, you can gather all this information and compare it. It's only by comparing real estate properties with the same information that you can truly determine which one is the best for you.

7.10 Tenants

Now that you have picked the perfect location and a great building that brings you a good investment return, it is time to find a tenant. Everyone has heard stories about terrible tenants who are noisy or completely trash a building. Although most of the time tenants are reasonable, we often focus on the minority who make someone's life miserable. For these reasons, some people don't want to invest in real estate as they are afraid of getting a bad tenant who damages the property or constantly calls them to fix problems. They only focus on the bad aspects of being a landlord and give up without even trying to find a solution to rectify these problems. As you will see below, there are many different ways you can avoid those issues in the first place.

7.10.1 Your property and mindset

As just mentioned, you often hear stories from landlords with terrible tenants, but you don't often hear the other side of the story. There is a well-known saying for real estate investors: "We get the tenant that we deserve."

As a landlord, if you don't put in any effort, give your tenant a building in terrible condition, don't pick up the phone when problems occur, or don't want to do any essential maintenance, the chances are you will end up with a bad tenant. If you don't provide the bare minimum, why would your tenant bother to make any effort for you? It is logical that bad property and lousy management result in bad tenants. This is not to say that you won't have any issues if you always act well, but if you offer poor services, don't be surprised when you get poor tenants.

You must remember that your tenant is a customer and not your friend. You have to treat your rental property like a business. And like any business, you must try to keep the best relationships with your customers and go the extra mile for them. However, you must draw the line on some aspects of your business and ensure your tenant follows them. Whenever you deal with your tenant, you must show professionalism, be organized, follow the law to the letter, and be clear with the rules. Then, whenever there is a misstep with those rules, you must immediately react in a professional manner to prove that you are on top of everything and won't get bullied.

7.10.2 How to pick the right tenant

To find a tenant, you have to make your property available through a specialized renting property website or through an agent who should select the best tenant for you. There is no such thing as an ideal profile for a tenant as it depends on the type of real estate you are renting. If you are renting a studio to a student, your tenant won't have a tenant history, salary, or stable financial situation. But you can interview their parents and get a guarantee from them.

Keep in mind that, depending on the country you live in, there are some questions you can ask and some you legally cannot. You must ensure that you follow the law strictly and only ask pertinent questions as a landlord: What is your job? What is your salary? Do you live with a family? Do you smoke? Do you have pets?

7.10.3 How to avoid problems

An ideal way to deal with problems is to avoid them in the first place by creating systems or having your rental set up in such a way that those problems can't occur. As an example, let's say that you rent an apartment and the water is calcareous. If your tenant doesn't regularly maintain the faucets, sinks, and shower, they will be damaged over the long run and you might have to replace them. Instead of counting on a tenant to do their job, you should consider installing a softener to improve the water quality and radically increase your water infrastructure's lifespan. Then, whether or not your tenant does their part correctly, your water infrastructure will last much longer.

If you don't want to be woken up at every hour by your tenant, be very clear that you can only be contacted during office hours and that you always answer within 24 hours. Only give an emergency phone number for real emergencies: fires, flooding, and so on. Honestly, even in those cases, there is probably nothing much you can do, except call the fire station.

Write a clause in the lease contract that prohibits pets on your property if you can. That way, you avoid having your tenant's pets damage your property or being too noisy for the neighbors.

Of course, every rental property is different. You have to look at your place and see what kinds of problems could happen and how you can set up things so that they don't.

7.10.4 How to plan for problems

How best to deal with actual problems? Most of the time, being a landlord means solving the same kinds of issues. The good thing is that you can plan in advance for problems and already have your solution ready. Then, when problems do happen, you simply have to refer to the solutions you have already prepared. This allows you to respond more effectively and prevent your emotions getting in the way.

- If there is a leak or your facilities don't work, give your tenant a list of phone numbers of handymen living nearby who could solve those issues if you can't do it yourself: a plumber, an electrician, a locksmith, a heating specialist.

- If your tenants don't pay on time, have a reminder set to check with them. If the problem persists, you might need to consider the type of legal action you have to take. You can have warning letters and eviction notices ready in advance for that purpose.

- In case your tenants damage the property, make sure that the lease contract is properly signed when the tenant moves in and that you have a documented lease report with pictures showing the state of the property when the tenancy started.

- In case your tenant loses their house keys, always have a backup set ready for them.

Aside from these examples, you should try to figure out the problems you will most likely face as a landlord for the type of property you have and prepare a solution for them.

7.11 Going further

You have to run your real estate like a business and you have to run it the way you want. If you decide that you are the one doing all the fixing, then you will indeed do that. If you decide to outsource all of it, you can do that instead, but you have to account for those extra expenses from the beginning.

Now that you have a basic understanding of what lies ahead, it is time for you to take action. The contents of this book are a firm foundation for you to build on, but they are by no means exhaustive. There are many excellent inexpensive resources: talk with people who have already invested the same way you plan to do, visit some places you might be interested in buying, listen to podcasts, get hold of books about real estate, watch videos online, and take seminars.

If you are looking for great insights into real estate, I suggest taking advantage of BiggerPockets. They have books, podcasts, YouTube videos, and a forum on real estate. You can get a lot of valuable information from their website: https://www.biggerpockets.com/.

If you are truly committed to doing the necessary work, real estate investing could be a tremendous experience and a first-class source of passive or active income in the future.

Chapter 8

Gold and Other Precious Metals

Since the dawn of humanity, gold has been considered an investment opportunity and widely used just about everywhere as a means of payment, precious raw material, safe haven, and jewelry. In this chapter, I explain the basics of gold investment, why people invest in it, what type of investment you can make, and how to invest in it. Although the information mainly focuses on gold, it can also apply to other precious metals such as silver, palladium, or platinum.

8.1 The basics

Before considering investing in gold, you must understand the basics. A common term you will hear is "ounce." Gold coins, silver bars, and other precious metals are often sold in ounces, and there are two types of ounces.

- The troy ounce (t oz or oz t.) weighs 31.1 grams
- The regular ounce weighs 28.35 grams

You must be aware of this difference, as it represents about 10% of the total weight. Gold is traditionally weighed in troy ounces, but some sellers list their product in ounces instead of troy ounces to mislead their potential customers and make their gold look like a bargain when it actually weighs less.

Another term you should know is "karat" which refers to gold purity. When used in jewelry, 100% pure gold is equivalent to 24 karats. Each karat therefore represents 1/24 of the 100% purity. For example, a 12-karat gold ring contains 50% pure gold (12 ÷ 24 = 0.5), and a 20-karat gold ring contains 83% pure gold (20 ÷ 24 = 0.833). You rarely find 24-karat jewelry as pure gold is soft and can be scratched, damaged, or easily bent. Instead, jewelers often mix it with other metals such as copper, zinc, or silver to create the color, shape, and hardiness jewelers want. Don't confuse "karat" with "carat," which is used to measure the weight of gemstones such as diamonds. One carat weighs 0.2 grams.

Next, you need to understand how gold and other precious metals are priced. There are three main components.

- *Spot price*. The price of the precious metal itself. The spot price constantly changes as the market price of gold fluctuates. You can easily check the market price of gold and other precious metal online (www.bullionbypost.eu/gold-price).

- *Premium*. The price you pay for all the intermediaries handling the transaction and the work done to transform the precious metal into its final form, such as coins, bars, or jewelry. The premium price varies based on the work necessary to create the final product, the number of intermediaries, the margin the intermediaries take, the type and size of the product, and so on. Generally, the smaller the piece you buy, the higher the premium per unit. It costs far more to mint 100 1-ounce coins than a single 100-ounce bar. Therefore, the premium on a 1-ounce coin is higher than on a 100-ounce bar.

- *Taxes*. Like many investments, you often have to pay taxes for precious metals, but the tax rate differs in each country. If you plan to invest in gold and other precious metals, you should be aware of your country's legislation and taxation, as this might significantly impact your return and investment strategy.

8.2 What brings value to gold

There are various reasons to invest in gold and other precious materials: their scarcity, safe value, diversification, or because they represent a hedge against inflation and an investment opportunity. As an investor, you must always invest purposefully and determine if one of those reasons makes sense in your investment plan.

In today's economy, we are using fiat money, which is a currency not backed by physical assets but by governments and central banks. All fiat money ever created has evolved and been replaced over time, unlike gold and other precious metals that have been around for thousands of years. Gold is considered a safe value, a hedge against inflation and crisis, which is why central banks round the world keep massive gold reserves.

According to the World Gold Council (2023), it is estimated that humankind has mined around 200,000 metric tons of gold over the course of its history (and about ⅔ since 1950). The United States Geological Survey (n.d.) evaluates the world's reserves at approximately 57,000 metric tons of economically minable gold.[1] Although gold has become harder to mine, its production has grown significantly over the years, and we are currently mining around 3,500 metric tons annually. At this rate, we will run out of gold within the next two decades. Even worse, current gold production is insufficient to cover demand, and it is estimated that around 25% of the annual gold supply comes from recycling jewelry and electronics. With gold reserves becoming scarcer, experts expect that gold prices will rise and gold recycling will have a critical role in its supply.

Although gold doesn't generate any income, it has historically grown in value and can act as a hedge against inflation or even as an investment opportunity. For example, from 2000 to 2020, the inflation rate in the United States was 2.1% on average, meaning that over 20 years the general price of goods and services increased by about 50%. In contrast, a troy ounce of gold cost $250 in 2000 and was traded at $1,750 in 2020, multiplying its value by seven. In this case, a gold investment not only served as a protection against inflation but also represented a great investment opportunity. Be aware that gold prices fluctuate significantly over the years and it is

---

[1] It is challenging to assess the planet's gold resources with precision since some places are considered economically minable at the current gold price, but more sites will be considered economically minable if the gold price increases.

not a guaranteed winning investment. If you bought gold in 1981 and kept it for 20 years, you would have lost money (Figure 8.1).

Figure 8.1 Gold price, 1974–2021

Gold has always been widely used in jewelry for its unique coloration and malleability. It doesn't tarnish or corrode over time while in contact with air or humidity. Its scarcity and price make it a symbol of power.

Gold is also generally used in electronics because of its density and its function as a heat conductor. Furthermore, gold is preferred to highly conductive metals like copper or silver because it doesn't oxidize or rust.

Finally, gold is a great way to diversify your portfolio from traditional assets like real estate or stocks. Many mutual funds have around 3% to 5% of gold in their portfolio as a hedge against inflation, protection in times of crisis, and diversification.

8.3 What form of gold to invest in

Gold comes in different forms and shapes, and people invented various creative ways to benefit from it. In this section, I describe the common ways people invest in gold and other precious metals. Of course, the type of investment you choose depends on your investment goals and why you have decided to invest in gold in the first place.

8.3.1 Coins

Coins are the most popular way to invest in gold and other precious metals as their value is standard, they are recognizable worldwide, and you can easily buy and sell them. There are three types of coins: bullion coins, proof coins, and uncirculated coins. Each has a different purpose. It is essential that you know the differences to determine which best fits your investment plan.

Bullion coins are the most common as they are mass-produced by the tens of thousands. They are punched from metal bars, cleaned, polished, and struck once. They generally have the advantage of being well known around the world, and you can easily find their market price online or through a broker. The most famous coins are the American Eagle, African Krugerrand, American Buffalo, Canadian Maple Leaf, and Chinese Gold Panda. These coins vary in size and purity; the American Buffalo is pure gold, while the American Eagle is 23 karats. As they are mass-produced, bullion coins have the lowest premium among all coins. If you want to invest in gold because of the material and you want something easily recognizable and marketable, famous bullion coins are the best choice for you.

Proof coins have the highest quality. They are hand-polished and struck twice to ensure the best quality possible. The coins are then carefully packaged in a capsule and often placed in a box with an official certificate of authenticity. The design of proof coins is the same as bullion coins, but the finishing could be different: shinier or having a mirror-like background. Proof coins were originally created to ensure their quality and design before mass-producing them. They are always made in a limited number and accompanied by a certificate of authenticity that states how many coins were struck and which number you own. As they are a limited edition, these coins are collectibles and come with a high premium. If you want to invest in coins for their collection value and want the highest quality and craftsmanship possible, then proof coins are a good choice.

Uncirculated coins are an intermediate between bullion and proof coins. They follow the same production process as the bullion coins and are struck only once. The finishing of these coins could be slightly better than bullion coins but not as good as proof coins. The main difference with bullion coins is that they come with an authentication certificate and are placed immediately in a protective capsule to preserve the coins' quality. They are rarer and have a higher premium than the bullion but usually a lower price than proof coins. So these coins are a good way to ensure excellent quality while staying within a budget.

8.3.2 Bars

Gold bars usually have a lower premium than bullion coins as it is much easier for refiners to mint bars rather than coins which requires more work. You can buy bars as small as 1 gram and sometimes up to 12.5 kilograms (but be ready to put down the price of a house to have the privilege of owning that kind of bar). When investing in bars, you should consider the following.

- *Size*. It is easier for a refiner to produce one gold bar of 100 grams than 100 gold bars of 1 gram. Furthermore, gold bars are generally packaged and there is a small cost for individual packages to consider. There will therefore be a lower premium per gram when you buy a heavier bar.
- *Brand*. Some refiners have a better reputation than others and have a higher premium on their bars.
- *Finishing*. Some refiners have unique designs on their bars, whereas others will be rough and simpler. This level of detail influences the premium you pay for your bar.

Regarding the size you should invest in, having the biggest bar to pay the lowest premium might not be the best strategy, as you have to think about the market liquidity. It is easy to find someone to buy a 10-gram gold bar for $650, but it is much harder to find someone willing to buy a 12.5-kilogram bar for $800,000 and more.

In addition, it is very tempting for the seller to create a fake bar or melt it and put a bar of iron in the middle, keeping the rest of the gold for themselves, and selling you the bar as if it was pure gold. Still, if you are considering investing in gold as a safe haven and to own something whose value is recognized worldwide, gold bars might be an excellent opportunity as the premium is much lower than for coins, and bar prices can be easily found online.

8.3.3 Digital gold

Instead of buying physical gold, you can buy digital gold from a mint or specialized company that safely stores it and can even sell it for you. Generally, the mint purchases and stores large bars and sells fraction ownership to different buyers. This method of buying gold is very convenient and there are many advantages.

- It is cost-effective, as you buy a fraction of a large bar and pay a low premium for your gold.
- It is very liquid, as you can buy and sell directly from the comfort of your home. The mint or platform you are buying from can generally repurchase it from you immediately, so you don't even have to worry about finding customers.
- You can buy gold in the dollar amount you want, say $50, instead of buying in a specific weight like an ounce.
- You don't have to worry about transportation, robbery, insurance, or finding a safe place to store your gold as everything is already taken care of.
- Buying from the mint or a reliable platform ensures you buy pure gold that isn't fake.

Of course, this convenience comes at a price.

- You pay various fees, covering purchase, storage, and sales, that you must check before investing as these can considerably reduce your long-term profit.

- You must buy from a reliable source, preferably a national mint backed by a government, to ensure you are not scammed.
- When buying digital gold, you obviously won't have access to the physical gold.

8.3.4 Jewelry

Another form of gold investment is jewelry. Many people buy jewelry to give to their loved ones, but some also buy it as an investment. This practice is quite popular in India where the idea is to invest while enjoying wearing your investment.

However, if you plan to invest in jewelry, be aware that the premium you pay is quite expensive as pieces are not always mass-produced and it requires a lot of work to design and create jewelry. Furthermore, if you resell your jewelry, it will most likely be melted down to recycle the material unless it is a famous piece from a well-known artisan or has historical value. Investing in gold jewelry is the most inefficient method as the premium you pay for gold bars and coins is much cheaper. But if you want to make a precious gift that can serve as a legacy for the next generation, it might not be a bad idea.

8.3.5 Financial assets

An alternative to purchasing physical gold is to invest in financial assets. Unlike physical gold, those assets can instantly be bought and sold in a couple of clicks while giving you exposure to gold and other precious metals.

Instead of buying yourself gold, an indirect way to benefit from it is to buy stocks of companies that deal with gold, like gold miners and refineries. As the business model of these companies is directly connected with the gold price, their stock price often fluctuates with it. These companies usually do well when the gold price is historically high. However, remember that not everything is directly related to the gold price. These companies have their own issues, goals, and management teams. They can still go bankrupt even if the gold price is high. You have to invest in them because you believe in the underlying business, not only because you believe in that sector. You must also consider the inherent safety and geopolitical risks related to gold mining that even the best company can't influence.

Rather than handpicking stocks, you can select ETFs and mutual funds that specialize in gold. These financial assets invest in stocks of gold companies, physical gold, derivatives, and so on. When investing in these assets, you ensure that you have diversified holdings in gold managed by professionals specializing in that field. You must be careful when you select your investment as they can be highly leveraged in derivatives of real gold. So although it can be quite profitable, it can also be risky.

I also need to mention that it is possible to invest in gold via futures and options. A futures contract is where you agree to buy gold in the future at a specific price. An option contract is where you agree to buy or sell gold at a specific price before a set date. Be alert that these are generally considered more speculative tools rather than long-term investments and require specialized knowledge and expertise.

8.4 Where and how to get your gold

Gold is an expensive metal, and there are many people and organizations that specialize in creating counterfeits and are flooding the market with fake gold. As such, the safest way to purchase physical gold is to buy it directly from the mint and refiners to ensure it is legitimate. Many refiners have physical shops and official websites where you can buy gold and have it delivered to a safe location. In addition, these deliveries are generally insured to avoid any nasty surprises.

You can buy and sell your gold in a physical shop from certified resellers. The main advantage is that you can see and touch the gold. Furthermore, you have a variety of choices from different brands. However, these shops charge you an additional premium.

Alternatively, you can buy your gold from many platforms and professional resellers. However, you must ensure that they are reliable intermediaries and that they aren't selling fake gold. So I advise against this strategy and suggest you buy directly from the source whenever possible.

If you are a collector of rare coins, you must go through shops and auction houses. Once again, these coins can be very expensive and you must ensure that you have their quality and origin certified.

8.5 Gold collections

If you are more of a collector and you love to own rare things, there are various factors you should be aware of that give value to a gold collection.

First, there is desirability. When investing in a coin collection, you target a specific niche market. You must determine if there is a niche market of people interested in the collection you want to start. If you are a *Star Wars* fan, you might fall in love with the R2D2 1-ounce gold coin. However, remember that not everyone likes *Star Wars*; and among fans, not all are interested in buying collectible coins. You will always be able to find someone interested in buying an American Gold Eagle or Maple Gold Leaf because those are standard coins. Collectibles, on the other hand, are for collectors; it's a niche market and you must be certain that you will find many prospective buyers.

Next, consider scarcity and mintage. The mintage is the number of coins the mint produces for a particular series. For example, the 1-ounce silver Lion of England in the Royal Tudor Beasts collection had a mintage of 7,010, which means that number of coins were struck for the series. Collectible coins are always released in limited numbers. If you are thinking about starting a collection, you should always be aware of the supply that will be released on the market. If the mint is going to release 100,000 coins or 1,000 coins, the coin's potential desirability will be quite different.

To increase the popularity of coin collections, mints create limited edition series where one or two coins of the collection are released yearly. However, this strategy doesn't always work; some coin collections never become popular and their demand quickly drops. As a collector, it may be difficult for you to find interested buyers. The best way to determine if a coin will be popular is to check on specialized forums. If a series comes out and people start to talk and obsess about it, there is a good chance it will continue to be popular.

If you like to collect and are an amateur in fine art and history, you might also be interested in buying rare gold coins that have an important historical provenance. Those coins can be bullion, uncirculated, or proof coins and can be sold for a high premium. However, it is a very niche market as only those people passionate about this collection are willing to pay the price.

By nature, rare coins are challenging to find. This scarcity could be intentional when a mint produces very few coins, hoping to create a frenzy for a limited supply and charging a high price. It could also be unintentional when the coins almost disappear from circulation. For example, 180,000 Double Eagle 1927-D $20 coins were struck, but the US government recalled the few that were sold because of the onset of the Great Depression. There are now only a couple in circulation and their value is estimated at $1.3 million and above.

A recent example of a successful coin collection is the Queen's Beasts series from the British Royal Mint that came out from 2016 to 2021. Every year the Royal Mint struck two coins representing the 10 Queen's Beasts heraldic statues erected in the Queen's honor during her coronation at Westminster Abbey in 1953. This collection was a great success and got a lot of attention on social media and specialized forums. In 2021, when the series was completed, the most popular coin of the series was the 2-ounce silver Griffin coin of 2017, selling for up to $200 on the secondary market, which is about 10 times the spot price. It might seem excessive, but that's how attractive the coin became in only three years.

When determining the value of a coin, one critical aspect to consider is its condition. The condition is graded on a 70-level Sheldon scale subdivided into three categories.

- Levels 1–49 are for circulated coins. Level 1 is for almost unidentifiable and very poor-quality coins. Level 49 is for excellent coins that only present minor imperfections.

- Levels 50–58 are for uncirculated coins that have been very well preserved and most likely never left their protective capsule.

- Levels 60–70 are for Mint State (MS) coins. These coins have the same quality as when coming out of the mint. Proof coins are supposed to be in perfect condition; however, they might differ from each other in very small details, only visible with an eight-fold magnification.

The value of your collection very much depends on its condition. That's why you must preserve and protect the coins by encapsulating and keeping them safe in a box.

8.6 Going further

Various factors can motivate you to invest in gold and other precious metals. Whatever your reasons, you have to make sure that it makes sense in your investment plan.

- If you are looking for a short- to mid-term opportunity because you believe that the gold price is very low and might increase in the future, investing in financial assets like stocks or ETFs might present a great investment opportunity for you as they are very easy to buy and sell, and there are low fees. On the other hand, buying physical gold and selling it six months later is a lot of work as you must store it, find a customer, and deliver it.

- If you are looking for safe insurance in case of a huge crisis, physical gold like bullion coins and bars could be an excellent opportunity.

- If you want to create a legacy, something to pass on to your heirs, then coins and bars might be interesting. Whether you want to create a collection or buy rare ones depends on you. In any case, the precious metal will always have value.

- If you are a collector looking to own something special with the best craftsmanship possible, then investing in proof or rare coins might be a good opportunity.
- If you want to diversify your portfolio and you have got a lot of physical, non-liquid assets like real estate, then investing in financial products like gold may be appropriate for you. It offers you the flexibility to buy and sell almost instantly.

When investing, you must do a lot of research. There are a lot of forums, blogs, and websites that can provide you with valuable articles and information.

- Coinweek. This website is primarily focused on rare coins, paper money, and other articles that will interest numismatists (www.coinweek.com).
- The Silver Forum. You can find a lot of discussions about the latest and most popular collections. You can also ask questions to a large community that will happily help you (www.thesilverforum.com).
- Bullion by Post. I like to use this website when I want to look at the current price of precious metals. It is very convenient and you can change the currency (www.bullionbypost.co.uk/gold-price/).
- World Gold Council. This website gives you a lot of useful information about gold as well as a beginner's guide that might be useful for your investment (www.gold.org).

If you are a beginner about to make your first purchase, I would advise you to look at the official mints in your country, including the following.

- Britain: The Royal Mint (www.royalmint.com)
- United States: United States Mint (www.usmint.gov)

- Canada: The Royal Canadian Mint (https://www.mint.ca/en)
- France: La Monnaie de Paris (www.monnaiedeparis.fr/fr)

For your first purchase, it's easier to look at local opportunities as they might exempt you from taxes and duties.

You can sell your gold and collections in various ways.

- *Retail*. You can directly sell your gold to collectors at conventions, markets, or on forums and websites such as eBay. Although it is time-consuming, it's the best way to sell your gold at market price.
- *Specialized shops*. You can sell your gold at specialized shops. It is convenient as you can most likely sell them in large quantities at once, but be aware that the price they give you will be lower than if you sell directly to collectors as they need to make a profit when reselling it.
- *Auctions*. If your collection is truly valuable and you have some rare pieces, it might be worth participating in public auctions. If your collection gets traction, the price could go through the roof. Be aware that you need to pay fees for those services.
- *Mints*. Official mints often provide an opportunity to buy back your gold and other precious metal. Although they will likely take out a portion of the premium, you won't have any problem to sell them in bigger quantity, which can save you a lot of time.

Finally, you should also pay particular attention to what percentage of your portfolio gold and other precious metal should have. Many fund managers believe that it is generally considered safe to have 5–10% of your portfolio in other assets such as gold. Once again, it depends on your personal situation, needs, and what you want to achieve in the future, but gold and other precious metals are good candidates to play a diversification role in your portfolio.

Chapter 9

Collectibles

This part of the book may be controversial, as many people won't consider a collection as a reliable investment. However, there is no denying that some collections are worth a fortune. For example, the nine Fabergé eggs of the Malcolm Forbes collection sold in 2004 for $50 million; Elizabeth Taylor's jewelry collection sold in 2011 for $116.8 million; and a collection of 22 Swiss watches sold in 2015 for $6.1 million. Those collections are, of course, inaccessible for most people, and it is unreasonable to think that a cheap collection could be worth a fortune overnight.

Most of us have memories of things we collected as children, whether they were rocks, playing cards, dolls, or a Lego set. We collected objects to have fun. For a passionate person, it could be to learn more about their passion or nostalgia. And for an investor, it is a means of diversifying their portfolio or making a profit.

In this chapter, we consider a collection as a group of one type of object that has been gathered together, but we also include individual artifacts or objects that have significant value. It covers what brings value over time to a collection, which collection to start, how to value a collection, where to buy and sell a collection, and some examples of the rise and fall of famous collections.

9.1 What brings value to a collection

Collecting objects for an investment purpose differs from collecting them as a hobby, and you always have to keep that purpose in mind. When investing, your primary goal is not to have the best collection or a complete set at any cost. Instead, your main goal is to make the most of your investment. You have to weigh the risk and possible reward of your investment.

Successful and expensive collections usually have common characteristics. Identifying those characteristics helps you determine if a collection has investment potential or if it should just be considered a hobby.

The first element has to do with supply and demand. If something is rare, cannot be produced anymore, and has a high demand, the chances are that this object is very desirable and people are willing to pay a high price for it. Collections of fine wine are sold for fortunes: a bottle of Château Mouton Rothschild from 1945 was sold for $343,000. As only a few bottles are left and this particular bottle is in demand, prices can skyrocket.

Scarcity is an important characteristic that can define the value of a collection. However, an object must be desirable and in demand to increase in value; it is not only because something is scarce that people are interested in it. For example, a rare collection of gums chewed by Winston Churchill might be unique, but it doesn't mean anyone will be interested in buying it.

It is essential to acknowledge that people might be interested in a collection for a while and that the current demand might be a passing fashion. One day, everyone may rush and queue at shops to get them, but after a while people get bored and go after the next shiny thing. This was the case for Beanie Babies in 1995 when everyone wanted these teddy bears and some even sold for more than $5,000. However, with the emergence of Pokémon cards and Furbies, Beanie Babies declined in popularity. Now only the most valuable ones are still worth something, but nothing like the price they used to fetch. So when starting a collection, you should always determine the rarity of the collection, if there is a short supply of the objects, a sustainable demand for them, or if it is only a passing fad.

Next, when selling an artifact or collection, the condition is critical and this can be the difference between a worthless object or a treasure. When collecting objects of a certain value, experts can usually evaluate their condition and determine a price. Of course, the better the condition the more valuable the object is. Some grading systems exist for standard collections like coins, as we saw earlier, but also for cards and stamps. For example, collectible cards can be graded and protectively sealed by specialized companies like Professional Sports Authenticator (PSA) or Beckett Grading Services (BGS). These companies have a scale grading system from 1 being in very poor condition to 10 being in perfect condition. At present, PSA 10 Charizard first edition Pokémon cards have been sold for more than $400,000, but a PSA 8 Charizard sold for about $10,000, and the only difference between those two cards could be as simple as one white spot or a tiny scratch on the back of the card.

Having your collection graded by experts gives your prospective customer the insurance of a certain level of quality. With this insurance, they might be more willing to buy your collection than an unrated one. However, it could also be a double-edged sword if your collection turns out to be of a lower quality than you expected.

When it comes to antiques, they can always be a bit damaged and people might think that it's a good idea to restore them to pristine condition. Unfortunately, that's not always the case, and some people make that mistake. Sometimes restoring an item drastically decreases its value as it loses a bit of its identity. Some items are better staying original. Suppose you own an antique and are thinking about restoring it, you must be very careful and check online and with experts if it will increase its value or not.

If you have a collection, you must do everything you can to preserve it. Every collectible coin has to be encapsulated; every card has to be sealed; jewelry has to be stored in special boxes; even the packaging of some unopened box figurines might have value and have to be preserved in a bigger box. Every object requires particular attention, and you must research the best ways to protect and ensure your collection stays in the best condition.

If it comes in a set, a complete collection is often more valuable than the price of individual pieces put together, as it is more difficult to come by an entire collection rather than individual pieces. However, if having a complete collection would cost you much more than you can afford for this particular investment, then it is not worth taking the risk of jeopardizing your financial future.

Provenance is the value of time, storytelling, and the previous owner. Objects have a life on their own, and some are associated with important events or belonged to someone who had a significant role in history. That's why people like to collect them. It could be handwritten letters by Napoleon, Elvis Presley's clothes, Jimi Hendrix's guitars, guns from the Second World War, and so on. These collections have great potential as some passionate people would pay a lot of money for them. But it is a niche market that only attracts a few people compared to more traditional collections such as coins or stamps. When you invest in a niche market, only people who are passionate about these collectibles truly see and appreciate their value. In other words, fewer people are willing to buy from you. If you invest in a niche market, I would advise you to join some kind of enthusiasts' club or online community. That's the best way to engage in that community, learn from your passion, and meet experts in your field as well as prospective buyers and sellers.

Authentication also brings more value to a collection. It is very appealing for counterfeiters to make fakes and sell them for a fortune. It's the main issue in collecting items, especially objects that have had historical significance or belonged to someone very famous. Some fakes are so well made that they are indistinguishable from the genuine article. You can come in contact with all sorts of fake objects: fake silver or gold coins, counterfeit signatures or paintings, or fake pictures. There is always a risk when buying a second-hand collectible item. However, if you have the item certified by a reputable source, it could increase its value or, at the very least, remove any doubt that the collectible is genuine.

Finally, the intrinsic value of an object is the material and work necessary to create it. If an artist had to work for a month on a painting, then it makes sense that its price is high. Gold and silver coins are expensive because of their core material. On the other hand, the intrinsic value of a mass-produced plastic toy or sheet of paper is low. This doesn't mean you shouldn't buy a stamp or a trading card because their intrinsic value is only worth the price of paper and printing. It's just an interesting perspective to take into consideration. Even if your collection doesn't take off, you have the object's intrinsic value and material that are at least worth something.

9.2 What collection to start

You can invest in countless collections with some having more lucrative potential than others. The choice of depends on your interests, budget, and risk tolerance. As you spend a lot of time researching them, you must be passionate to invest in a collection. Here are some examples of popular collections.

- *Coins*. As we have seen, collectibles and rare coins are prevalent. There are many books, websites, and experts you can refer to.
- *Stamps*. Like coins, stamps are very popular investments and gather passionate people worldwide.
- *Art*. Many of the wealthiest people invest in art such as paintings and sculptures to diversify their portfolio.
- *Wine*. For wine enthusiasts, this is a great way to finance their passion. We explore wine investment in the next chapter.
- *Books and comics*. First editions of rare books and comics can be extremely valuable if they're in good condition.
- *Watches, handbags, cars, shoes, and other luxury items*. Investing in luxury articles made by well-known brands requires much capital. It's a niche market, but the people involved most likely have a lot of money to spare. Some luxury collections are only accessible to well-established and well-known collectors, and those items are highly sought-after.
- *Toys and trading cards*. *Star Wars* figurines, Barbie dolls, Pokémon trading cards, baseball cards, and so on. Although some of these collections can be speculative, they can be very valuable for an avid collector.

These are only a few examples, and many other collectibles represent excellent investment opportunities. Keep in mind that collecting items can be highly speculative, especially with newer collections. You should therefore undertake due diligence.

9.3 Evaluating, buying, and selling a collection

If you are serious about investing in a collection, you need to be able to evaluate it. Each collectible item has its market and features. There are various ways you can get useful information and buy collectibles.

- *Online marketplaces.* You can start your research by looking at online marketplaces such as eBay, Craigslist, or Amazon. These websites are a convenient way to size up the market and determine the price of a particular item. Even if you don't plan to buy from them, you can quickly access the market value of the items you are looking for. Be aware that some items are easier to find in specific marketplaces so you need to figure out which marketplace is more appropriate for your particular collection.
- *Official websites.* If you are looking for items from a particular brand, their official website is the best way to get information and purchase the item before it hits the secondary market.
- *Online communities.* There are forums, websites, and social media groups dedicated to specific types of collections. These communities are an important source of information and a good way to connect with potential buyers and sellers.
- *Auctions.* These are the places to be for collectors. They're exciting, you can meet a lot of people, and they're a good way to find collectible items. There are physical or online auctions. If you are targeting a specific niche, you might have to look at specialized auctions.

- *Specialty stores.* Depending on the item you collect, there are specialized collectible shops in every big city. They can be a good opportunity for you to find particular items.
- *Collectors' clubs, fairs, and conventions.* Many collections are sold from hand to hand. Meeting collectors in specialized clubs, fairs, and conventions is therefore a useful way to learn more about market trends and have remarkable findings.

When buying collectible items, it's essential to be careful and do your research. You should try to verify the item's authenticity, check its condition, and be aware of its market value. You should also be mindful of any red flags that could potentially prove that an item is fake. Additionally, it's advisable to consider the fees and commissions associated with buying and selling through a middleman.

9.4 The rise and fall of famous collections

When considering investing in collectibles, you must recognize that the demand for a particular collection can be a passing trend. You should carefully research and determine if the price you pay today is fair or if it will go down as people lose interest. Many collections have risen and fallen in that fashion, and you must learn from those lessons so that you won't get burned yourself.

If you were a child in the United States in the early 1990s, you were probably aware of the marketing frenzy related to Beanie Babies. These teddy bears were introduced in the market in 1994 by Ty Warner. Originally, they sold for $5 in stores, but they rapidly increased in price to hundreds or even thousands of dollars for the rarest on the secondary market. Warner was a genius marketer who controlled the supply by creating limited editions of Beanie Babies or even destroying stocks. People were fighting in stores to get their hands on the precious teddy bears and sell them on the secondary market. The frenzy was so high that in 1997 eBay sold more than $500 million worth of them. Unfortunately, everything started to fall apart in the early 2000s when people grew tired of the bears and started to look for the next big thing. The prices on the secondary market plummeted and only the rarest Beanie Babies are still worth anything today.

The price people are willing to pay for some items in a collection can sometimes appear ludicrous. You might think this is a recent trend, but let me assure you that our ancestors also had their fair share of following trends. One infamous episode took place in the seventeenth-century Dutch Republic when tulips were first introduced from the Ottoman Empire. The buying and selling of bulbs became very popular as people were excited about getting rare colored tulips that could be sold for a fortune. As everyone saw the price increase, more people invested, bought, and sold bulbs. In what has been described as "tulip mania" and "the madness of crowds," people were going into debt, paying a year's salary, and exchanging land to get their hands on rare bulbs. And then in 1637 the bubble exploded, and the bulbs' price fell precipitously and never recovered. Fortunes were made but also lost because of this episode.

Now instead of giving an example of a recent collection that has collapsed, I offer a case of a collection that may or may not fall. In 1996, Satoshi Tajiri introduced the video game Pokémon to the world. It was an instant hit and kids of that generation were absolutely crazy about it. Pokémon was everywhere: an animated series, T-shirts, toys, and the most popular trading cards. The collectors' market for Pokémon cards has grown and been very popular over the last few years as people are willing to pay enormous sums for them. A 1995 Pokémon Japanese Topsun Charizard Blue Back card sold for $493,230 at auction in 2021; a Blastoise card sold for $360,000 the same year; and a rare 1999 Pokémon Base Set Shadowless Holo Charizard card sold for $420,000 the following year. Needless to say, those kinds of numbers are mind-blowing for a simple playing card. However, when looking at the historical price tags of some cards on Card Ladder (a website specializing in card trading, https://www.cardladder.com/), we clearly see a downward trend. Will Pokémon card collections last over the long term or will they fall as well? Honestly, only time will tell.

What we can conclude from these tragic episodes is that people are likely to fall into a herd mentality. When you buy an item, you must know if you are buying it at an inflated price because everyone is crazy about it or if you are buying it at a fair price.

9.5 Going further

When considering investing in a collection, the critical part is to always remember that it is for an investment purpose. So many people get carried away by their passion and don't think about the investment. If you are collecting as a hobby, that's fine, but don't integrate it into your investment plan in that case. On the other hand, if you truly are collecting as an investment, you always have to look at it with the eyes of an investor and safeguard that it fits your plan.

When deciding which collection to start, you must make sure there is a good demand for it and it is a topic you love, something you can study or talk about for hours without getting tired of it. If you are planning to start a common collection such as stamps, coins, or cards, the good thing is that there are many tools, books, and websites that can help you gather information on these topics. However, if you are getting into a niche collection, information is more difficult to find and you have fewer people to buy from and sell to.

With all this in mind, should a collection be your primary investment? Probably not, and it should only represent a small part of your portfolio. However, it could be a hobby that turns out to be profitable. Remember that the key to success when creating a collection is to view it as an investment, and like any investment, you should weigh the risk and potential reward.

Chapter 10

Wine and Other Alcohol

Wine is an alternative to traditional investments that could be a means for enthusiasts to diversify their portfolios. Unlike discussions elsewhere in the book about specific assets that might be a more central element of your portfolio, this chapter focuses on people who love wine and would like to learn how to benefit from it while financing their passion.

To consider wine investment, you must understand the characteristics of a good bottle of wine and what brings it value over time. Otherwise, you may invest in a bottle that disappoints you. Once you know what makes a good investment wine, we look at the factors you must consider when investing, and finally, we discuss in further detail how to invest in wine. Although this section focuses on wine, much of the content could apply to other fine alcohols like whisky, brandy, rum, or premium beers.

10.1 What brings value wine and other alcohol

Have you ever wondered why some bottles of wine are priced at $10 and some at $100? After all, they both contain fermented grape juice. Here you will find some answers about the factors influencing the price of a bottle of wine.

To start with, there is the name, origin, and appellation. A bottle of wine is directly priced on the basis of the renown of its vineyard. You can therefore find average quality wines that sell for a premium because of their house's fame. You can also find high-quality wines that are undervalued because they come from lesser-known houses. Wine appellations also play an essential part in their value. Appellations are legal enactments that guarantee the geographical origin and production process of a bottle. If a wine has a famous appellation like Bordeaux, it can claim a high premium. If a vineyard is located in a neighboring region and cannot claim that prestigious appellation, even if the quality, environment, and production process are the same, it might be priced lower because of the lack of an appellation.

The vintage is the year the grapes are harvested. Every vintage wine is unique because weather and climate conditions differ from year to year and impact the taste. So a wine's vintage plays a key role in its price. A key criterion that defines a good vintage is sunshine. If grapes enjoy plenty of sunny days, they have more chance to develop their taste. But if the weather is too hot, too cloudy, or too rainy, the harvest might produce a bad vintage. It is a delicate balance that can't be controlled, so excellent vintage wines are challenging to find and are highly priced, even more than older wines with lower-quality vintage. As it is tied to a local climate, vintage is specific to regions. You shouldn't therefore assume that a good vintage for one bottle of wine is good for another. Although vintage might not affect the price of mass-produced wine, it has a much greater impact on premium wine produced in limited quantity, such as Bordeaux Grand Cru. As an investor, you must buy good vintage wine and avoid wine from a bad year as it will seriously affect the return on your investment over time. For example, although it is younger, a Château Lafite Rothschild 2000 is 50% more expensive than a Château Lafite Rothschild 1999 as the former vintage is excellent for Bordeaux wines.

Famous wine critics and labels can also influence the price of a specific bottle of wine. If a bottle gets the praise of well-established critics and certification from famous awards, its price will rapidly increase. In the wine community, positive critics and awards are guarantees for buyers that those wines are of good quality and could represent an investment opportunity.

Like any product, wine prices fluctuate with supply and demand. As a vineyard can only produce a limited amount each year, the supply is finite, and of course the number of available bottles decreases over time as they are consumed. In other words, good-quality wines with high demand and low supply are expensive.

There is a common misconception that the older a bottle of wine the better it gets. On the contrary, most bottles of wine are meant to be drunk within five years, and only a small percentage of the production is designed to age well over five or 10 years. These are premium bottles produced in smaller quantities and are therefore more expensive. Wine is a complex drink that contains many elements: alcohol, acids, phenolics, and so on. Those elements gradually evolve and change the wine's structure, taste, and even coloration. Over time, tannins tend to fall and become sediment at the bottom of the bottle. The taste becomes smoother, rounder, and less harsh. The coloration can also change due to slow oxidation: white wines often become darker with age while red wines get a more tinted brown color. Some wines are designed for aging and will only show their best taste after several years. As it is more difficult to find these bottles of wine, they tend to be more costly.

When investing in wine, you should select bottles that will age well, such as premium Bordeaux, Barolo, Grand Cru Burgundy, or Rioja Gran Reserva. To ensure the best results, you should always research or ask the producer how many years a bottle can be aged.

10.2 Factors to consider when investing

Investing in wine can be quite profitable. According to the Liv-ex Fine Wine 100 index (the industry-leading benchmark that tracks fine wine prices, https://www.liv-ex.com/news-insights/indices/), prices rose by roughly 30% from 2020 to 2022. But you should be aware that such indexes cover thousands of wines. Like the stock market, some individual bottles outperform and some underperform. Here are some important factors to consider when investing in wine.

In many respects, a bottle of wine can be considered a collectible, and as with other similar items it is advisable to keep the original packaging intact. It is even better to buy an entire case of wine as it will keep its value and you might be able to sell the whole case at one go.

It is also better to buy premium products from well-known and established houses that age well rather than purchase cheap wine hoping for the best. The price you pay for a bottle is a determining factor in your investment's future profit. Many people can afford to age ordinary bottles of wine that cost $10 and sell them a couple years later, but fewer people can afford to age premium bottles that cost $100. Think about it: if the return on investment is the same, it is much more practical to buy fewer bottles with a high premium than many average bottles for the same return. For example, if you buy and store 10 bottles of $100 wine that will double in price after 10 years, you can sell them all for $2,000 and get a $1,000 profit. On the other hand, you would need to buy and store 100 bottles of $10 wine that would also double in price after 10 years to get the same return. It would take much more space, time, and effort to sell them for the same profit.

The best way to invest in wine is to check the quality yourself and visit the producer. You would most likely get the wine at a lower price since you don't go through an intermediary, you ensure you don't buy counterfeits since you have it from the source, and you might even have the chance to talk with the winemaker who could advise you on which wine would be a great investment opportunity. However, buying wine directly from vineyards might be challenging if you live far away. In that case, you should buy from specialized distributors and retailers that can help make your selection. But be conscious that fine wine is a lucrative business and there are many counterfeit premium bottles on the market, so you must make sure you buy from a reliable source.

You must store your wine properly. The traditional way is to keep it in a cellar where it can age in the best conditions.

- *Light.* Wine must be protected from direct contact with light as ultraviolet light can attack some of its organic components.
- *Humidity.* Wine must be kept in a constant humidity of around 75%. If it is too dry, the cork might dry up and the wine might

oxidize and turn into vinegar. If it is too wet, the label might be damaged and mold can appear on the bottle.

- *Temperature.* Wine must age at a constant temperature of around 13°C. If it is too hot, the flavor might be cooked. If it is too cold, it might lose its aroma.

When storing a bottle, you should always place it horizontally as this ensures that the cork stays humid and the wine can breathe. If you don't have a cellar or can't store your wine in such conditions, you shouldn't invest in wine. You don't want to wait 10 years only to realize your investment is lost because you didn't store it properly.

When you are ready to sell your wine, you must find the right buyer. An excellent way to meet people with the same interest is to be part of a wine club. You can participate in events and wine tastings where you have the chance to meet enthusiasts, restaurant sommeliers, and other professionals potentially interested in buying your wine.

You can sell your wine at auctions where many investors worldwide have the means to buy the best-quality wine. However, you have to pay high commission fees for that service. An alternative is to sell online via auction websites. However, I would advise looking at national or regional websites to limit transportation costs and risks.

To make your selection, consider all the factors that give value to a bottle that we outlined earlier: name, origin, appellation, vintage, critics, supply, and age.

10.3 How to invest in wine

A popular way to finance wine consumption is to buy everything in double quantities. Whenever you purchase a bottle or a case of wine that can be aged, buy one for your own consumption and one as an investment that you will age for some years.

Each bottle of wine ages and gains value differently, but if you can pick bottles that increase in value by about 10% every year by paying attention to the factors we have outlined earlier, then you can sell your investment bottle for double the price after eight years and cover the cost of the first bottle. There is of course no guarantee of a return on investment and it is a long process that takes a lot of time to research, buy, age, and find the right person to sell wine to. This strategy is not to dramatically increase your wealth but more to finance your passion and learn while doing it.

If you don't have a cellar or don't want to deal with the tedious process of having to store and sell your wine, you can still invest by using the services of a wine portfolio manager. They keep track of market trends, advise on the storage period of the wine you select, and are up to date on the market price. They can also take care of the research process, logistics, storage, purchase, and selling. They are able to create a diversified portfolio with wines from different regions, excellent premium vintage bottles with significant potential for the future, and more affordable bottles that could present good returns on investment. However, those services come at a price and you have to pay storage and commission fees that you must check before investing.

10.4 Going further

If you are passionate about wine and looking for physical assets that could diversify your portfolio without taking too big a portion of it, wine investment is a good opportunity. It is a compelling way to finance your passion, obtain insights, and meet people with the same interest.

I strongly suggest you have a look at the Better Tasting Wine website for first-class advice on selection, investing tips, tasting, and everything else you could imagine about wine (http://www.bettertastingwine.com/lessons.html). You should also look at the most famous marketplace for wine investment: Liv-ex (London International Vintners Exchange, www.liv-ex.com/news-insights/). In this exchange, fine wine prices are published and bottles can be bought and sold like stocks and bonds from anywhere in the world. There are also interesting tools and indexes that track market trends, such as the Liv-ex Fine Wine 100 and the Liv-ex Fine Wine 1000 (mentioned earlier) that can help in your investment research. You can also check out market trends and interesting articles at Seven Fifty Daily (https://daily.sevenfifty.com/category/articles/) and Wine Spectator (https://www.winespectator.com/).

Investing in wine is not a get-rich-quick scheme; you will most likely hold and age a bottle for years before selling it. You should always do your homework, keep track of the market, work with trustworthy partners, and buy good-quality wine. To increase your potential return, you should invest in wine that has high-value potential: good origin, appellation, great vintage, positive critics and awards, and high demand. You should also take particular care when aging your wine and find the right person to sell it to. Finally, the best thing about investing moderately is that even if you get it wrong and your bottle doesn't appreciate as much as you wanted, you can still drink and enjoy it.

Chapter 11

Art

Very few things can give us such a variety of emotions as art. Some fall in love with a piece, while others hate it. Some are enraged by the audacity of an artist, while others are indifferent to what they create. Some artworks make us reflect, dream, or stand in awe. In other words, art creates emotions and passions that are highly subjective to the person who experiences it.

Due to this subjectivity, investing in art feels distant or obscure for many people and seems like a shaky prospect at best. Despite this, artworks have regularly outperformed the stock market index. Contemporary artwork has offered an annual return of 14% over the last 25 years, according to the Citi Global Art Market chart. Although those numbers only reflect the best-performing artists who sell at auction, it does give you an idea of why many people are attracted by art investment. This chapter aims to help you navigate art investment by explaining how to value art, where to buy and sell, how to invest in it, and what art collection to start.

11.1 What brings value to art

As we have said, art is very subjective. You might sometimes wonder why some pieces are worth millions of dollars when non-experts believe a child could do the same. There is so much of a gray area in the art world that it is challenging to get a reliable and predictable return on your investment. Nonetheless, there are some key characteristics that are common to valuable art and can help you pick good investment opportunities.

The price of the material and the number of hours used to research, plan, and execute a piece of art play key roles in determining its base price. As such, it seems logical that a three-meter-high marble sculpture made over a year would cost more than a simple paper sculpture made in a day. It also seems logical that an artist who has worked for 20 years and is considered an expert in their craft would produce higher quality art than someone just out of art school. This experience and expertise have a cost that will be accounted for in the final price of the work.

The price of a piece of art also depends on what other work by the same artist is selling for. If a painting sold for $10,000, it's logical that a similar one from the same artist would cost about the same. Work from well-known artists often appreciates over time by going from one collector to another at auction. If a famous collector buys a piece of art from a blue-chip artist for $1 million, then decides to sell it at auction years later, they will expect its price to have appreciated over time. The term blue chip is often used to refer to well-established companies or artists. In other words, they are considered safe bets to invest in.

Like any collectible, the condition is critical in evaluating a piece of art, especially historical pieces. If a canvas is torn or a sculpture damaged, their prices will be negatively affected. On the other hand, an old artifact in perfect condition could be worth a lot because it is rare to find such a piece in that condition. In other words, if you acquire any kind of art, you must preserve it and keep it in the best possible state.

Some pieces of art have a significant history—either a pivotal work that brought an artist fame or a piece that defines a new era or genre. Like historical artifacts, art gains value depending on who created and owned the work. So while a piece of art by a famous artist generally commands a high price, the same applies when someone famous purchases a work, owns it for a while, and then sells it. If you combine both factors, you can expect a significant increase in price. This was the case for *Tower of the Koutoubia Mosque*, painted by Winston Churchill in 1943 after attending the Casablanca Conference with Franklin D. Roosevelt. It was a pivotal moment in the war as the two leaders demanded the unconditional surrender of the Axis powers. The painting was bought in 2011 for just under $3 million by Brad Pitt and reportedly gifted to his wife Angelina Jolie, who then sold it for $11.5 million (£8.3 million) in 2021 after a dramatic nine-minute bidding battle.

Supply and demand always plays a crucial role in pricing an item and this is also the case with art. If an artist is in demand, the price rises; conversely, the price falls if a famous artist floods the market. There is a saying that artists only get rich after they die, which is unfortunate for the artist in question. But there is a certain market logic at play since the artist won't be able to produce any more work. Furthermore, after a couple of years on the market, the artwork will have had time to change hands and eventually appreciate in price. Another critical point is that most of the artist's life is already known and, therefore, there's less risk of ruining their reputation, as is unfortunately the case for many artists.

11.2 Where to buy and sell

There are several ways you can buy art. One traditional way is to visit a gallery or a dealer and see if there's anything that interests you. At a gallery, you get to see work from several artists and you can talk with gallerists and curators, which helps you learn more about the art market or a specific artist. You can also create long-lasting relationships with professionals who are able advise you about new investment opportunities on the market.

Artists often sign contracts with a gallery or a dealer to sell their art. As such, they usually have negotiating power and can reduce the price of some pieces by 5% or 10%. When you buy art, the gallery receives a commission that can be as high as 50% of the price you pay. The gallery therefore has an incentive to sell it for as much as possible.

Something peculiar about the art world for the uninitiated is that you might not be qualified to be a buyer for specific pieces. Even if you go to a gallery and are ready to buy the asking price in cash, some artists can refuse you as they would prefer their art to go to a famous collector who will sell it years later at a higher price. It might be frustrating, but it is in the artist's interest that their work is bought by a well-known collector as this might increase the price of future pieces. Some famous artists prefer to lose a sale rather than compromise their future value. If that's the case, you should not take it personally and look for another piece or another gallery.

When an artist sells through an auction, gallery, or agent, they have to deduct a commission from the final price. Some artists therefore choose to sell their art directly from their studios to save on the commission. If you have the chance to connect with an artist then that might be the best way to invest as you won't pay any commission either. In addition, you have the opportunity to learn more about an artist you like and they might contact you for other pieces.

Another alternative is participating in art fairs or conventions. They take place worldwide and showcase art from various galleries. This is an opportunity to network, meet professionals from the industry, and see what is trending in the art world.

Finally, one excellent way to buy art is to go to auctions. There are, of course, physical auctions, but also online auctions that you can access from your computer. Some auctions specialize in a specific kind of art or collectibles, while others are general and showcase a great variety of items. Auctions can be an opportunity to find art at a lower price as some artists or collectors might need cash and have to sell their work in a hurry. Going to an auction also gives you a feel for the market price of some pieces. If you have an interest in a particular artist and you have the chance to see some of their art sold, you will have a better grasp of the market price for their art. Auctions offer networking opportunities too since you can meet artists, gallery owners, art critics, curators, and collectors.

11.3 How to invest in art

When we think about investing in art, the first thing that comes to mind is to invest in a superb canvas or a beautiful sculpture made by a master. But art comes in various shapes and forms, and technology has drastically changed how we invest in art.

There are many types of physical art to buy: sculptures, paintings, ceramics, prints, illustrations, photography, and so on. The type of art you invest in depends on your specialization and interest. The biggest advantage of owning physical art is that you get the chance to enjoy it yourself. At the other end of the spectrum, you can invest in digital art. There are a lot of new exciting opportunities that technology offers. In that regard, we will have a closer look at non-fungible tokens in the next chapter.

Alternatively, you could invest in art funds and fractional art. Art is expensive, and there isn't an exchange-traded fund or mutual fund you can invest in to create a diversified art portfolio. Very few people can afford artwork from masters that costs hundreds of thousands or even millions of dollars. So it's quite difficult to create a diversified art portfolio. If you don't have that kind of money, you can still buy fractional ownership in a piece of art from companies such as Yieldstreet, Maecenas, and Masterworks. These companies give you the opportunity to invest in blue-chip artists by buying fractional ownership of their artwork, like owning shares of a company in the stock market. These companies take care of everything: buying the artwork, insuring it, storing it, maintaining it, and giving you a share of the profit when selling it.

This is an opportunity to only allocate a fraction of your capital to multiple blue-chip artists without having the responsibility to store, insure, and sell the piece of art. However, there are a few things you need to take into consideration. First, as mentioned earlier, artworks are notoriously illiquid, and although you can buy a share in individual pieces very easily online, you must be prepared to hold them for a long time. Second, you won't have control over what happens to the artwork. If you have connections and would like to sell the artwork at an auction, the decision is not up to you. Finally, there are fees the platform charges you on an annual basis to cover their maintenance costs and they take a commission on the sales.

11.4 What to buy

Selecting a good investment is hard, and buying early from rising stars and hoping to hit the jackpot is risky. Just because an artist is popular now doesn't mean that they will be in the future. As a result, many investors prefer to invest in pieces from well-established artists. Although it's more expensive, those pieces are also better known and there is a market for them. In addition, other collectors are already buying and are interested in their work, in contrast to a rising star who has to build their reputation and gain collectors.

Investing in art is a long-term prospect. You have to ensure that you can conserve and keep your art in good condition. It also takes a while to find the right buyer willing to pay the asking price. And you need to consider any fees you have to pay to sell your art through auctions or galleries.

There is an abundance of art, but if you truly want to make money, you need to become an expert and know what you are talking about. Instead of buying from various genres, I would suggest specializing in a specific genre that could offer significant investment opportunities.

11.5 Going further

Art investment can be a first-class prospect if you are passionate about it and already have a diversified portfolio of traditional resources such as financial assets, real estate, or gold. Art investment is also an illiquid asset and will take time to sell, so you must ensure that you can store and conserve it properly.

Before investing, you must study the market carefully, get art subscription magazines, and read blogs and books about art in your particular area of expertise. You should also create a network with artists, gallerists, curators, negotiators, collectors, and so on. These people are sources of valuable information and they can buy or sell you art. Remember, there is no guarantee of a reliable return when investing in art. You must think about it as a way to diversify your portfolio, one that could potentially get you a great return while enjoying the art you own.

Chapter 12

Cryptocurrency and Non-fungible Tokens

Like many people, you have most likely heard of cryptocurrency. Some believe it is the future of our economy and others believe it is not worth anything. Even if you don't want to invest in cryptocurrency, it is still interesting to understand why there is so much fuss and why some people are so vocal about it. This chapter helps you understand what cryptocurrency is, introduces the leading cryptocurrencies, shows why people invest in them, and how to invest and benefit from them. We also have a closer look at another application of blockchain technology: non-fungible tokens.

12.1 What is cryptocurrency?

Cryptocurrency is a digital money built on blockchain technology. The blockchain is a database shared on a computer network, making the cryptocurrency decentralized, which means it is not controlled by one institution but by the system itself. Cryptocurrency is currently the most famous use of blockchain technology, although there are already some other promising applications like NFTs.

You might wonder why people make such a fuss about digital money when we are already using fiat money, such as US dollars or euros, and we are making bank transfers without any issue. The main reason for this enthusiasm is that cryptocurrencies promise to solve some of the shortcomings of fiat money.

- Corruption is an unfortunate reality in most countries as cash and some bank transfers are not easily traceable. Blockchain technology can discourage corruption because every cryptocurrency exchange can be traced, making it much more difficult to hide money where everyone can see it.

- Many banks have obscure conditions and charge high fees when transferring money overseas or exchanging currencies. And those transfers can take days. Cryptocurrency transaction fees are comparatively meager when trading (especially for large transactions) and transfers are instantaneous.

These are only some of the examples of solutions provided by cryptocurrencies. However, they also pose many challenges.

- Most cryptocurrencies are highly volatile. It is common to see cryptocurrencies like Bitcoin lose or gain 30% of their market value over a period of a month or less. If you live paycheck to paycheck, you might face significant issues if you receive your salary in cryptocurrency.

- Cryptocurrencies are technologies. Like any technology, they could be replaced by a better one and investors are wary about investing everything in a technology that could be obsolete in a couple of years.

- All activity around crypto is consuming huge amount of energy, negatively impacting the environment. In 2022, it was reported that Bitcoin mining consumed more energy than Norway. Although many investors want crypto companies to use renewable energy sources, it is only the case for a relatively small proportion of the traffic.

12.2 Types of cryptos

At present, there are over 23,000 cryptocurrencies, which is a large panel to choose from if you are interested in investing in them. The number of coins grows every day because the technology evolves and improves. For now, let's describe some of the most famous cryptos.

Satoshi Nakamoto (2008) describes the invention of Bitcoin as a system for electronic transactions relying not on trust, but a peer-to-peer network using proof-of-work to record transactions. Bitcoin was the first cryptocurrency ever created and although technology and cryptocurrency have improved a lot since then, Bitcoin is by far the most prominent cryptocurrency in the world today, with a total market capitalization of about $560 billion.

It isn't easy to come up with something concrete regarding the future value of Bitcoin. Some detractors say that it's worth nothing, in contrast to many advocates who say that one Bitcoin could be worth $200,000 or even $1 million within five years. The issue with those high valuations is that most advocates don't even come up with a clear explanation of how they calculate these figures. I prefer the view of some investors like Cathic Wood who at least presents a logical explanation, stating that if institutional investors start allocating 5% of their funds to Bitcoin, it could be worth over $500,000 in the future.

There is an interesting anecdote dating from 2010, at the beginning of Bitcoin, when Laszlo Hanyecz purchased two pizzas for BTC10,000 (Deka 2022). At that time, it was worth about $41. In today's value, it is about $200 million (not including tips). So that was quite an expensive meal!

If Bitcoin is considered the gold of cryptocurrency, then Ethereum is the silver. It is the second biggest cryptocurrency with a total market capitalization of about $250 billion. Ethereum was created in 2015 by Vitalik Buterin, inspired by Bitcoin; this technology can be used for transactions and recording assets. It is also programmable and people can build applications on its blockchain. That's a big difference between these two assets as it allows the creation and use of smart contracts to build and deploy decentralized applications on its network without a middleman. For example, you can use this technology to receive payment of royalties. As Ethereum describes itself: "While Bitcoin is only a payment network, Ethereum is more like a marketplace of financial services, games, social networks and other apps that respect your privacy and cannot censor you" (Ethereum n.d.)

Cardano is the first cryptocurrency to be built on a proof-of-stake blockchain platform which works fundamentally differently than the proof-of-work to record transactions on the blockchain.

- *Proof-of-work*. This used to be the traditional way all cryptocurrencies operated. Miners must solve complex cryptographical puzzles to create a new block and write the transaction on the blockchain. Those blocks of cryptocurrencies reward miners, but the computing power necessary to mine them has drastically increased over the years.
- *Proof-of-stake*. This is considered an improvement on the proof-of-work system. Instead of having powerful computers mining on the blockchain, staking is about putting your cryptocurrency aside, locked for a specific period to contribute to the blockchain. Unlike proof-of-work, proof-of-stake does not reward new blocks of cryptocurrencies as mining does, but a share of the transaction fee. This operation is much more cost-effective and less energy-intensive.

This was an important innovation in the crypto sphere. Even Ethereum changed from a proof-of-work to a proof-of-stake model in 2022. This technology is considered more efficient and doesn't require active work to record transactions on the blockchain.

12.3 Why invest in cryptos

There are various reasons to invest in cryptocurrency.

- *Future potential*. People usually invest in cryptocurrencies because they believe in the underlying technology. They think it could be a vital tool in the future that could benefit humanity as a whole. For this reason, by investing early in this technology, they hope they will get some of the profit from any future revolution.

- *Diversification.* Investing in crypto is a way to diversify your portfolio from traditional investments such as stocks, real estate, or gold.
- *Capital appreciation.* People who hold crypto assets for the long-term hope that they will grow in value over time. Additionally, cryptocurrencies are highly volatile and people trade them to try to make a profit.
- *Low transaction fees.* People buy cryptocurrency to transfer funds from anywhere in the world for an insignificant fee.
- *Create additional revenue.* It is possible to create passive income by staking or mining specific coins. We discuss this further below.

12.4 How to benefit from crypto investment

Investing in cryptocurrency is a wild ride as it is a highly volatile asset. However, many people believe in the long-term value of this technology and think its value will appreciate over time. They hope they can buy it at a low price and sell it later at a much higher valuation.

Another way to benefit from cryptocurrency is to be an active player in the system by contributing to the blockchain. For the time being, there are two main ways people can contribute.

- *Mining.* This is for cryptocurrency that requires proof of work to record transactions. When mining, you need specialized tools dedicated to this work. Although you can technically do it from any device with computing power connected to the internet, this is inefficient and will most likely cost you more in energy than the potential reward. You can see examples online of people mining with their personal computers, phones, and even PlayStations or Tesla cars.

- *Staking*. When staking, you show proof of ownership and commit your coins to the blockchain. You will be rewarded with new coins that you can pledge to the blockchain or cash out. Be aware that you will need to commit your coins for a specific period and won't be able to cash them immediately. It can be frustrating if the crypto coin you have chosen falls and any return you get from your investment doesn't outweigh that loss.

Both methods require significant investments, which is why professionals have taken over most mining and staking activities. You must ensure you understand the financial risk of what you are doing as the rewards are not as significant as they used to be.

Like other assets, many financial tools allow you to invest directly or indirectly in crypto. For example, you can buy stocks in a company that specializes in crypto mining or deals with cryptocurrency. In that case, it is similar to buying shares in a gold mining company that benefits from a price increase in gold. Alternatively, you can invest in an ETF and other mutual funds that specialize in crypto investment. This strategy can help you create a diversified portfolio in the crypto sphere.

12.5 How to invest in crypto

Here are the steps you can follow to invest in cryptocurrency.

- *Research and select your coin*. The first step is to do due diligence and research the market. As mentioned earlier, there are more than 23,000 types of coins. You should ensure you are not falling for a scam and select coins that align with your investment goals.
- *Select a reputable crypto exchange*. Once you have selected the coins you want to invest in, you must choose a crypto exchange that allows you to buy them. You should select a reputable exchange that trades the cryptocurrency of your choice. Today's most popular exchanges are Binance,

Coinbase, and Kraken. Be alert to the fact that even crypto exchanges that were considered safe and backed with millions of dollars from leading institutional investors have gone bust. In 2022, the second largest crypto exchange, FTX, filed for bankruptcy because of fraud allegations. Although the company's liquidation is in progress and assets worth $7.3 billion have been retrieved, it is already clear that the users will only get some of their money back.

- *Create and fund your account.* After you have selected the crypto exchange, you need to set up your account and transfer money via a bank, credit card, or PayPal.
- *Buy cryptocurrency.* You are now ready to invest and can buy cryptocurrencies.
- *Transfer your cryptocurrencies to a crypto wallet.* Once you have bought your cryptos, you can decide to transfer them to a crypto wallet to ensure they are safe. A crypto wallet is basically a safe that will store your public and private keys. A public key is the identification number of your crypto wallet, allowing you to receive cryptocurrency. It is the equivalent of your bank account number—everyone can see your public key, but nobody can access it without the security code. A private key is proof that you own the crypto wallet—it's the safety key that gives you access to your crypto wallet. It is the equivalent of the security code for your bank account.

There are many crypto wallets available such as MetaMask, ZenGo, and Exodus. You can have hot wallets that are connected to the internet and cold wallets that aren't connected to the internet.

12.6 Scams

Unfortunately, many crypto projects turn out to be scams. A lot of people have lost their entire life savings to these scams, so it is essential only to allocate a fraction of your portfolio that you are willing to use for crypto projects.

There isn't a foolproof method that can definitively tell you if a crypto project is a scam. But there are some red flags you can easily spot.

- *Too good to be true.* When a crypto project advertises a guaranteed return on investment of 20% or even more it is most likely a scam. To put this into perspective, Bernie Madoff, who created a $65 billion fraud and the biggest Ponzi scheme in history, reportedly promised a return on investment of 9%. In other words, there is no investment that can guarantee that absurd level of return.
- *Not many holders.* If a crypto project has only a handful of people holding most of the coins, this is a big concern for its future viability as it will be highly dependent on the willingness of those few holders.
- *Illiquidity.* There is often an issue with small coins when it is not possible to sell because there is simply no demand for them on the market.

If you are interested in learning more about crypto scams, I recommend watching videos from the YouTube channel Coffeezilla, where the author unveils and confronts many crypto scams (https://www.youtube.com/channel/UCFQMnBA3CS502aghlcr0_aw).

12.7 Non-fungible tokens

Following the crypto revolution, another type of asset came about using blockchain technology called an NFT. This is a unique digital asset recorded on the blockchain. It cannot be exchanged for another (thus the name), unlike a dollar bill or even a Bitcoin. You can create an NFT of anything: a picture, drawing, music, video, or even a meme on the internet.

When people look at an NFT, they often imagine it as a picture, when in reality it's not. An NFT is a line of code written on the blockchain that proves you own an asset. It is comparable to a certificate of ownership—if you own a car, the certificate of title for a vehicle (also known as an automobile title or pink slip) proves that it is yours and that you haven't stolen it.

Many digital artists immediately saw the potential of this technology as it enables them to sell ownership of their art, which was previously seen as something easily duplicable without having to pay for it. Furthermore, it allows for the application of smart contracts that can deliver royalties to the NFT creators for any future transactions of this NFT. As a result, many artists, such as Snoop Dogg, have been very vocal in promoting NFTs and creating their own projects. Here are some examples of famous NFTs.

- *Everydays: The First 5000 Days.* This NFT represents the work of the artist Beeple, who created a new NFT every day for 5,000 days. He then gathered the collection together and created a unique NFT. For many people, it was the first time they had heard of an NFT, and it sold for $69.3 million.
- *Bored Ape.* This NFT project features 10,000 pictures of cartoon-like apes that were generated by an algorithm. By owning a Bored Ape NFT, you become a member of the Bored Apes Yacht Club (BAYC) and can access private chat, special events, and so on. Many celebrities, such as Justin Bieber, Eminem, and Paris Hilton, are part of the club.
- *The First Tweet.* Jack Dorsey is the founder of Twitter and decided to create an NFT of the first Tweet ever done on the platform. This NFT was eventually sold to the crypto entrepreneur Sina Estavi for $2.9 million. After a while, he tried to sell it back and was hoping to get $48 million for it, but he only got a top bid of $6,800.

Unfortunately, as of today, many NFT projects have drastically decreased in value and many investors lost money in the process.

12.8 What gives value to an NFT

People see much value in NFTs. Some are built with specific functionalities, such as access to a virtual world or game, smart contracts that give royalties to their creator, or they can be used as a key to access certain content. People can value those utilities, making the NFT more desirable.

One factor that brings the most value to an NFT is the person who creates it and the community behind it. If the person is well known and already has an extensive fan base, the NFT can skyrocket in value. Whether it is for a game, artwork, or a series of images, an NFT project is driven by the people who believe in it. In addition, if an NFT is owned and promoted by many celebrities, it will be highly valued.

Supply and demand also plays a key role in valuing an asset. If there is a limited supply of an item that is highly desirable its price will skyrocket. Like many other assets, the general market mood and demand for an asset can affect its price. According to Raynor de Best (2023), the number of sales and sales value for NFTs reached a peak at the end of 2021. Since then the price and number of sales of NFTs have only dropped.

12.9 How to invest in NFTs

Here are the steps you can follow to invest in NFTs.

- *Research and select your NFT.* The first step consists of finding an NFT project that interests you. Many popular platforms exist, such as OpenSea, Rarible, and Nifty Gateway, where you can browse NFTs. Alternatively, you can look at popular NFT projects on their own platforms.

- *Get a crypto wallet and fund it.* To invest in NFTs, you must have a crypto wallet. Your wallet permits you to buy Ethereum or Cardano, which then will allow you to purchase NFTs.

- *Browse and buy NFTs.* Once you have funds in your wallet, you can browse different NFT marketplaces and buy the NFTs you are interested in. You can also bid for NFTs that are up for auction.

12.10 Going further

Should you invest in cryptocurrencies or NFTs? As always, it depends on your situation and investment plan, and no single answer suits everyone. There is no denying blockchain technology's great future potential. However, there still needs to be definitive proof that it will happen. In addition, cryptocurrencies and NFTs have only been around for a couple of years in contrast to all the other investment assets that have been available for decades or centuries.

If you are looking to diversify your portfolio, are willing to take big risks, are looking for very long-term investments, are very interested in blockchain technologies, and truly believe in its potential, then it makes sense to allocate a fraction of your portfolio to it. But you must only invest what you are willing to lose.

The crypto coin or NFT project you select depends on you and your investment plan. Do not take any recommendations on faith because you like someone, especially if it is a celebrity promoting a project (most don't know anything about it and are just paid to promote it). Whatever people say about crypto, don't trust anyone implicitly, and especially any promise of a return.

There are many active communities on social media. When investing, you should get involved in the community of the coin or NFT project you are interested in. This can help you have more information on the project and where it is going in the future.

If you would like to access the blockchain, you can use the following website: https://blockchain.info/. There you can find information on all major cryptocurrencies, research transactions, and wallets.

Finally, be careful to safeguard all your access codes. There are many stories of people losing access to their crypto wallets because they forgot their private keys. Have a physical and digital backup safely stored to ensure that nobody can copy them and you won't forget them. Nothing is worse than knowing your own a fortune and not having access to it. Although some companies now specialize in retrieving those access codes from people who forget them, there is never any guarantee, just a sliver of hope that it might not be lost forever.

Chapter 13

Investment Plan

13.1 Framework for an investment plan

Now that we have been through all the individual components of your investment plan, it is time to put them together. I believe that if a plan is too complicated nobody will follow it; this is especially true if the plan takes years in the making. Honestly, to be effective and have any chance of success over the years, an investment plan must be simple and shouldn't take up more than one or two pages.

That's why the investment plan I am giving you follows the structure of this book. It's a simple four-step framework.

- Create your objectives and evaluate their costs
- Evaluate and optimize your situation
- Design your portfolio
- Create your plan

Let's go into more detail.

13.1.1 Create your objectives and evaluate their costs

As we saw in Chapter 1, the first step of your investment journey is to determine where you are heading by fixing your goals. You can use the SMART framework to help you create effective goals that will be specific, measurable, achievable, realistic, and time-bound. Once you have defined your SMART goals, you must determine what you need to achieve them: cost, knowledge, skills, experience, certification, and so on.

13.1.2 Evaluate and optimize your situation

The second step is evaluating your situation with the assets you own and the liabilities you owe. You can use Table 13.1 as a model to write these down and their respective cash flow.

Table 13.1 Investment plan: assessment of assets and liabilities

Assets ($)			Liabilities ($)			
Assets	Market value	Cash in	Debts	Interest (%)	Remaining debt	Cash out
Total assets			Total liabilities			

Once you have gathered this information, you can take a step back and analyze your situation, as demonstrated in Chapter 2. After assessing your assets and liabilities, you do the same with your income and expenses. You can find a more detailed version of Table 13.2 in Chapter 2.

Table 13.2 Investment plan: income and expenses

Income ($)			Expenses ($)		
	Month	Year		Month	Year
Salary			Housing		
			Transport		
			Subscriptions		
			Living expenses		
			Finance		
Total income			Total expenses		

There are many ways you can save money, and I propose the following order to help you structure your approach.

- Refinance all your loans
- Pay off your highest interest rate debts
- Create an emergency fund
- Minimize the expenses that don't change your habits
- Reduce expenses that do change your habits

In addition, I recommend opening a separate bank account dedicated to investment, where you will automatically save a fixed percentage of your earnings every month (preferably on the day you get paid).

13.1.3 Design your portfolio

The third step is to determine what types of investment will help you achieve your goals. You should only invest in assets that make sense in your overall strategy and create a portfolio that helps you reach your objectives. This book divides investments into nine categories: career, business, financial assets, real estate, gold and other precious metals, collectibles, wine and other alcohol, art, and cryptocurrency and non-fungible tokens. You must determine which investments are suitable for your path and create a portfolio that can help you attain your goals. As we have seen in Chapter 3, you can aim to create different types of portfolios such as growth, income, conservative, value, balance, or mix to reach your goal.

13.1.4 Create your plan

When investing over the long term, you know well in advance what skills you need or research you must do. The last step of your investment plan is therefore to write what you're going to do this year to achieve your goals: what investments you will make, how you will save money, what you are going to study, and so on. You should review and update your plan at least once a year to ensure that you are on track to reaching your goals.

This framework is, of course, only a suggestion, and I recommend you articulate your plan in the best way that suits your needs. Now let's have a look at two concrete examples.

13.2 Case study 1

Let's take the hypothetical case of a young couple living and working in Belgium. They have both finished their studies; Clotilde is a lawyer working for a firm and Jonathan is a vet working at an animal hospital. Let's apply the four-step framework to their case.

13.2.1 Create objectives and evaluate costs

Clotilde and Jonathan have an ambitious dream for their future and have created the following SMART goal they would like to pursue. "We would like to own and rent a multi-family house within 10 years." Specifically, they want to purchase a multi-family home with three units where they will live in one and rent the others. They believe that in ten years it would cost about $600,000 to buy and renovate the type of house they are looking for. They therefore contact a banker who informs them that they need a $60,000 down payment.

13.2.2 Evaluate and optimize the situation

Table 13.3 is a simplified version of Clotilde and Jonathan's financial situation.

Table 13.3 Case study 1: assessment of assets and liabilities, year 0

Assets ($)			Liabilities ($)			
Assets	Market value	Cash in	Debts	Interest (%)	Remaining debt	Cash out
Cash and savings	500		Credit card debt	10	4,000	400
Car	10,000					
Total assets	10,500	—	Total liabilities		4,000	400

Clotilde and Jonathan are young, they don't have many significant assets, and they are also fortunate as they don't have student loans, but a simple credit card loan. Although they have good salaries for their age and location, Clotilde and Jonathan have a lot of expenses that can be optimized (Table 13.4).

Table 13.4 Case study 1: income and expenses, year 0

Income ($)			Expenses ($)		
	Month	Year		Month	Year
Salary 1	2,000	24,000	Housing	1,200	14,400
Salary 2	2,000	24,000	Transport	700	8,400
			Subscriptions	400	4,800
			Living expenses	1,000	12,000
			Finance	500	6,000
Total income	4,000	48,000	Total expenses	3,800	45,600

13.2.3 Design the portfolio

To reach their goal, Clotilde and Jonathan have decided they need to invest in a growth portfolio to accumulate enough cash for their down payment. Their investment strategy will mainly focus on savings, investing in their respective careers, and in a growth ETF.

13.2.4 Create the investment plan

It would take Clotilde and Jonathan 25 years at their current savings rate to accumulate $60,000 for the down payment. To reach their goal, they need to radically increase their savings rate. So for this year, they will focus on building a solid financial foundation by constantly saving and reducing their expenses, paying off their credit card debt, and creating an emergency fund. In the meantime, both are going to seminars, reading books, and networking to improve their skills and careers. They will also start to study the stock market and prepare to invest.

Let's fast forward a bit and have a look at their updated investment plan after one year.

13.2.5 Create objectives and evaluate costs

Clotilde and Jonathan's objective is unchanged: "We would like to own and rent a multi-family house within nine years." For the time being, they still believe that it would cost about $600,000 to buy and renovate the type of house they want.

13.2.6 Evaluate and optimize the situation

Next, when evaluating and optimizing their situation, they produce a new assessment of assets and liabilities (Table 13.5) and income and expenses (Table 13.6).

Table 13.5 Case study 1: assessment of assets and liabilities, year 1

Assets ($)				Liabilities ($)			
Assets	Market value	Cash in	Debts	Interest (%)	Remaining debt		Cash out
Emergency fund							
Savings	5,000						
5,400							
Car	9,000						
Total assets	19,400	—	Total liabilities		—		—

Table 13.6 Case study 1: income and expenses, year 1

Income ($)			Expenses ($)		
	Month	Year		Month	Year
Lawyer's salary	2,100	25,200	Housing	1,200	14,400
Vet's salary	2,100	25,200	Transport	400	4,800
			Subscriptions	300	2,400
			Living expenses	800	8,400
			Finance	300	3,600
Total income	4,200	50,400	Total expenses	3,000	36,000

Clotilde and Jonathan's financial situation has radically improved after one year. They are able to pay off their credit card debt by regularly saving and reducing their expenses.

13.2.7 Design the portfolio

As they have beens focusing mainly on building a solid financial foundation, they couldn't invest any money yet. But they now have the stock market knowledge and savings to be able to start investing in a growth portfolio.

13.2.8 Create the investment plan

For the next couple of years, Clotilde and Jonathan will undertake three things.

- Continue working on their careers.
- Keep 50% of their remaining savings in cash.
- Invest 50% of their savings in the Vanguard Growth ETF (VUG). They select this ETF because it focuses on a growth company, has a low expense ratio and good historical performance.

Now let's fast forward and look at their updated investment plan in year five.

13.2.9 Create objectives and evaluate costs

"We would like to own and rent a multi-family house within five years."

13.2.10 Evaluate and optimize the situation

Although their cost of living increased and they had to sell their old car to buy a new one, Clotilde and Jonathan continue to save and invest diligently while keeping their expenses under control (Tables 13.7 and 13.8).

Table 13.7 Case study 1: assessment of assets and liabilities, year 5

Assets ($)			Liabilities ($)			
Assets	Market value	Cash in	Debts	Interest (%)	Remaining debt	Cash out
Saving account	30,000					
ETF investment	40,000					
Emergency fund	5,000					
Car	10,000					
Total assets	85,000	—	Total liabilities		—	—

Table 13.8 Case study 1: income and expenses, year 5

Income ($)			Expenses ($)		
	Month	Year		Month	Year
Lawyer's salary	2,500	30,000	Housing	1,300	15,600
Vet's salary	2,500	30,000	Transport	500	6,000
			Subscriptions	300	3,600
			Living expenses	900	10,800
			Finance	400	4,800
Total income	5,000	60,000	Total expenses	3,400	40,800

During the last four years, Clotilde and Jonathan were able to save on average about $15,000 per year. They invest 50% of their savings in the Vanguard Growth ETF (VUG). This investment paid off handsomely as they invested a total of $30,000 and their investment is now worth $40,000.

13.2.11 Design the portfolio

Clotilde and Jonathan have saved $30,000 in a separate bank account and have a $40,000 investment in an ETF.

13.2.12 Create the investment plan

Because of their high savings, they have enough funds to pay the down payment for their dream house five years earlier than their original objective.

13.3 Case study 2

John and his wife Belinda are both working as employees. They are 50 years old and getting closer to retirement. Although the country they live in offers a pension scheme, they would like to be safe and acquire assets that will create enough passive income so they can live without needing the pension scheme when they retire. They are also thinking about starting a silver coin collection to gift to their grandchildren as a legacy.

13.3.1 Create objectives and evaluate costs

"We want to acquire assets that will create passive income to compensate for our living expenses when we retire in 15 years." Currently, the couple's living expenses are $2,000 per month and, accounting for inflation, they expect those living expenses to be around $2,500 per month in 15 years.

"We want to gift to each of our four grandchildren a silver coin collection worth about $2,000 within 10 years." As they have four grandchildren, the collection of coins should be worth a total of $8,000.

13.3.2 Evaluate and optimize the situation

John and Belinda are in a great position as they don't have any debt and are able to save 50% of their income. They currently don't have any income-generating assets, but they will actively work toward that goal (Tables 13.9 and 13.10).

Table 13.9 Case study 2: assessment of assets and liabilities, year 0

Assets ($)			Liabilities ($)			
Assets	Market value	Cash in	Debts	Interest (%)	Remaining debt	Cash out
Cars	20,000					
Stocks	10,000					
Emergency fund	15,000					
Savings	5,000					
Total assets	50,500	—	Total liabilities			

Table 13.10 Case study 2: income and expenses, year 0

Income ($)			Liabilities ($)		
	Month	Year		Month	Year
Salary 1	2,000	24,000	Housing	1,200	14,400
Salary 2	2,000	24,000	Transport	100	1,200
			Subscriptions	100	1,200
			Living expenses	500	6,000
			Finance	100	1,200
Total income	4,000	48,000	Total expenses	2,000	24,000

John and Belinda have a great financial foundation and savings rate, but they don't yet have any assets that generate income for them.

13.3.3 Design the portfolio

As their main objective is to create passive revenue, John and Belinda will need to create an income-generating portfolio that allows them to compensate for their living expenses when their retire. To achieve this goal, they have decided to invest in real estate and stocks that pay dividends.

13.3.4 Create the plan

This year, John and Belinda will immediately invest and change that situation.

- They plan to make their first real estate investment and acquire a studio.
- They have already invested in stock and have great knowledge to pick up value stock. They will now focus on finding value stocks that distribute dividends.
- They don't know much about silver investment, so they will have to study the market and see what options they have.

Fast forwarding a year, let's have a look at their situation.

13.3.5 Create objectives and evaluate costs

"We want to acquire assets that will create passive income to compensate for our living expenses when we retire in 14 years." The expected cost hasn't changed, and John and Belinda still need to acquire assets that will generate about $2,500 of passive income every month.

"We want to gift to each of our four grandchildren a silver coin collection worth about $2,000 within nine years."

13.3.6 Evaluate and optimize the situation

During the year, the market value of John and Belinda's cars reduced by about 10%. They sold $10,000 worth of stocks to use as a down payment to buy a $100,000 studio. They saved $24,000 during the year that they invested as follows: $800 to start the silver coin collection and $23,200 to buy stocks that provide a bit more than a 5% dividend (Table 13.11).

Table 13.11 Case study 2: assessment of assets and liabilities, year 1

Assets ($)			Liabilities ($)			
Assets	Market value	Cash in	Debts	Interest (%)	Remaining debt	Cash out
Studio	100,000	7,800	Mortgage loan	2	90,000	7,200
Stock	23,200	1,200				
Silver collection	800					
Cars	18,000					
Emergency fund	15,000					
Savings	10,000					
Total assets	19,400	9,000	Total liabilities		90,000	7,200

The newly acquired studio's rent is $650 per month and they pay about $600 per month for the mortgage payment, which increases their housing expenses. They have also slightly increased their living expenses (Table 13.12).

Table 13.12 Case study 2: income and expenses, year 1

Income ($)			Expenses ($)		
	Month	Year		Month	Year
Salary 1	2,000	24,000	Housing	1,800	21,600
Salary 2	2,000	24,000	Transport	100	1,200
Studio	650	7,800	Subscriptions	100	1,200
Dividend	100	1,200	Living expenses	700	8,400
			Finance	200	2,400
Total income	4,750	57,000	Total expenses	2,900	34,800

13.3.7 Design the portfolio

John and Belinda's portfolio is already working well and fulfilling its purpose by generating a steady income. Although most of the studio's rent goes to pay the mortgage, it's only a temporary situation, and their goal is to be out of debt when they retire. Regarding their silver investment, they have heard of the success of the Queen's Beast series, they have decided to invest in the new Royal Tudor Beasts collection 1-ounce silver proof coin (see Chapter 8). It's a collection of 10 different coins. They sign up for the subscription program and will receive two different coins a year for $100 each. As they want four complete collections, it costs them $800 per year, which they will pay each year until their collection is complete at the end of year five. They hope the Royal Tudor Beast collection will be as successful as the Queen's Beast series. Their expected cost is $1,000 and they hope they can sell it for $2,000 once the collection is complete.

13.3.8 Create the investment plan

For the next couple of years, John and Belinda plan to invest in three main ways.

- Continue the silver coin collection for their grandchildren.
- Save 50% of their cash in a separate bank account to be able to buy another studio in a couple of years.
- Use 50% of their savings to invest in dividend stocks.

Let's fast forward to year five and have a closer look at John and Belinda's situation.

13.3.9 Objectives

"We want to acquire assets that will create passive income to compensate for our living expenses when we retire in 10 years." The expected cost has increased, and they need to acquire assets that will generate about $2,600 of passive income every month.

"We want to gift to each of our four grandchildren a silver coin collection worth about $2,000 within five years."

13.3.10 Evaluate and optimize the situation

A lot happened over the last couple of years. John fell sick and was hospitalized following a car accident he was responsible for. As they were saving an average of $24,000 per year over the last four years, where 50% was invested in the stock market and 50% saved in a bank account, an important part of their savings was used to pay for his hospital bill and a new car. Fortunately, they had saved a lot of money over the last couple of years, and it was not a big problem to come up with the funds (Table 13.13).

Table 13.13 Case study 2: assessment of assets and liabilities, year 5

Assets ($)			Liabilities ($)			
Assets	Market value	Cash in	Debts	Interest (%)	Remaining debt	Cash out
Studio	110,000	7,800	Mortgage loan	2	65,000	7,200
Stocks	85,000	4,250				
Silver collection	8,000					
Cars	28,000					
Emergency fund	5,000					
Savings	8,000					
Total assets	244,000	12,050	Total liabilities		65,000	7,200

John and Belinda's combined salaries have slightly increased over the years. In addition, they still receive an average 5% dividend from their stock investment. All their living costs have slightly increased but are still manageable (Table 13.14).

Table 13.14 Case study 2: income and expenses, year 10

Income ($)			Expenses ($)		
	Month	Year		Month	Year
Salary 1	2,100	25,200	Housing	1,800	21,600
Salary 2	2,100	25,200	Transport	150	1,800
Studio	700	8,400	Subscriptions	150	1,800
Stock dividend	354	4,250	Living expenses	750	9,000
			Finance	200	2,400
Total income	5,254	63,050	Total expenses	3,050	36,600

13.3.11 Design the portfolio

Although their savings have suffered, John and Belinda's income-generating portfolio did its job and provided a good income. They have also reached their second goal with the silver collection. It cost them a total of $4,000, but as the collection is complete it is now worth $8,000 on the secondary market. They can now gift the collection to their grandchildren five years earlier than they thought.

13.3.12 Create the investment plan

For the next ten years, John and Belinda plan to do the following.

- Save about $10,000 per year to be able to buy a second studio for when they retire.
- Invest the remainder of their savings in dividend stocks.

Finally, let's see the situation at year 15 and determine whether John and Belinda reached all their goals.

As you can see in Table 13.15, they now have two studios, bringing in a total rent of $19,200 per year, without having to pay for any mortgage. In addition, their stock investment increased in value over the years on top of delivering a constant 5% dividend of about $12,500 per year. Their average monthly passive income is about $2,642, which is above their objective of $2,600.

Table 13.15 Case study 2: assessment of assets and liabilities, year 15

Assets (\$)			Liabilities (\$)			
Assets	Market value	Cash in	Debts	Interest (%)	Remaining debt	Cash out
Studios	220,000	19,200				
Stocks	250,000	12,500				
Cars	20,000					
Emergency fund	10,000					
Savings	5,000					
Total assets	505,000	31,700	Total liabilities		—	—

Although their savings took a dent a bit earlier, they managed to invest and reach their goal. The secret to their success is their high savings rate and constant investing.

13.4 Alterations to your plan

Remember that this is only a plan; it won't necessarily work exactly as you want. But keeping it in mind will make a big difference between you and the average investor. When writing your plan, you have to make a lot of assumptions. Some will be accurate while others miss their target. This is to be expected as no one can predict the future. But as long as your assumptions are logical, prudent, and backed up by a lot of research, you should be well prepared.

As we have seen in the case studies, you must remain adaptable and adjust your plan when things don't go as you predicted. Along with your plan, you have to adjust your schedule. As with everything in life, nothing goes exactly according to plan. You shouldn't be obsessed about this for any reason. If you can't find good real estate at a reasonable price, it is perfectly acceptable to wait until you do. You may not find anything as good at first, but if you wait patiently for the right opportunity, rather than rushing into an uncertain investment because you feel pressured by time, perhaps you will find something even better. If it gets you closer to your goal, that's what matters.

Once you have written your plan, you have to check it periodically; I would advise doing so each month. It will only take you a few minutes as you assess your progress and check if you are on track. And if you are lagging behind, you can see if your plan needs some readjustment.

13.5 Going further

It's now your turn to write an investment plan. I strongly advise you to put it on paper, as it makes your plan more tangible. Although I propose a specific structure in this book that I believe should be suitable for most people, I don't know your personal situation and you should use a structure that fits your needs and objectives.

In any case, you can complete the following in this book or you can also download it on the resource page of our website: http://www.kevinponcelet.com.

13.5.1 Create objectives and evaluate costs

....
....
....

13.5.2 Evaluate and optimize the situation

Assets ($)			Liabilities ($)			
Assets	Market value	Cash in	Debts	Interest (%)	Remaining debt	Cash out
Total assets			**Total liabilities**			

Income ($)			Expenses ($)		
Income	Month	Year	Home	Month	Year
Salary			Housing		
			Transport		
			Subscriptions		
			Living expenses		
			Finance		
Total income			**Total expenses**		

....
....
....

13.5.3 Design your portfolio

....
....
....

13.5.4 Create your plan

....
....
....

Chapter 14

Conclusion

This book's main purpose is to be a guide to help you grow your wealth over time and achieve your goals. It's the book I wish I had in my hands when I started my journey, and I hope it helps you understand the basics of investing better. Whether you plan to invest in the stock market, your career, real estate, a business, or other assets, I hope the book brings you valuable knowledge and the inspiration to help you get closer to your financial dream.

I don't believe in giving any specific investment advice, such as a particular stock pick that will suit everyone's needs and objectives, and I think I have been quite clear about the reasons why. Each individual has different situations and circumstances, and there isn't one single path to wealth in order to achieve your objectives. The journey you choose is a reflection of who you are and I believe it's the same with the investments you make. The beauty about investing is that you can adapt your investment strategy to yourself and your needs. You can be very proactive and decide to be behind everything. Equally, you can decide to have a more passive approach where you create a system, and you look at your money grow without your active management.

Although many see investing as something very complicated or boring, it doesn't have to be. Nonetheless, it's very understandable that people can feel overwhelmed by the task ahead. What to invest in? What to buy? Is it safe? And countless other questions. It's the reason why I suggest creating an investment plan with the following structure.

- The first step of your investment journey is to define your objectives and determine clearly where you are heading. To help you create goals, you can use the SMART framework, which is an effective tool to help you see the path ahead and what you need to navigate it.

- Once you know what you are looking for, you must evaluate and optimize the resources you have on hand to ensure you start your journey with a solid foundation. For this, you need to crack the numbers and lay down all your assets and liabilities as well as your income and expenses. In doing so, you gain awareness of where you stand, what's missing in your portfolio, and how you can optimize and reduce your current expenses.

- Then you must decide on the types of investments you will make. You must design a portfolio that helps you achieve your objectives. You can invest in your career, a business, financial assets, real estate, or less common assets such as gold, art, collectibles, wine, cryptocurrencies and non-fungible tokens.

- The last step of your investment journey is to put everything together and create a concrete plan to achieve what you want. Ideally, you should make it as simple as possible in one or two pages. Keep in mind that it's a plan that will take years to achieve, and therefore you will need to revise and adjust it regularly.

Having a plan is great, but it's useless on its own if you don't take the necessary steps forward in your investment journey. You are the person responsible for your financial future and no one else. So it really is up to you to make the right moves.

On a final note, this book is the first edition, and I intend to write much more in the future about investing. If you like the content and are interested in making it better, please don't hesitate to contact us at to share your story and send us your feedback: hello@bulanpress.com.

Glossary

asset tangible or intangible resource with economic value that an individual or company owns

balance sheet statement of a company's assets, liabilities, and shareholders' equities at a specific date, showing what a company owns and owes

bear market state of the stock market when investment prices are going down

black swan rare event that could have terrible consequences on the stock market

blockchain database shared on a computer network, making cryptocurrency decentralized

blue chip well-established companies or artists considered safe bets to invest in

bull market state of the stock market when investment prices are going up

cash flow statement report showing the movement of cash in and out of a company during a specific period

compound interest snowball effect of profit made by reinvesting earnings into invested capital

cryptocurrency digital money built on blockchain technology

curriculum vitae document that highlights a professional and academic journey

exchange-traded fund financial asset that aims to replicate a specific index's performance by purchasing the same assets

fiat money government-issued and -recognized currency not backed by physical commodities

hard skill technical skill that helps complete specific tasks

house flipping real estate investment strategy of acquiring property that needs renovation, fixing it, and then selling it at a profit *house hacking* real estate investment strategy of finding ways to create an income from a building while living in it, often by renting it out

income statement report that lists a company's income and expenses during a specific period of time

index group of financial instruments that measures detailed data, tracks the performance of various companies, and provides a market indicator to compare portfolio performance

inflation general increase of price over time which results in a decrease in purchasing power

initial public offering process when a private corporation sells its shares to the public for the first time

interest rate proportion of a loan that is charged as interest to the borrower, typically expressed as an annual percentage of the loan outstanding

international securities identification number unique and unchanging 12-character alphanumeric code to identify assets worldwide

investing allocating resources and time to generate a profit and achieve a specific goal

liability debt that an individual or institution owes

market capitalization company's value on the stock market, calculated by multiplying the company's stock price by the total number of shares outstanding

mintage number of coins a mint produces for a particular series

mortgage loan designed to buy or refurbish real estate; it generally has a lower interest rate than other types of loans as it is considered safer for banks since the property purchased is used as collateral

mutual fund financial asset managed by an investment company that gathers money from many investors and uses it to create a diversified portfolio of various assets

portfolio ensemble of assets invested in, such as stocks, bonds, real estate, or art

principal amount of money lent to the borrower

private company company generally owned by a handful of people or institutions, with shares that can't be freely exchanged on the stock market

private key proof of ownership of a crypto wallet, the equivalent of the security code for a bank account

public company company that is publicly traded, with shares that can be freely exchanged on the stock market

public key identification number of a crypto wallet, allowing holder to receive cryptocurrency; the equivalent of a bank account number

real estate investment trust company that owns real estate and must distribute more than 90% of its taxable income to shareholders

shareholder private or institutional investor that owns a share of a company

shareholder's equity shareholder's ownership in a company

shares outstanding total shares held by all of a company's shareholders

soft skill skill that helps an individual interact with people and their environment to perform tasks

stock market physical or virtual place where investors exchange financial assets

ticker symbol unique set of characters used to identify a particular security traded on the stock market

token synonym for any cryptocurrency that doesn't have its own blockchain and is built on another coin's blockchain; Bitcoin and Ethereum are considered coins since they have their own blockchain

whale investor with a considerable amount of money who can potentially change the market mood by taking or selling huge positions

References

Best, Raynor de. 2023. NFT—Statistics and Facts. Statista, March 30. https://www.statista.com/topics/8513/nft/#topicOverview. Accessed 16 Apr 2023.

Bolles, Richard N., with Katharine Brooks. 2021. *What Color Is Your Parachute? 2022: Your Guide to a Lifetime of Meaningful Work and Career Success*. New York: Clarkson Potter/Ten Speed.

Clason, George S. 1989. *The Richest Man in Babylon*. London: Plume.

Collins, J. L. 2016. *A Simple Path to Wealth: Your Road Map to Financial Independence and a Rich, Free Life*. CreateSpace Independent Publishing Platform.

Damodaran, Aswath. 2011. *The Little Book of Valuation: How to Value a Company, Pick a Stock, and Profit*. New York: Wiley and Sons.

Deka, Chayanika. 2022. Bitcoin's Pizza Day 12th Anniversary: 2 Pizzas for 10,000 BTC. CryptoPotato, May 22. https://cryptopotato.com/12-years-since-a-florida-based-programmer-bought-2-papa-johns-pizzas-with-bitcoin/. Accessed 12 Apr 2023.

Doran, G. T. 1981. There's a S.M.A.R.T. Way to Write Management's Goals and Objectives. *Management Review* 70(11): 35–36. https://community.mis.temple.edu/mis0855002fall2015/files/2015/10/S.M.A.R.T-Way-Management-Review.pdf. Accessed 26 Mar 2023.

Elkins, Kathleen. 2020. Warren Buffett Warns against Carrying a Credit Card Balance: 'You can't go through life borrowing money at those rates.' CNBC, May 13. https://www.cnbc.com/2020/05/13/warren-buffett-cautions-against-carrying-a-credit-card-balance.html. Accessed 26 Mar 2023.

Ethereum. n.d. What Is Ethereum? https://ethereum.org/en/what-is-ethereum/. Accessed 12 Apr 2023.

Gardner, David, and Tom Gardner. 2017. *The Motley Fool Investment Guide: How the Fools Beat Wall Street's Wise Men and How You Can Too*, 3rd ed. New York: Simon & Schuster.

Gillespie, Lane. 2023. Bankrate's 2023 Annual Emergency Savings Report. Bankrate, February 23. https://www.bankrate.com/banking/savings/emergency-savings-report/. Accessed 12 Apr 2023.

Graham, Benjamin. 2005. *The Intelligent Investor*, rev. ed. New York: Collins.

Green, Rachael. 2023. 57% of Americans Can't Cover a $1,000 Emergency with Savings—Here's How You Can Prepare for Unexpected Costs and Build an Emergency Fund. DentalPlans, February 28. https://newsdirect.com/news/57-of-americans-cant-cover-a-1-000-emergency-with-savings-heres-how-you-can-prepare-for-unexpected-costs-and-build-an-emergency-fund-792842649. Accessed 26 Mar 2023.

Greenblatt, Joel. 2010. *The Little Book That Still Beats the Market*. New York: Wiley and Sons.

Kiyosaki, Robert T. 2018. *Rich Dad Poor Dad: What the Rich Teach Their Kids about Money That the Poor and Middle Class Do Not!*, rev. ed. Scottsdale, AZ: Plata Publishing.

Markowitz, Harry. 1952. Portfolio Selection. *The Journal of Finance* 7(1): 77–91.

Mayer, Christopher. 2018. *100 Baggers: Stocks That Return 100-to-1 and How to Find Them*. Baltimore, MD: Laossez-Faire Books.

Nakamoto, Satoshi. 2008. Bitcoin: A Peer-to-Peer Electronic Cash System. Bitcoin. https://www.bitcoin.org/bitcoin.pdf. Accessed 15 Apr 2023.

Pape, Scott. 2017. *The Barefoot Investor*. Milton, Qld: John Wiley and Sons.

PK. 2021. S&P 500 Periodic Reinvestment Calculator (with Dividends). DQYDJ. https://dqydj.com/sp-500-periodic-reinvestment-calculator-dividends/. Accessed 5 Apr 2023.

Stanley, Thomas J., and William D. Danko. 1996. *The Millionaire Next Door: The Surprising Secrets of America's Wealthy*. New York: Pocket Books.

United States Geological Survey. n.d. How Much Gold Has Been Found in the World? https://www.usgs.gov/faqs/how-much-gold-has-been-found-world. Accessed 13 Apr 2023.

World Gold Council. 2023. Above-ground Stocks. February 8. https://www.gold.org/goldhub/data/how-much-gold. Accessed 13 Apr 2023.

Further Reading

Address Maker. 2021. The 5 Factors of a Good Location. December 31. https://addressmaker.in/blog/the-5-factors-of-a-good-location/.

AirDNA. 2023. Home Page. https://www.airdna.co.

Allen, Alicia. 2020. The 7Ps of the Marketing Mix. Oxford College of Marketing, October 8. https://blog.oxfordcollegeofmarketing.com/2020/10/08/understanding-the-7ps-of-the-marketing-mix/.

Anderson, James. 2021. How Many Grams in an Ounce of Silver? SD Bullion, January 14. https://sdbullion.com/blog/how-many-grams-in-a-troy-ounce-of-silver.

ArtZolo. 2017. The Do's & Dont's While Investing in Art. September 29. https://www.artzolo.com/blog/art-investing-dos-and-donts.

Barrow, Colin. 2011. *Starting and Running a Business All-in-One for Dummies.* Chichester: John Wiley and Sons.

Berlinger, Joe, dir. 2023. *Madoff: The Monster of Wall Street.* Documentary Series. Netflix.

Better Tasting Wine. n.d. Common Asked Questions on Wine Storage. http://bettertastingwine.com/storage.html.

Better Tasting Wine. n.d. Vintage Guide: Good, Safe, vs. Bad Bets. https://www.bettertastingwine.com/vintage.html.

BiggerPockets. 2016. Calculating Numbers on a Rental Property [Using the Four Square Method!]. YouTube. https://www.youtube.com/watch?v=T_7vhsSBi7c.

BiggerPockets. 2018. 7 Tips for Managing Rental Properties. YouTube. https://www.youtube.com/watch?v=dXxYnLZ8AHU.

Blockchain. 2023. Home Page. https://blockchain.info/.

Bloomberg Originals. 2018. How Toyota Changed the Way We Make Things. YouTube. https://www.youtube.com/watch?v=F5vtCRFRAK0.

BluEntCAD. 2022. The 4 Types of Real Estate: What You Need to Know. March 21. https://www.bluentcad.com/blog/types-of-real-estate/.

Board of Governors of the Federal Reserve System. 2022. Federal Reserve Issues FOMC Statement. Press Release, March 16. https://www.federalreserve.gov/newsevents/pressreleases/monetary20220316a.htm#:~:text=The%20Committee%20seeks%20to%20achieve.

Board of Governors of the Federal Reserve System. 2023. Consumer Credit—G.19. https://www.federalreserve.gov/releases/g19/current/default.htm.

Bored Ape Yacht Club. 2023. Home Page. https://boredapeyachtclub.com/#/.

Bragg, Steven. 2020. Balance Sheet Definition. AccountingTools, November 3. https://www.accountingtools.com/articles/balance-sheet.

Britannica. 2019. Gold: Properties, Occurrences, and Uses. https://www.britannica.com/science/gold-chemical-element/Properties-occurrences-and-uses.

Bulbagarden. 2009. History of Pokémon. https://bulbapedia.bulbagarden.net/wiki/History_of_Pok%C3%A9mon.

BullionByPost. 2023. Gold Price: Track the Live Gold Price. https://www.bullionbypost.eu/gold-price/.

Burgess, Luke. 2018. Don't Chase Opportunities, Let the Opportunities Come to You. Energy & Capital, August 17. https://www.energyandcapital.com/articles/don-t-chase-opportunities-let-the-opportunities-come-to-you/77609.

Busby, Mattha. 2017. Revealed: How Gambling Industry Targets Poor People and Ex-gamblers. *The Guardian*, August 31. https://www.theguardian.com/society/2017/aug/31/gambling-industry-third-party-companies-online-casinos.

Business Queensland. 2022. The 7 Ps of Marketing. August 29. https://www.business.qld.gov.au/running-business/marketing-sales/marketing-promotion/marketing-basics/seven-ps-marketing.

Calculator.net. 2023. Investment Calculator. https://www.calculator.net/investment-calculator.html.

Calculator.net. 2023. Loan Calculator. https://www.calculator.net/loan-calculator.html.

Callahan, Chrissy. 2021. SMART Goals: Examples, Tips and More to Help You Get Started. Today, January 20. https://www.today.com/tmrw/what-smart-goal-how-system-could-help-you-stay-task-t205317.

Caplinger, Dan. 2022. What Is a Stock Market Index? The Motley Fool, October 18. https://www.fool.com/investing/stock-market/indexes/.

Caplinger, Dan. 2023. How to Invest in Index Funds. The Motley Fool, April 21. https://www.fool.com/investing/how-to-invest/index-funds/.

Cardano. 2023. Home Page. https://cardano.org/.

Carleton, Peter. 2019. Fiscal Quarter (Q1, Q2, Q3, Q4). InvestingAnswers. https://investinganswers.com/dictionary/q/quarter-q1-q2-q3-q4.

CAWBusiness. 2016. The Marketing Mix (Extended)—Simon Atack. YouTube. https://www.youtube.com/watch?v=oMZMrnNWY-A.

Centre d'Aide Airbnb. n.d. Frais de service Airbnb [Airbnb Service Fees]. https://fr.airbnb.be/help/article/1857/frais-de-service-airbnb?_set_bev_on_new_domain=1657609646_N2UwOTNiYzQyMjRk.

CFI Team. 2022. Notary. Corporate Finance Institute, December 22. https://corporatefinanceinstitute.com/resources/careers/jobs/notary/.

CFI Team. 2023. Dow Divisor. Corporate Finance Institute, January 22. https://corporatefinanceinstitute.com/resources/knowledge/trading-investing/dow-divisor/.

CFI Team. 2023. Cash Flow from Investing Activities. Corporate Finance Institute, March 13. https://corporatefinanceinstitute.com/resources/knowledge/accounting/cash-flow-from-investing-activities/.
CFI Team. 2023. Investment Portfolio. Corporate Finance Institute, March 16. https://corporatefinanceinstitute.com/resources/knowledge/trading-investing/investment-portfolio/.
CFI Team. 2023. Risk Tolerance. Corporate Finance Institute, March 20. https://corporatefinanceinstitute.com/resources/wealth-management/risk-tolerance/.
CFI Team. 2023. Income Statement—Income, Expenses, and Profit/Loss. Corporate Finance Institute, April 16. https://corporatefinanceinstitute.com/resources/knowledge/accounting/income-statement/.
CFI Team. 2023. SMART Goals: Specific, Measurable, Attainable, Realistic, Timely. Corporate Finance Institute, April 19. https://corporatefinanceinstitute.com/resources/knowledge/other/smart-goal/.
CFI Team. 2023. Cash Flow from Operations. Corporate Finance Institute, April 26. https://corporatefinanceinstitute.com/resources/knowledge/accounting/cash-flow-from-operations/.
CFI Team. 2023. Cash Flow from Financing Activities. Corporate Finance Institute, April 27. https://corporatefinanceinstitute.com/resources/knowledge/accounting/cash-flow-from-financing-activities/.
Chen, James. 2020. What Is an Investment Fund? Types of Funds and History. Investopedia, March 16. https://www.investopedia.com/terms/i/investment-fund.asp.
Chen, James. 2020. What Is the Dow 30, Companies in It, Significance. Investopedia, December 25. https://www.investopedia.com/terms/d/dow-30.asp.
Chen, James. 2023. Income Statement: How to Read and Use It. Investopedia, March 27. https://www.investopedia.com/terms/i/incomestatement.asp.
Chicago Humanities Festival. 2012. Philip Kotler: Marketing. YouTube. https://www.youtube.com/watch?v=sR-qL7QdVZQ.
Citi GPS. 2022. Global Art Market Disruption: Pushing the Boundaries. March 17. https://www.privatebank.citibank.com/insights/art-gps.
Cohébergement. n.d. Bail meublé étudiant: Un contrat de location de 9 mois [Student Furnished Lease: A 9-month Rental Contract]. https://www.cohebergement.com/blog/bail-meuble-etudiant-un-contrat-de-location-de-9-mois-82#:~:text=Pour%20que%20les%20choses%20soient.
Coinbase. n.d. Coinbase Wallet. https://www.coinbase.com/fr/wallet.
Conti, Robyn. 2023. What Is An NFT? Non-Fungible Tokens Explained. Forbes Advisor, March 17. https://www.forbes.com/advisor/investing/nft-non-fungible-token/.

Crypto. 2022. What Is a Crypto Wallet? A Beginner's Guide. April 26. https://crypto.com/university/crypto-wallets.

Daly, Lyle. 2023. How Many Cryptocurrencies Are There? The Motley Fool, April 19. https://www.fool.com/investing/stock-market/market-sectors/financials/cryptocurrency-stocks/how-many-cryptocurrencies-are-there/.

Daly, Lyle. 2023. What Is Staking in Crypto? The Motley Fool, April 21. https://www.fool.com/investing/stock-market/market-sectors/financials/cryptocurrency-stocks/what-is-staking/.

Danial, Kiana. 2023. *Cryptocurrency Investing for Dummies*. New York: John Wiley and Sons.

Davis, Chris, and Alana Benson. 2023. Index Fund vs. ETF: What's the Difference? NerdWallet, January 30. https://www.nerdwallet.com/article/investing/etf-vs-index-fund-compare.

Dekier, Łukasz. 2012. The Origins and Evolution of Lean Management System. *Journal of International Studies* 5(1): 46–51.

DeRosa, Anthony. 2021. Where to Search for Jobs: Finding Your next Opportunity. *Wall Street Journal*, January 19. https://www.wsj.com/articles/where-to-search-for-jobs-finding-your-next-opportunity-11605109352.

Desjardins, Jeff. 2015. How Are Silver and Gold Bullion Premiums Calculated? Visual Capitalist, December 3. https://www.visualcapitalist.com/how-silver-and-gold-bullion-premiums-calculated/.

Ebere. 2023. What Is an Investment Portfolio? Overview, How It Works, and How to Build One. Kiiky Wealth, February 24. https://kiiky.com/wealth/investment-portfolio/.

Eco Plus. 2016. Le fordisme [Fordism]. YouTube. https://www.youtube.com/watch?v=YXQfABp9a3E.

EHL Insights. n.d. 10 Questions to Ask Yourself When Choosing a Career. Hospitality Insights. https://hospitalityinsights.ehl.edu/questions-choosing-career.

EraGem. 2020. History & Explanation of Carat Weight. February 24. https://eragem.com/news/history-explanation-carat-weight/.

European Central Bank. 2021. Monetary Policy. August 14. https://www.ecb.europa.eu/ecb/tasks/monpol/html/index.en.html#:~:text=We%20are%20targeting%20an%20inflation.

Experis. 2021. 20 Tips for Great Job Interviews. https://www.experis.com/en/insights/articles/2021/05/25/20-tips-for-great-job-interviews.

Fernando, Jason. 2023. Bond: Financial Meaning with Examples and How They Are Priced. Investopedia, March 9. https://www.investopedia.com/terms/b/bond.asp.

Fernando, Jason. 2023. Market Capitalization: How Is It Calculated and What Does It Tell Investors? Investopedia, March 16. https://www.investopedia.com/terms/m/marketcapitalization.asp.

Fernando, Jason. 2023. Fiscal Quarters (Q1, Q2, Q3, Q4) Explained. Investopedia, April 5. https://www.investopedia.com/terms/q/quarter.asp.

Finviz. 2023. Stock Screener—Overview Mega Market Cap. https://finviz.com/screener.ashx?v=111&f=cap_mega&o=-marketcap.

Gay, Christina. 2016. 8 Wastes of Lean Manufacturing. MachineMetrics, January 25. https://www.machinemetrics.com/blog/8-wastes-of-lean-manufacturing.

Glassdoor Team. 2021. How to Negotiate Your Salary. Glassdoor, July 7. https://www.glassdoor.co.uk/blog/guide/how-to-negotiate-your-salary/.

Gold Price. 2010. Gold Price History. https://goldprice.org/gold-price-history.html.

GrayStake. 2019. 7 Techniques de 'house hacking' [7 'House Hacking' Techniques]. December 27. https://www.millenial-independant.com/investissement/immobilier/house-hacking/.

Grimes, William, and Robin Pogrebin. 2015. How to Buy Art: A Beginner's Cheat Sheet. *New York Times*, May 7. https://www.nytimes.com/2015/05/08/arts/design/how-to-buy-art-a-beginners-cheat-sheet.html.

Guardian, The. 2022. Man Who Paid $2.9m for NFT of Jack Dorsey's First Tweet Set to Lose Almost $2.9m. April 14. https://www.theguardian.com/technology/2022/apr/14/twitter-nft-jack-dorsey-sina-estavi.

Gwen PROF. 2018. OST et fordisme [OST and Fordism]. YouTube. https://www.youtube.com/watch?v=hROMDbkCeoU.

Half, Robert. 2023. How to Negotiate Salary after You Get a Job Offer. RobertHalf, April . https://www.roberthalf.com/blog/salaries-and-skills/be-ready-for-salary-negotiations-with-these-8-tips.

Hayes, Adam. 2022. Growth Stock: What It Is, Examples, Growth Stock vs. Value Stock. Investopedia, January 10. https://www.investopedia.com/terms/g/growthstock.asp.

Hayes, Adam. 2022. Tulipmania: About the Dutch Tulip Bulb Market Bubble. Investopedia, November 22. https://www.investopedia.com/terms/d/dutch_tulip_bulb_market_bubble.asp.

Hayes, Adam. 2023. Cash Flow Statement: How to Read and Understand It. Investopedia, April 5. https://www.investopedia.com/terms/c/cashflowstatement.asp#:~:text=What%20Is%20a%20Cash%20Flow.

Headley, Susan. 2022. Coin Grading Made Simple. The Spruce Crafts, April 20. https://www.thesprucecrafts.com/coin-grading-made-simple-768384.

Headley, Susan. 2022. Top 10 Most Valuable U.S. Coins Found in Pocket Change. The Spruce Crafts, June 27. https://www.thesprucecrafts.com/most-valuable-coins-in-pocket-change-768897.

Herrity, Jennifer. 2023. Guide: How to Choose a Career. Indeed, March 11. https://www.indeed.com/career-advice/finding-a-job/how-to-choose-a-career.

Hetler, Amanda. 2023. 10 Common Cryptocurrency Scams in 2023. WhatIs, April 19. https://www.techtarget.com/whatis/feature/Common-cryptocurrency-scams.

Heyford, Shauna C. 2022. How to Achieve Optimal Asset Allocation. Investopedia, February 19. https://www.investopedia.com/managing-wealth/achieve-optimal-asset-allocation/?utm_campaign=quote-yahoo&utm_source=yahoo&utm_medium=referral.

Higginbotham, Daniel. 2021. How to Choose a Career. Prospects, May. https://www.prospects.ac.uk/careers-advice/getting-a-job/how-to-choose-a-career.

Hurree. 2020. What Are the 7Ps of the Marketing Mix? YouTube. https://www.youtube.com/watch?v=OF4w862D0s4.

Hwang, Inyoung. 2023. A Brief History of the Stock Market. SoFi Learn, March 15. https://www.sofi.com/learn/content/history-of-the-stock-market/.

iDealwine. n.d. Château Lafite Rothschild 2004 (Rouge). https://www.idealwine.com/fr/prix-vin/385-2004-Bouteille-Bordeaux-Pauillac-Chateau-Lafite-Rothschild-1er-Grand-Cru-Classe-Rouge.jsp.

Indeed Editorial Team. 2023. Job Search: 6 Ways To Find Your Next Job. Indeed, March 21. https://www.indeed.com/career-advice/finding-a-job/best-ways-to-find-a-job.

Insider Business. 2021. How the Beanie Babies Frenzy Collapsed | Rise and Fall. YouTube. https://www.youtube.com/watch?v=OuD0h5I-NrQ&t=292s.

International Precious Metals. n.d. The Most Valuable Coins In Circulation: Quarters, Dimes & More. https://www.preciousmetals.com/blog/post/the-most-valuable-us-coins-in-circulation.html.

Investopedia Team. 2021. Modern Portfolio Theory: What MPT Is and How Investors Use It. Investopedia. https://www.investopedia.com/terms/m/modernportfoliotheory.asp#citation-1.

Investopedia Team. 2022. Index Fund vs. ETF: What's the Difference? Investopedia, October 24. https://www.investopedia.com/ask/answers/033015/whats-difference-between-index-fund-and-etf.asp#:~:text=What%20Is%20the%20Difference%20Between.

Investor's Business Daily. n.d. Supply and Demand. https://www.investors.com/ibd-university/can-slim/supply-demand/.

Jackson, Anna-Louise. 2023. What Is Earnings Season? Why Is It Important? Forbes, January 30. https://www.forbes.com/advisor/investing/what-is-earnings-season/.

Johnson, Matt. 2018. How to Grade Pokemon Cards for PSA | Pokemon Grading Scale. PSA Collector, August 2. https://www.psacollector.com/how-to-grade-pokemon-cards/.

Johnston, Matthew. 2023. Top S&P 500 Index Funds. Investopedia, February 15. https://www.investopedia.com/articles/markets/101415/4-

best-sp-500-index-funds.asp?utm_campaign=quote-yahoo&utm_source=yahoo&utm_medium=referral.

Kagan, Julia. 2023. What Is a Mortgage? Types, How They Work, and Examples. Investopedia, March 27. https://www.investopedia.com/terms/m/mortgage.asp.

Kagge, Erling. 2015. *A Poor Collector's Guide to Buying Great Art*. Berlin: Gestalten.

Kanbanize. 2021. 7 Wastes of Lean. https://kanbanize.com/lean-management/value-waste/7-wastes-of-lean.

Karus, Martin. 2021. How Much Gold Is There Left to Mine and What Happens If Gold Runs Out? Tavex, September 13. https://tavex.fi/en/how-much-gold-is-there-left-to-mine-and-what-happens-if-gold-runs-out/#:~:text=According%20to%20the%20US%20Geological.

Kastrenakes, Jacob. 2021. Beeple Sold an NFT for $69 Million. The Verge, March 11. https://www.theverge.com/2021/3/11/22325054/beeple-christies-nft-sale-cost-everydays-69-million.

Kenton, Will. 2022. Cash Flow from Investing Activities Explained: Types and Examples. Investopedia, June 22. https://www.investopedia.com/terms/c/cashflowinvestingactivities.asp.

Koch, Richard. 2018. *The 80/20 Principle: The Secret of Achieving More with Less*. New York: Currency.

Koepp, Brent. 2023. Top 24 Most Expensive & Rarest Pokemon Cards Ever Sold. Dexerto, March 30. https://www.dexerto.com/pokemon/top-5-most-expensive-pokemon-trading-cards-1395031/.

Krebiehl, Anne. 2016. What Happens as Wine Ages? Decanter, November 3. https://www.decanter.com/learn/advice/what-happens-as-wine-ages-340685/.

Krebiehl, Anne. 2018. What Really Happens as Wine Ages? Wine Enthusiast, October 9. https://www.winemag.com/2018/10/09/what-happens-wine-ages/.

Kurtuy, Andrei. 2023. The Ultimate Guide to Job Hunt—Land Your Next Job in 2023. Novorésumé, January 4. https://novoresume.com/career-blog/how-to-find-a-new-job-easy.

Kurtuy, Andrei. 2023. Should You Include a Picture on Your Resume or CV in 2023? Novorésumé, March 21. https://novoresume.com/career-blog/including-photo-on-resume.

Laurence, Tiana, and Seoyoung Kim. 2021. *NFTs for Dummies*. New York: John Wiley and Sons.

Levy, Adam. 2022. ETF vs. Index Fund: What Are the Differences? The Motley Fool, June 29. https://www.fool.com/investing/how-to-invest/etfs/etf-vs-index-fund/.

Levy, Adam. 2022. Why Should You Use Crypto? The Motley Fool, September 20. https://www.fool.com/investing/stock-market/market-sectors/financials/cryptocurrency-stocks/benefits-of-cryptocurrency/.

Lewis, Michael. 2022. Top 10 Most Valuable Types of Collectibles in the World. Money Crashers, November 2. https://www.moneycrashers.com/most-valuable-expensive-types-collectibles/.

Liu, Berlinda, and Gaurav Sinha. 2022. SPIVA® U.S. Scorecard. https://www.spglobal.com/spdji/en/documents/spiva/spiva-us-year-end-2021.pdf.

Liv-ex. n.d. Liv-ex Indices. https://www.liv-ex.com/news-insights/indices/.

Love Money. 2017. The World's Most Valuable Collections Ever Sold. October 3. https://www.lovemoney.com/galleries/68018/the-worlds-most-valuable-collections-ever-sold?page=1.

Ma Cave à Vin. 2017. Comment Stocker Son Vin? Ma Cave à Vin [How to Store Your Wine? My Wine Cellar]. December 14. https://www.ma-cave-a-vin.fr/blog/2017/12/comment-stocker-vin/#:~:text=Privil%C3%A9giez%20un%20stockage%20en%20pleine.

Malhotra, Deepak. 2014. 15 Rules for Negotiating a Job Offer. Harvard Business Review, April. https://hbr.org/2014/04/15-rules-for-negotiating-a-job-offer.

Management Meditations. n.d. Lean Management Is ... https://www.lmmiller.com/what-is-lean-management/.

Mass Live Media. 2020. Why You Need the 7 P's of Marketing. March 25. https://www.masslivemedia.com/the-7-ps/.

McCabe, Ashleigh. 2022. 7Ps of the Marketing Mix: The Acronym Sent to Streamline Your Strategy. Hurree, October 11. https://blog.hurree.co/blog/marketing-mix-7ps.

McClure, Ben. 2022. Modern Portfolio Theory: Why It's Still Hip. Investopedia, November 28. https://www.investopedia.com/managing-wealth/modern-portfolio-theory-why-its-still-hip/.

McKay, Dawn Rosenberg. 2022. How to Make a Career Choice When You Are Undecided. The Balance, September 13. https://www.thebalancecareers.com/steps-to-choosing-career-525506.

McKeever, Vicky. 2021. There's a 'Unique' Opportunity in Art, Which Has Beat the S&P 500 over 25 Years, Asset Manager Says. CNBC, May 27. https://www.cnbc.com/2021/05/27/there-are-unique-opportunities-in-art-says-one-asset-manager.html.

McLaughlin, Emily. 2023. Lean Management. TechTarget, March. https://www.techtarget.com/searchcio/definition/lean-management#:~:text=Lean%20management%20is%20an%20approach.

MetaMask. 2019. Home Page. https://metamask.io/.

Midwest Bullion Exchange. 2019. What Is the Difference between an Ounce and a Troy Ounce? August 29. https://privatebullion.com/blog/troy-ounce-vs-ounce/.

Mind Tools Content Team. 2009. Frederick Taylor and Scientific Management. Mindtools. https://www.mindtools.com/pages/article/newTMM_Taylor.htm.

Mr. Money Mustache. 2023. Home Page. https://www.mrmoneymustache.com/.

Mugleston, Pete. 2023. Mortgages: How Much Can You Borrow? Online Mortgage Advisor, April 26. https://www.onlinemortgageadvisor.co.uk/mortgage-affordability/how-many-times-wage-borrow-mortgage/.

Nareit. 2019. What's a REIT (Real Estate Investment Trust)? https://www.reit.com/what-reit.

NASDAQ. 2023. Home Page. https://www.nasdaq.com/.

NASDAQ. 2023. TotalEnergies SE (TTE) Dividend History. https://www.nasdaq.com/market-activity/stocks/tte/dividend-history.

Nationwide Coin & Bullion Reserve. 2020. What Is the Difference between Proof Coins & Uncirculated Coins? April 6. https://nationwidecoins.com/what-is-the-difference-between-proof-coins-uncirculated-coins/.

New Money. 2022. How Many Stocks Should Be in Your Portfolio? (Buffett, Lynch, Pabrai Explain). YouTube. https://www.youtube.com/watch?v=SZE1Ep5KTPU.

Nifty Gateway. 2023. Home Page. https://www.niftygateway.com/.

Nikolovska, Hristina. 2020. Cigarette Prices by State in 2020. Balancing Everything, July 16. https://balancingeverything.com/cigarette-prices-by-state/.

Nobel Prize. 1990. Press Release: The Sveriges Riksbank Prize in Economic Sciences in Memory of Alfred Nobel 1990. October 16. https://www.nobelprize.org/prizes/economic-sciences/1990/press-release/.

Nova, Annie. 2018. Another Challenge in Retirement? Student Loans. CNBC, November 14. https://www.cnbc.com/2018/11/14/more-older-people-are-bringing-student-debt-into-their-retirement.html.

O'Brien, Shauna. n.d. The Complete Guide to REIT Taxes. Dividend. https://www.dividend.com/dividend-education/the-complete-guide-to-reit-taxes/.

O'Connell, Brian. 2022. Mutual Funds: What They Are & How They Work. Seeking Alpha, March 25. https://seekingalpha.com/article/4434117-what-is-a-mutual-fund.

Ocean Cleanup, The. 2022. 80% of River Plastic Comes from 1000 Rivers. https://theoceancleanup.com/rivers/.

Ontario Securities Commission. 2021. 3 Factors That Affect Bond Prices. June 22. https://www.getsmarteraboutmoney.ca/invest/investment-products/bonds/3-factors-that-affect-bond-prices/.

OpenSea. 2021. Home Page. https://opensea.io/.

Organizational Communication Channel. 2017. Classical Management Theory. YouTube. https://www.youtube.com/watch?v=d1jOwD-CTLI.

Palumbo, Jacqui. 2021. Rare Winston Churchill Painting Sold by Angelina Jolie Smashes Auction Record. CNN, March 2. https://edition.cnn.com/style/article/winston-churchill-christies-sale-auction-record/index.html.

Pan, Jing. 2021. Cathie Wood's $500K Bitcoin Call Is Already Happening—How to Ride the Wave to Half a Million. Yahoo Finance, October 30. https://finance.yahoo.com/news/cathie-woods-500k-bitcoin-call-120000814.html#:~:text=%E2%80%9CIf%20we.

Partena Professional. 2019. Create an SPRLU. November 18. https://www.partena-professional.be/fr/nouvelles/creer-une-sprlu.

Penn State Extension. n.d. Collectables Project. https://extension.psu.edu/programs/4-h/opportunities/projects/communication-and-expressive-arts/collectables.

Plain Bagel, The. 2021. Fractional Shares Explained—Everything You Need to Know about Sharing Shares. YouTube. https://www.youtube.com/watch?v=P3oZOg9yRuY.

Poon, Linda. 2019. The Rise and Fall of New Year's Fitness Resolutions, in 5 Charts. Bloomberg, January 16. https://www.bloomberg.com/news/articles/2019-01-16/here-s-how-quickly-people-ditch-weight-loss-resolutions.

Professional Sports Authenticator. 2023. Home Page. https://www.psacard.com/.

Randall, Kaylee. 2019. What Makes Art Valuable? The Collector, August 11. https://www.thecollector.com/what-makes-art-valuable/.

Rao, Narayana. 2021. Illustrations of Success of Scientific Management - Bricklaying Improvement by Gilbreth. Industrial Engineering Knowledge Center, May 17. http://nraoiekc.blogspot.com/2013/08/illustrations-of-success-of-scientific_4.html.

Rarible. 2023. NFT Marketplace for Your Community. https://rarible.com/.

Reiff, Nathan. 2023. The Top 25 Stocks in the S&P 500. Investopedia, April 5. https://www.investopedia.com/ask/answers/08/find-stocks-in-sp500.asp.

Reimann, Nicholas. 2021. Madoff Ponzi Scheme Victims Receiving More than $500 Million in Repayments, Feds Say. Forbes, September 16. https://www.forbes.com/sites/nicholasreimann/2021/09/16/madoff-ponzi-scheme-victims-receiving-more-than-500-million-in-repayments-feds-say/?sh=5cfa967d12ad.

Renterverse. 2023. Apartment vs. Condo: What's the Difference? March 27. https://www.apartments.com/blog/difference-between-renting-an-apartment-or-condo.

Ritchie, Joshua. 2022. Stock Market History. Intuit Mint Life, January 31. https://mint.intuit.com/blog/investments/the-history-of-the-stock-market/#:~:text=The%20first%20stock%20exchange%20in.

Robert Walters. n.d. Top Tips to Structure Your CV. https://www.robertwalters.com.au/career-advice/cv-and-interview-tips/top-tips-to-structure-your-cv.html.

Robillard, Hunter. n.d. Wine Portfolio Management: Why You Need it & Best Practices. Vinovest. https://www.vinovest.co/blog/wine-portfolio-management.

Rosen, Andy. 2023. Proof of Work vs. Proof of Stake: The Biggest Differences. NerdWallet, February 10. https://www.nerdwallet.com/article/investing/proof-of-work-vs-proof-of-stake#:~:text=The%20main%20difference%20between%20proof.

Rosenberg, Matt. 2020. The 5 Sectors of the Economy. ThoughtCo, January 28. https://www.thoughtco.com/sectors-of-the-economy-1435795.

Royal Mint. n.d. Bullion & VAT Explained. https://www.royalmint.com/invest/discover/invest-in-gold/value-added-tax-on-investments/.

Royal Mint. n.d. DigiGold. https://www.royalmint.com/digital-investments/digigold/.

S&P Dow Jones Indices. n.d. What Is an Index? https://www.spglobal.com/spdji/en/research-insights/index-literacy/what-is-an-index/.

Sharma, Sumit. 2019. Balance Sheet Items. WallStreetMojo, May 15. https://www.wallstreetmojo.com/balance-sheet-items/.

Sherman, Fraser. 2021. About Different Stock Markets. Chron, December 17. https://smallbusiness.chron.com/different-stock-markets-13350.html.

SkillsYouNeed. 2011. The 7 Ps of Marketing Mix. https://www.skillsyouneed.com/lead/7-marketing-ps.html.

Smith, Andrew. 2022. Robert Kiyosaki Warns to Beware of "Fake Money." The Coin Republic, December 12. https://www.thecoinrepublic.com/2022/12/12/robert-kiyosaki-warns-to-beware-of-fake-money/.

Smith, Jemma. 2021. How to Write a CV. Prospects, April. https://www.prospects.ac.uk/careers-advice/cvs-and-cover-letters/how-to-write-a-cv.

Smith, Kevin. 2016. Supply and Demand Examples in the Stock Market. How The Market Works, January 18. https://education.howthemarketworks.com/supply-and-demand-examples-stock-market/.

Statista. 2023. Average Number and Value of Completed NFT Sales on the Ethereum Blockchain up to November 29, 2022. https://www.statista.com/statistics/1265353/nft-sales-value/.

Stephanis, Brittany, and Robert Leslie. 2021. The Rise and Fall of Beanie Babies, Which Made Ty Warner a Billionaire but Now Are Nearly Worthless. Business Insider, August 9. https://www.businessinsider.com/rise-and-fall-beanie-babies-ty-warner-2021-8.

Strickler, Elizabeth. 2021. NFTs, the Metaverse and the Future of Digital Art. TED. YouTube. https://www.youtube.com/watch?v=oupHYHv_me0.

Sumagaysay, Levi. 2020. Airbnb IPO Raises at Least $3.5 Billion, Challenging DoorDash and Snowflake for Largest IPO of the Year. MarketWatch, December 10. https://www.marketwatch.com/story/airbnb-ipo-raises-at-least-3-5-billion-challenging-doordash-and-snowflake-for-largest-ipo-of-the-year-11607564401.

Tardi, Carla. 2023. Financial Portfolio: What It Is, and How to Create and Manage One. Investopedia, April 25. https://www.investopedia.com/terms/p/portfolio.asp.

Tasting Book. n.d. Lafite-Rothschild 2000: Château Lafite-Rothschild. https://tastingbook.com/wine/chateau_lafiterothschild/lafiterothschild_2000.

Tehranian, Kayvon. 2021. How NFTs Are Building the Internet of the Future. TED. YouTube. https://www.youtube.com/watch?v=2206a87-GcQ.

Thune, Kent. 2022. Major Market Indexes List. The Balance, January 26. https://www.thebalancemoney.com/major-market-indexes-list-2466397.

Tom. 2020. Airbnb Host Fees: How Much Is Airbnb Charging You? An Up-To-Date Guide. Host Tools, December 11. https://hosttools.com/blog/airbnb-rentals/airbnb-host-fees/.

Tom. 2021. Is Airbnb Profitable for Hosts? Everything You Need to Know. Host Tools, July 9. https://hosttools.com/blog/airbnb-rentals/is-airbnb-profitable-for-hosts/?swcfpc=1.

Tuchman, Mitch. 2017. 5 Warren Buffett Quotes for Anyone Who Thinks They Can Pick Stocks and Get Rich Like He Did. MarketWatch, August 11. https://www.marketwatch.com/story/the-5-times-warren-buffett-talked-about-index-fund-investing-2017-04-28.

Turits, Meredith. 2020. How to Create a Business Budget for Your Small Business. NerdWallet, October 30. https://www.nerdwallet.com/article/small-business/how-to-create-a-business-budget.

Turner, Brandon. 2015. *The Book on Rental Property Investing: How to Create Wealth and Passive Income through Smart Buy & Hold Real Estate Investing*. Denver, CO: Bigger Pockets.

tutor2u. 2016. PESTLE Analysis Explained. YouTube. https://www.youtube.com/watch?v=sP2sDw5waEU.

tutor2u. 2016. SWOT Analysis Explained: Business Strategy. YouTube. https://www.youtube.com/watch?v=7JmDXDZYx0s.

Tyson, Eric. 2021. *Investing for Dummies*, 9th ed. New York: John Wiley and Sons.

U.S. Bureau of Labor Statistics. 2023. CPI Inflation Calculator. https://www.bls.gov/data/inflation_calculator.htm.

U.S. Inflation Calculator. 2023. US Inflation Calculator. https://www.usinflationcalculator.com/.

U.S. Securities and Exchange Commission. n.d. Bonds. https://www.investor.gov/introduction-investing/investing-basics/investment-products/bonds-or-fixed-income-products/bonds.

U.S. Securities and Exchange Commission. n.d. Mutual Funds. https://www.investor.gov/introduction-investing/investing-basics/investment-products/mutual-funds-and-exchange-traded-1#Benefits.

United States Mint. n.d. What's the Difference between Bullion, Proof, Uncirculated, and Circulating Coins? https://catalog.usmint.gov/coin-differences.html.

Wamala, Yowana. 2023. What Does It Mean to Refinance a Loan? ValuePenguin, March 7. https://www.valuepenguin.com/loans/refinancing-a-loan-what-it-means.

Wine Folly. 2016. Wine Vintages and Why They Matter (Sometimes). September 12. https://winefolly.com/deep-dive/wine-vintages-and-why-they-matter/.

World Bank. 2023. GDP (Current US$). https://data.worldbank.org/indicator/NY.GDP.MKTP.CD?most_recent_value_desc=true.

World Gold Council. 2023. Historical Demand and Supply. January 31. https://www.gold.org/goldhub/data/gold-demand-by-country.

World Gold Council. 2023. Above-ground Gold Stocks. February 8. https://www.gold.org/goldhub/data/above-ground-stocks.

WTSO. 2018. What Happens to Wine When It Ages. February 6. https://www.wtso.com/blog/what-happens-to-wine-when-it-ages/.

Yahoo Finance. 2023. Amazon.com, Inc. (AMZN) Stock Price, Quote, History & News. https://finance.yahoo.com/quote/AMZN?p=AMZN&.tsrc=fin-srch.

Youth Central. n.d. How to Write a Cover Letter. https://www.youthcentral.vic.gov.au/jobs-and-careers/applying-for-a-job/what-is-a-cover-letter/how-to-write-a-cover-letter.

ZenGo. 2023. Home Page. https://zengo.com/.